JOSEPH

University of Nebraska Press
Lincoln

JOSEPH

Portraits through the Ages

ALAN T. LEVENSON

The Jewish Publication Society
Philadelphia

The author would like to thank the provost, the
dean, the vice president for research, and the chair
of the History Department at the University of Oklahoma for their support of this project and for their
assuming the costs of this index.

Library of Congress Cataloging-in-Publication Data
Names: Levenson, Alan T., author.
Title: Joseph : portraits through the
ages / Alan T. Levenson.
Description: Philadelphia : The Jewish
Publication Society, [2016] | Includes
bibliographical references and index.
Identifiers: LCCN 2016015314
ISBN 9780827612501 (cloth : alk. paper)
ISBN 9780827612938 (mobi)
ISBN 9780827612945 (pdf)
Subjects: LCSH: Joseph (Son of Jacob)
Classification: LCC BS580.J6 L485 2016
DDC 222/.11092—dc23 LC record available
at https://lccn.loc.gov/2016015314

Set in Iowan Old Style by Rachel Gould.

To Hilary and Ben

CONTENTS

ACKNOWLEDGMENTS

This book emerged from eighteen years of teaching Bible to the students at the Siegal College of Jewish Studies in Cleveland, Ohio. Most of these students were serious adult learners; some were educators seeking their master's degree; fewer were students from Israel or the former Soviet Union who had never finished their undergraduate degree for one good reason or another. In this context depth trumped coverage, and my classes usually covered one book of the Torah or a small unit such as the five holiday scrolls, the post-Exilic prophets, and so on. In the case of "Joseph" I must have been pleased enough to tell Marc Lee Raphael of the College of William and Mary. Marc, always encouraging, suggested that I organize my questions and observations in publishable form. The result was *The Story of Joseph: A Journey of Jewish Interpretation*, a one-hundred-page study guide, long out of print. I thank Marc for his initiative, and for thirty years of encouragement and good counsel.

I would have let "Little Jo" alone except that I began to notice the appearance of a slew of fine guides on how to read the Bible, biblical biographies, and biographies of biblical books in a series entitled Jewish Lives. So I proposed this project to Rabbi Barry Schwartz, director of the Jewish Publication Society, who thought the idea of showing Joseph not only as he appears in the primary text of Genesis 37–50, but also in subsequent traditions, would be a welcome addition to this literature. Rabbi Schwartz supplied me with a title and much good-humored encouragement along the way. I wish to thank Rabbi Schwartz and Carol Hupping, managing editor at JPS, who read this manuscript with great care and suggested many improvements.

I did not think the task of turning a readers' guide into an accessible book would be difficult, but I was wrong. Producing this work required considerable reading and rereading of sources. Above all I underestimated the difference between producing a stream of useful questions about a biblical text and offering a portrait of a biblical and postbiblical figure as complex as Joseph.

Fortunately this project also turned out to be a labor of love. In Cleveland former colleagues Roger Klein, Moshe Berger, and Lifsa Schachter set me straight on a number of issues. Karen Spector read the entire manuscript to insure accessibility— she has performed this service twice now for book projects of mine, and I am duly grateful. A summer class offered at Case Western Reserve / Siegal Lifelong Learning Institute in Cleveland reminded me how varied judgments, even contemporary Jewish judgments, of a biblical character can be. I thank Brian Amkraut, Alanna Cooper, and Sheryl Hirsch for their invitation, and my dear friend Sid Good for hosting me, as always, when I return to my home away from home.

The Schusterman Center for Judaic and Israel Studies, the Department of History, and the Religious Studies Program at the University of Oklahoma have provided an optimal environment for research and writing, something not to be taken for granted in an era when "academia" is a much-maligned profession. The College of Arts and Sciences and the Provost's Office at OU generously granted me a sabbatical to complete this project. Everyone at OU knows and appreciates the leadership of President David Boren; among many other events, we have shared our thoughts at several "Holiday Lights" ceremonies. In my eight years at OU I have received constant encouragement from two history chairs, Robert Griswold and Jamie Hart. Norman (Noam) Stillman, the founder of the program I now have the honor of directing, has supported this project from the outset. My colleague Dan Snell commented extensively on my concluding chapter, which deals with ancient Egypt. I spent enjoyable hours looking over illustrations of the Joseph narrative with Mariah Aschbacher. David Vishanoff in Religious Studies gave me some great sources on Joseph in Islam—my sincere apologies to Mariah and David that I did not use more of the material they gave me. I also want to thank Charles Kimball, director of the Religious Studies program at the University of Oklahoma, for his exceptional guidance of that program and his unfailingly collaborative manner.

The young, overwhelmingly Christian students at the University of Oklahoma could not be much more different than the adult Jewish students I taught in Cleveland, but many of them know their Bible, and most of them evidence considerable intellectual curiosity in seeking new ways to unlock its meaning. Special thanks are due to the students in my Hebrew Bible and Genesis through Jewish Eyes classes. Valarie Harshaw, the Schusterman Center's administrator, scanned more Joseph-related articles than she cares to remember, and I thank her for her time and effort.

This book represents a modern Jewish historian's second foray into Bible scholarship, and I would once again like to record my gratitude to scholars actually trained in the field. Fred Greenspahn, Lester Greenspoon, Scott Noegel, and S. David Sperling kindly answered questions to which I ought to have known the answer. Numerous reviews of *The Making of the Modern Jewish Bible* (2011) were exceptionally helpful in thinking about this book. In several emails after his H-Judaic review appeared, Professor Alan Cooper of the Jewish Theological Seminary was willing to patiently explain what I did and did not get right about modern Jewish Bible scholarship. An Association of Jewish Studies panel dedicated to this earlier book in December 2012 likewise provided valuable correctives and different perspectives from the ones I forwarded. I thank Professors Jon D. Levenson, Shuly Rubin Schwartz, and Susannah Heschel for their insights on that occasion. Fred Greenspahn alerted me to several recent sources of which I had been unaware and steered me away from some faulty understandings of the older scholarship. Intrepid Bible scholars including Zev Farber, Mark Leuchter, Lisa Wolfe, Rachel Havrelock, and Eva Mroczek generously shared their far more rigorous approaches to biblical material and biblical characters. Students and colleagues at Ludwig Maximilians Universität (Munich), Graduate Theological Center (Berkeley), Oklahoma City University, University of Tulsa, University of Texas, and Case Western University raised many excellent questions and gave me many suggestions for further inquiries. For the many shortcomings that remain after all this guidance, I have nobody to blame but myself.

Let me raise a dilemma common to academic acknowledgements: Is there any way to thank the scholars of the past to whom any reader of the Bible is most indebted? It is absurd (and pompous) to thank Rashi and his successors, yet the medieval commentators are obviously indispensable. The same must be said of course of the mainly anonymous authors of the midrashic collections that preceded the medieval commentators. Closer to our own times, with families and students who might conceivably read these pages, I note Nehama Leibowitz (1905–97), whose incomparable work revealed the dynamics of Jewish biblical interpretation (*parshanut ha-miqra*) and showed where small exegetical disagreements reveal major interpretative differences. The *Encyclopedia of Biblical Interpretation* by Menachem Mendel Kasher (1895–1983) culled many sources indispensable for those of us who are enthusiastic Bible readers, but not so well versed in Oral Torah. Louis Ginzberg (1873–1953) and Henrietta Szold (1860–1945) wove many sources into a running "rabbinic Bible" paralleling the original. That work,

Legends of the Jews, remains a model of elegance, erudition, and testimony to the exegetical imagination. Finally, perhaps surprisingly, I owe an enormous debt to Thomas Mann's four-volume *Joseph and His Brothers*. When I had trouble imagining a scene or a character, nobody came to my aid more reliably than Mann. I have many heroes among scholars still at work: it will be clear enough from the following pages who they are.

My wife, Hilary, and my son, Benjamin Ze'ev, will be used to this sentiment by now: I love you both.

February 2016 / Adar Rishon 5776

INTRODUCTION

I have a deep affection for the Joseph narrative. And so do many others, including Johann Wolfgang von Goethe, Thomas Mann, and Isaac Bashevis Singer, who praise Joseph as one of the greatest stories of all times. That is an extraordinary claim given that the biblical text of Joseph comprises just thirteen chapters (Genesis 37–50), making Joseph the most sustained narrative in Genesis, but still a very small work. The literary genius of Joseph will get much attention in the following pages, hopefully fostering an appreciation of the interpreters of Joseph from biblical times until today. But this book cannot be an exhaustive survey of Joseph traditions; that would require more learning and more patience than I possess—and many, many more pages.

A reader might expect an inquiry into the historical Joseph. I devote relatively meager space to this issue for the simple reason that little can be said about Joseph with certainty. This is a portrait, not a biography.[1] We are not dealing with a David or Solomon, both acknowledged by ancient texts, who left physical remains for archaeologists to argue about, or even a multilayered biblical account that can be read against itself, as historians read conflicting contemporaneous documents. The Bible's account of David and Solomon contains histories, counterhistories, a pious retelling in Chronicles, and an awareness of other sources, now lost, but once available for inspection.

The biblical account of Joseph contains none of these features. Recovering the historical Joseph turns out to be elusive, and frankly, not critical, although I will survey some of the biblical historians' best efforts at this in my last chapter. Whether Joseph was fact or fiction, he was certainly real for the writers of the Bible and for subsequent interpreters.

I lean heavily in this book on "traditional" Jewish authors whose views about the divine origins of Torah I do not share. What I do share seems to me more important: a sense that we stand before a text that becomes richer with continued reading. The rabbinic dictum "the Torah was written in the language of human meanings" and the suggestion to "turn it and turn it again, for everything is contained within in" have served me well as a teacher for decades, and my students, both pious and skeptical, seem to be as untroubled as I am by this apparent contradiction in enthusiastically using commentators with very different views of Torah and its nature. The most famous rabbinic guides (Rashi, Rashbam, Abraham ibn Ezra, Nachmanides) may be found within these pages. Alongside them the reader will find a number of modern scholars of various backgrounds and religious orientations. Some scholars find the methods of traditional readers and contemporary historical-critical ones fundamentally incompatible.[2] I usually find them complementary, answering different kinds of questions, with both camps bringing out aspects of the text not evident on first glance. This triangulation, or blending, of the Bible itself, the traditional commentators, and modern scholarship found throughout this book is intentional and represents a straightforward application of my teaching method to the printed page.[3]

The Bible has been accepted by millions as literal truth for centuries, so I strive to be clear about what is actually written in the Bible and what comes later. Theologically, for many readers, the Bible rests on a higher plateau than its commentaries, and I try to honor that sensibility. But I clearly do *not* want the Bible, including Joseph, to stand on its own, as some Protestant Reformers desired. The divide between the Bible and its commentators and the divide between Jewish and Christian approaches to Scripture are interrelated. Of the many axioms of Jewish interpretation, the fundamental dichotomy between Written Torah and Oral Torah is paramount. Put simply, rabbinic Judaism did not believe that the revelation God gave Moses at Mount Sinai exhausted the message of Scripture, which was to be discovered anew by every generation of interpreters.[4] By contrast, for traditional Christians the single most important key to unlocking the meaning of the Old Testament was the New Testament.[5] These dichotomies, with all they imply, made traditional Jewish and Christian exegesis different, despite a shared veneration of the Scripture.[6] Although the isolation of Jews from non-Jews has often been exaggerated, it remains true that midrash, Talmud, and the medieval rabbis worked mainly in Jewish languages, drew mainly from Jewish sources, and proceeded mainly via Jewish exegetical practices.[7]

My incorporation of post-Enlightenment, modern readers of all religious backgrounds requires, therefore, a word of explanation. Today's mainstream Bible scholars agree that disciplinary demands regarding evidence, awareness of one's own religious beliefs, and the contested nature of texts and translations ought to guide one's scholarly views. A person's religious convictions, or lack of same, ought to be bracketed out when engaging in modern scholarship. My inclusion of non-Jewish modern commentators derives from the premise that modern Bible scholarship, where conducted by Jews, however observant, conforms to the standards of the profession. Whether or not Jewish Bible scholarship retains distinct tendencies, and I have argued elsewhere that it does, academic conversations about the Bible can no longer be denominationally defined.[8] The portrait of Joseph found in these pages may be *a* Jewish portrait, but it cannot be *the* Jewish portrait, nor even an exclusively *Jewish* portrait, and so I have consciously tried not to take sides between traditional and modern approaches.

I believe that Joseph can be read on many levels. I reject Spinoza's view that the Bible applies to only one place, one time, and one people, and that biblical obscurities reflect error rather than depth.[9] As a personal drama, Joseph's rise from slavery to majesty offers an ancient spin on the universal rags-to-riches theme. Joseph's character develops from abrasive youth to wise old age, but he remains a cryptic figure, no doubt rooted in his difficult upbringing. As a family drama, the abuse of a brother and his sale into slavery, his long separation, and his ultimate reconciliation with his brothers cannot be surpassed. The reunion of father and son in Gen. 46:29–30 and Jacob's pained recollection of the departed Rachel in Gen. 48:7 count among the most touching moments in Scripture. For the talmudic-era sages and modern scholars alike, the rending and repairing of the family occupies the heart of this narrative.

A rabbi friend of mine asked why I did not simply excise the "Egyptian" material that some modern readers find less interesting? But I think ignoring the Egyptian part of the Joseph story, the national part, would be a mistake. To begin with we must acknowledge that the transition between Genesis and Exodus could have been accomplished in a few verses. Instead we have Joseph starring in a captivating chain of events bringing Israel down to Egypt and paving the way for a family drama to become a national drama. This transition constitutes another layer of this tale. As we will see, the biblical narrator draws the details of settlement, tribal fates, and burial of the last Patriarch (Jacob-Israel) with great care. Joseph's physical remains, mentioned three times, became a major theme for later writers. Finally, as a theological meditation, Joseph seems as if written for today. Unlike in earlier Genesis narratives, as Jack Miles writes, "in the story of Joseph . . . the Lord God is neither active nor articulate."[10] Yet the absence of divine miracles and utterances, as well as the emphasis on human agency, contrasts with the gradually unfolding sense of the characters and the readers alike that God somehow controls the tale's outcome. In brief, Joseph is accessible, intriguing, and thought provoking. Ironically the relative paucity of legal material in Joseph, as in most of Genesis, only contributes to the accessibility of Joseph to a general audience.[11]

Roads Not Taken: Historical and Source Criticism

What did the biblical authors know and when did they know it? William Dever's clever title raises questions many have asked about the Joseph narrative.[12] Some scholars have argued that Joseph tells the story of the Hyksos conquest of Egypt, regarded as a national scandal by the Egyptians—from an Israelite point of view.[13] That the rise to prominence of an "Asiatic" such as Joseph took its inspiration from a period in ancient Egypt when foreigners ruled cannot be discounted; that Asiatics served Egyptian households is solidly documented. But all historians believe that the Joseph story comes from a later time than Egypt's Second Intermediate period. The erstwhile confidence that Genesis reflected traditions of the mid-second millennium BCE has evaporated. Even if there were an Abraham, Isaac, and Jacob, the narratives about them were written at a later date and reflect later concerns. Other scholars date Joseph from the United Monarchy (eleventh to tenth centuries BCE).[14] Still others, focusing on the prominence of Judah, believe the period after the Assyrian exile (722–721 BCE) offers the most natural setting.[15] Egyptologist Donald Redford concludes that the Joseph tale comes from a much later period.[16] Redford's position has been judged extreme, but so has the conception that these events were related to Moses at Sinai about a figure that lived four hundred years earlier. Settling this matter has not proven critical for Jewish exegetes, who have paid more heed to the meaning of the past than to its historicity.[17]

Who wrote the Joseph story? Historicity did not drive rabbinic inquiries into the text—neither did questions regarding authorship. Tradition assumed that Moses wrote the Torah at God's behest, but this presupposition rarely cramped rabbinic exegetical style. The early rabbis freely noted variations of style, word choice, authorial voice, and even language. In the modern world academics took these observations and concluded that the Bible was authored by a variety of hands over the course of several centuries. Source-critical Bible scholarship—sometimes known as the Documentary Hypothesis—posits four basic sources (called J, E, P, and D) at work in the Pentateuch. "D," for "Deuteronomist," appears mainly in the book that bears its name and in the histories that follow (Joshua–2 Kings). Source critics maintain that the other three sources (J=Jahvist, E=Elohist great mid-twentieth century, and P=Priestly) may all be found in Genesis 37–50. Regarding Joseph, a practitioner of source criticism wrote, "An achievement of such literary excellence should be, one would naturally expect, the work of a single author. *Yet, such is definitely not the case.* While P's part in the story of Joseph is secondary and marginal, J and E are prominently represented throughout, each in his own distinctive way."[18]

The consensus holds that Joseph reflects Northern traditions, and may even intend to counterbalance the Southern, Judean emphasis of the Jacob cycle. Richard Elliott Friedman's bestselling *Who Wrote the Bible?*, a thorough application of the source-critical method, devotes only a few pages to the Joseph story. Within these pages, however, Friedman attributes: the conflicting traditions concerning Schechem, the God-names invoked in the naming of Jacob's children, the promotion of Ephraim over Manasseh, and the exculpatory roles given to Reuben and Judah to the conflict between the Southern, pro-Judah "J" source and the Northern-Ephaimite, pro-Joseph, "E" source. Of course source criticism constitutes merely one method of biblical criticism, especially well-designed to identifying textual components.[19] With respect to the Joseph cycle, I agree with those scholars who find the source-critical approach must be combined with other modern approaches that yield a more prismatic reading of scenes and characters.[20]

Modern scholars point to the reluctance of the master editor

of the Torah, called "Redactor," abbreviated as "R," to abandon well-preserved traditions. The Redactor, perhaps Ezra the
Babylonian, fifth century BCE, had a well-wrought story in
Joseph and found a suitable place for it. Two important Northern tribes (Ephraim and Manasseh) passed down the Joseph
tale, and the editor of the Bible hated to chop a venerable tale
in the "final cut." The fall of the Ten Tribes, formerly led by
the Ephraimites, enabled Judahite revisions of the narrative
that highlighted Judah's role (JE). Later still, whether before
or after the exile, the Priestly author(s) added those infamous
genealogical notices (Gen. 46:8–27) as well as other asides
that often baffle contemporary readers. In academic perspective, then, the reasons for the preservation and prominence of
Joseph are essentially political.[21] In traditional Jewish perspective, in contrast with contemporary scholarship, the final form
of the Bible, the Torah especially, was simply a given, which
provided the starting point for commentaries determined to
wrest every nugget of moral and religious instruction from the
text. The scholarly goal of the rabbis was not to get behind
the text, but rather to get into it. And there can be no arguing with the fact that the Bible we have—rather than its component pieces—exerted its extraordinary influence through
the ages. On the integrity of the text, I champion a utilitar-
ian approach. Rather than try to exclude as later accretions
the story of Tamar and Judah in Genesis 38, the Mrs. Potiphar
episode in Genesis 39, the theophany to Jacob in Genesis 46,
or Jacob's address in Genesis 49, it makes more sense (to me)
to see how the text we have had for over two millennia fits
together. One particular objection to this approach ought to
be acknowledged: namely, that by avoiding questions about
authorial development of the Joseph text in favor of focusing
on the received text, I am trying to insinuate some kind of
crypto claim about revelation.[22] I am not. I accept the author(s)
of Joseph as human but do not think the particular process of
authorship should determine my reading.

The question of the genre of the Joseph text has been raised by some as an argument against using a literary approach—we do not know the genre, so how can we assess the Bible's literary nature? Is Joseph an oral saga? A fairy tale? A novella? The question of genre has proven to be a matter of scholarly debate; the question begs comparison of Joseph with other texts, ancient and modern.[23] A quick glance at some Egyptian literature indicates the presence of parallels.[24] The story of Potiphar's wife (Genesis 39) has a resemblance to "The Tale of Two Brothers," a thirteenth-century BCE Egyptian text that involves a younger brother falsely accused of rape by the elder brother's lascivious wife. The scenes in Pharaoh's court and the details of Joseph's agrarian policies abound with details of Egyptian life. In "The Tradition of Seven Lean Years," a text of uncertain antiquity, a famine is resolved when Pharaoh receives guidance from the god Khnum in a dream. This recalls the role of Joseph as dream interpreter in Genesis 41. "The Instructions of Amenhotep," "The Teaching of King Merikare," and "The Maxims of Ptahhotep" offer examples of Egyptian "Instructional" or Wisdom Literature, akin to Proverbs, which some modern scholars, beginning with Gerhard von Rad, consider the best description of Joseph's genre.[25] As with questions of historicity and authorship, lack of agreement about literary genre has not hampered subsequent readers.

Joseph beyond Genesis

Joseph fades from the Bible after Genesis. Despite two passages relating to the disposal of Joseph's earthly remains in Exod. 13:19 and Josh. 24:32, and brief mentions in Psalms, Samuel, and Chronicles, Joseph is reduced mainly to his role as progenitor of the "House of Joseph," that is, the important northern tribes of Ephraim and Manasseh. The prophets ignore Joseph as an individual, though Ezekiel movingly invokes the competition and reconciliation of Joseph and Judah. Even Psalm 105 seems odd in focusing on Joseph's rulership rather than on his relationships:

He [God] called down famine on the land
And cut short their daily bread.
But he had sent on a man before, them
Joseph who was sold into slavery;
He was kept a prisoner with fetters on his feet
And an iron collar clamped on his neck.
He was tested by the Lord's command
Until what he foretold came true.
Then the king sent him and set him free,
The ruler of nations released him;
He made him master of his household
And ruler over all his possessions,
To correct his officers at will
And teach his counselors wisdom. (Ps. 105:16–22)[26]

Yet Joseph's "comeback" in two late biblical books and in early postbiblical literature suggests that he was never a forgotten character in ancient Israel. So does a text in Matt. 2:13–15, by an anonymous but Jewishly learned author who bestows the name Joseph on the New Testament's most consequential dreamer.[27] The overall themes of diasporic dangers, achieving success in the courts of foreign kings, and overcoming false accusations invite comparison between the Joseph narratives and the biblical Daniel and Esther. Joseph interprets dreams that baffle the gentiles; Esther and Daniel make a didactic point out of preserving their Jewish loyalties. The story of Joseph profoundly shaped these books,[28] and in chapter 5, "Joseph from Rags to Riches," I turn to the allusions to Joseph in both Daniel and Esther at greater length.

Judging Joseph: The Hellenistic World

Commentary on Joseph began in the Bible itself, and changing circumstances gave rise to a renewed interest in Joseph. By the period of early Rabbinic Judaism and early Christianity, most Jews lived in the diaspora and under gentile rule—the groundwork for Joseph's comeback had been laid. Four works in particular testify to the potential of the Joseph story to engage readers in this era.[29] *Jubilees*, an artful retelling of Genesis, and a best seller among the Dead Sea sectarians, probably dates back to the second century BCE. *Jubilees* portrays Joseph as an innocent victim of his brothers' envy and later on as a just ruler of the Egyptians. *Testaments of the Twelve Patriarchs*, also originating in the late second century BCE, expatiates on Joseph's virtuous refusal of Potiphar's wife, Benjamin's virtue, the malice of the sons of the handmaids, and more. For this author or authors, Joseph stands as a major figure in Jewish antiquity. The *Testaments* of both Simeon and Zebulon tellingly use the death of Joseph, who died before his older brothers, as their supposed points of reference. *Joseph and Asenath*, a Greek romance, was probably written in Egypt around first to second centuries CE. It may or may not be a Jewish missionary tract. The dramatic rejection by Asenath of the gods of Egypt preceding her marriage to Joseph and her affirmation of the God of Israel serves as the tale's theological core.

In the second half of the first century CE, the historian Flavius Josephus portrayed his biblical namesake as the very model of Greco-Roman virtue. Since Josephus essentially retold the Bible in his *Antiquities*, his additions to and evasions from Scripture are particularly interesting. Even the Dead Sea Scrolls, whose profoundly unworldly and parochial perspective might have led to neglect of the worldly and cosmopolitan Joseph, make him a prominent character. Classicist Erich Gruen has identified a common thread in these retellings of Joseph in the Hellenistic and Roman eras: enormous pride in Jewish attainments and values.[30]

Judging Joseph: The Rabbis

Rabbinic explorations of Joseph's character will occupy our attention throughout this book. In midrash and Talmud the story of Joseph was seen as every bit as worthy of discussion as other parts of the now fully canonized Torah.[31] Considering that Judaism does not count him among the three Patriarchs,[32] it is striking that Abraham, Isaac, and Jacob together receive twenty-three chapters in all, while Joseph is the focus of nearly thirteen. The Soncino translation of Midrash Rabbah on Genesis 37–50 runs 233 pages! Early on Joseph wins the accolade "tzadik," a righteous man. The justification for this verdict is primarily his sexual restraint with Potiphar's wife. But tzadik does not mean perfect. Like most biblical figures, Joseph comes in for some sharp criticism. Midrash Rabbah on Genesis, usually dated to the fourth century CE, bristles with criticism of Joseph as well as lauding him with praise—this seems to me a striking difference from the Hellenistic sources and the Church Fathers. The Church Fathers construed Joseph as a prefiguration for Jesus, and as a flawless model of Christian life, overlooking the darker sides of Joseph's character.[33]

Medieval Jewish commentary is so outstanding an achievement that it is often taken for Jewish commentary in general. No one has exerted as much influence on Jewish understandings of the Bible as Rashi (Rabbi Shlomo Yitzhak, 1040–1105).[34] He was a pedagogue and anthologizer of genius who developed the interlinear Torah commentary, and selectively deployed midrashic collections. His clear explanations of the Bible's meanings dominated elementary Jewish education for centuries. Rashi's successors in Bible commentary often take him as their starting point, including his own grandson, Rashbam (Rabbi Samuel ben Meir, 1080–1160). Rashbam championed *peshat*, the plain-sense reading of the verse, understood in context and in accordance with grammatical rules.[35] A contemporary of Rashbam's, Abraham ibn Ezra (1089–1164), was born in Toledo but wandered to Rome and then to England. Ibn Ezra combined the intellectual traditions of the Jews in the Islamic world, who employed the linguistic similarities of Arabic and Hebrew to good effect, with advances made in Europe.[36] For many Nachmanides (Moshe ben Nachman, 1194–1270) represents the acme of medieval Jewish Bible commentary. He takes issue with his predecessors ("loving correction" toward Rashi, "open rebuke and hidden love" toward ibn Ezra) and combines a philosophical acumen rivalling Maimonides' with mystical insights drawn from developments in Kabbalah.[37] A final, obvious observation seems in order. Just as midrash did not end, but morphed into collections of midrashim, mystical texts, liturgical guides, and more, so too Bible commentary became a self-generating enterprise connecting the medieval tradition to today's commentators.

Judging Joseph: Modern Bible Scholarship

Since this book is not very interested in uncovering the historical background, or in determining the narrative sources components, two arenas in which modern scholarship excels, the reader may ask: what can the toolkit of contemporary scholarship contribute to postbiblical and medieval readings? My short answer sounds like a Zen koan. We are modern people and need modern readings to relate to the text. To take one example, Maurice Samuel, a superb belletrist, impugns Joseph's dealings with his brothers in Genesis 42–45 to a degree that even the most critical premodern rabbi would find uncomfortable. To call Joseph the Righteous a sadist, as Samuel does, goes beyond medieval bounds.[38] Literary scholars such as Robert Alter, Meir Sternberg, and Ilana Pardes offer extended readings of stories and characters in a format quite different from the interlinear style of midrash or Rashi. Biblical historians such as Nahum Sarna and Gary Rendsburg explain Joseph in light of ancient Near Eastern evidence as well as comparative methods, and with the understanding that the Bible did not speak to its readers as a history book does. Other modern readers that we will meet in the chapters that follow bring other insights from the worlds of psychology, feminist analysis, and political science.

Joseph is complicated figure, drawn with the Bible's celebrated mix of exposition and silence. For those people content to simply parrot biblical verses or reduce biblical figures to stereotypes, I do not think this book will be attractive. For readers willing to entertain the idea that the character of Joseph has deepened and grown over the centuries, and continues to do so, I hope that this work will serve as an enjoyable guide. You likely have your own ideas about Joseph already; by the end of this book you will have more, and will meet commentators along the way that you find congenial—or uncongenial.

Although this book follows the Joseph story from beginning to end, it highlights particular aspects of Genesis 37–50. Chapter 2 deals with Joseph as dreamer, chapter 5 with Joseph's ascent, chapter 7 with Joseph and Judah's jockeying for position. I examine "minor" incidents and characters (e.g., chapter 3 on Tamar, chapter 4 on Mrs. Potiphar, chapter 8 on Jacob's mention of Rachel in Gen. 48:7). Chapters 9–11 treat the underappreciated denouement of the Joseph story and the transition to Exodus.

But we begin in chapter 1 with Genesis 37, the opening of the Joseph narrative and the beginning of the weekly Torah portion, Va-yeshev. My favorite dictum on the relationship between the Bible and its commentaries comes from the novelist Thomas Mann. His words may be taken as tongue-in-cheek, as serious, or as both:

> Since when, however, one might ask, does a commentary compete with its text? And then: is not a discussion of the "how" as worthy and important in life as the transmission of the "that"? Yes, is not life first truly fulfilled in the "how"? It should be remembered that before a story can even be told it must first tell itself, and indeed tell it in the kind of detail of which life alone is the master, detail that lies beyond any narrator's hope or prospects of attaining it. He is able only to approximate such detail by serving the "how" of life more faithfully than the lapidary spirit of the "that" has deigned to do.[39]

1

Joseph

Favored Son, Hated Brother

The conception, birth, and naming of Joseph signals the arrival of a special character. Rachel is described in scripture as an *"akarah,"* properly translated as "barren woman," but more whimsically rendered as "a woman who eventually gives birth to a terrific baby boy." Sarah and Rebecca bore this appellation, and so will many female heroes later in the Bible, including Hannah and Samson's unnamed mother.[1] In this case Rachel suffers years of conflict with her sister and co-wife, Leah; fruitlessly seeks Jacob's intercession through prayer as his father, Isaac, did for Rebecca; and even attempts primitive fertility treatments in the form of mandrake plants (*dudaim*) purchased from Leah in exchange for Jacob's company at night. Do any of these means employed by Rachel work? No, they do not.[2] Dan and Naphtali, Rachel's two children through Bilhah her handmaid, do not seem to assuage her bitter feelings. After a last burst of child bearing by the fecund Leah, the biblical text turns, matter-of-factly, to what *does* work:

> Now God remembered Rachel; God heeded her and opened her womb. She conceived and bore a son, and said, "God has taken away [*asaf*] my disgrace." So she named him Joseph [*yosef*], which is to say, "May the Lord add [*yosef*] another son for me." (Gen. 30:22–24)

Rachel produces a boy and, as it were, double-names him.

Her first name addresses the removal of shame entailed by producing a male heir; her second name is a request for another son. Unlike name changes, double-naming at birth in the Bible is rare and in this case is fraught with destiny.[3] The Hebrew verbs *asaf/yosef*, if connected to the newborn child, may be imaginatively rendered as "one who is taken away, and added back with increase," not a bad summary of Joseph's life story. As usual for biblical naming speeches, the text says much about the namer as well as the named. Here, at the birth of her firstborn, Rachel expresses the demanding nature that makes her such a suitable spouse for the similarly characterized Jacob.[4] Rachel's prayer for a second son will be fulfilled with the birth of Benjamin, but it will cost Rachel her life. (We will turn to the death and burial of Rachel much later in this book.) Although she is mentioned in the Joseph story proper for one verse only (Gen. 48:7), it is a most poignant one. Her presence, moreover, hovers over the Joseph narrative as the departed mother of two favored sons and as the absent maternal figure that might have guided Joseph in his formative years.

The birth of Benjamin involves an at-birth renaming. Aware that she is dying, Rachel calls the child Ben-oni (child of my suffering), but Jacob immediately renames him Benjamin, "son of the South" or "son of my right hand." This name suggests strength, as does Jacob's valedictory in Genesis 49 and so do the tales of Benjamin's progeny later in the Bible. But Genesis 37–50 presents Benjamin merely as a cipher for Joseph. Benjamin gets no spoken lines; this biblical technique often highlights that the figure is an object acted on rather than an acting subject.[5] Benjamin's subsequent status as Jacob's favored son, the youngest son, Rachel's son, makes him a perfect surrogate for Joseph.[6] This device allows the biblical narrator to test the brothers' spiritual growth and fraternity on the one hand; the limits of Joseph's forgiveness and fraternal feelings on the other hand. Not only is Benjamin silent in Genesis 37–50; we are never told how Benjamin feels about his situation at home in Canaan or before the vizier Joseph in Egypt. The eighteenth-century painting by Girodet de Roucy-Trioson in which Benjamin recognizes Joseph is a wonderful imaginative leap that underscores the connection of the full brothers.[7]

Commentators through the ages found much to say about Genesis 37, a magnificent model for anyone interested in how to start a story. The first verse contains an element of tension between permanence and impermanence, between tranquility and disturbance. "Now Jacob was *settled* in the land where his father had *sojourned*, the land of Canaan." Settling and sojourning (or "wanderings," as *gorei* might be rendered) could be understood as synonyms, but the language here suggests a difference nuance. The rabbis questioned whether Jacob really thought he was entitled to more peace than the peaceful Isaac.[8] As one midrash muses, "When the righteous seek to dwell in peace in this world, Satan comes and opposes them, saying, 'It is not enough for them that so much is prepared in the coming age, they want to live in peace in this world!'"[9] Foreshadowing and reversals stud this chapter from stem to stern: Jacob will not find peace in Canaan; he will not even end his days in Canaan. Joseph will enjoy most-favored-son status from the onset, will end this chapter in a pit (*bor*), and will then return to his destined state.

Talking About My Generations

Commentators have lavished even more attention on the second verse than the first. Gen. 37:2 reads, "This, then, is the line of [*v'eleh toldot*] Jacob: At seventeen years of age Joseph tended the flocks with his brothers, as a helper to the sons of Bilhah and Zilpah." The New Jewish Publication Society translation (NJPS) is wonderful: it is used throughout this book. But every translation (and translator) makes choices. In this case NJPS separates the names "Jacob" and "Joseph" by five words, where the original has them in succession, and introduces a paragraph break after "This, then, is the line of Jacob."[10] This successful attempt at clarity on the part of the translators obscures a clear problem for the reader of the Hebrew original (*v'eleh toldot Yakov Yosef*).[11] The opening constitutes a well-established genealogical formula, "so and so begat so and so," which appears nine other times in Genesis. What ordinarily follows is a listing of the sons in age order. In other words the verse ought to read, "This, then, is the line of Jacob: *Reuben*." Why does the Bible fail to render the genealogical list and then turn to Joseph's story? This anomaly demands explanation.

One midrash contends that since Jacob's family was saved only as a result of Joseph's being in Egypt, the fates of Jacob and Joseph were inextricably linked.[12] By this logic placing their names consecutively makes narrative sense. Another midrash suggests that the uncanny similarities between the lives of Jacob and Joseph justified the variation from the formula. Here are some of the obvious parallels: Jacob and Joseph were both children of mothers who suffered infertility and difficult pregnancies (Rebecca and Rachel, respectively). They were both threatened by their brothers. They were both exiles. They both experienced alienation from their families and then reunited with them. They both had offspring in a foreign land. Other similarities between father and son enumerated by this midrash have fewer bases in the text, including my students' perennial favorite—that Jacob and Joseph were both born circumcised. The rabbis recoiled from the idea that the patriarchs might have been uncircumcised, yet, unlike with Abraham and Isaac, there is no biblical narration of their circumcisions. Even excluding more far-fetched midrashim, the likening of the fates of Jacob and Joseph has much to commend it.[13]

Much later both Jacob and Joseph announce in the same words, "I am about to die." Although "gather" is a mundane word, it is also the root of Joseph's name, and it is used twice in the Jacob's deathbed scene. Life and death seem also at play in Gen. 45:26, when Jacob's sons tell him that "Joseph is yet alive," preceding the announcement that "the spirit of their father Jacob revived" (Gen. 45:27) and Jacob's declaration that "Joseph my son is yet alive" (Gen. 45:28). Although Judah uses the phrase *"nafsho k'shurah nafsho"* (his soul is bound up with his soul; Gen. 44:30) to connect Jacob with Benjamin, who is called the son of his old age, Benjamin is often a stand-in for Joseph, and this seems to be the case here. Jacob's soul (*nefesh*: life breath) is bound up with Joseph's too.

But one may ask if all that "likening" is a sufficiently technical answer to our question: why the variation of the genealogical formula? Rashi endorses the midrashic solution linking and likening the fates of Jacob and Joseph but reads *v'eleh toldot* less literally than "generations" or "line." Instead Rashi reads this phrase as "this is the story" or "this is the history," another common use of the word *toldot* in the Bible. It is worth noting here that much rabbinic literature did not have the burden of translating the text—the rabbis assumed the superiority of the Hebrew text over any versions or languages and commented in Hebrew as well.[14] Famously Rashbam rejected his grandfather's solution to the problem contained in this verse (Gen. 37:1). Rashbam considered *v'eleh toldot* a formula indeed, only one completed in the genealogies of Gen. 46:8–27 and Genesis 49. More globally Rashbam considered the entire Joseph cycle anticipatory background, allowing Moses to declare, "Your ancestors went down to Egypt seventy persons in all" (Deut. 10:22).[15] Rashbam's position may strike readers here as forced, but it expresses Rashbam's principled support of *peshat*, a mode of reading Bible that struck twelfth-century practitioners as being more precise than the age-old mode of midrash.[16]

The Elder Shall Serve the Younger

If, however, we follow the midrash and Rashi in their likening of Jacob and Joseph in Gen. 37:2, we have a link to the most prominent topic of this opening chapter: the brothers' hatred toward Joseph, enumerated briskly, almost clinically, by the Bible:

v. 2 Joseph is a tattletale: "And Joseph brought bad reports of them to their father."

v. 3 Joseph is Jacob's declared, open favorite: "Now Israel loved Joseph best of all his sons, for he was the child of his old age."

v. 3b Joseph gets a visible symbol of that favoritism: "and he made him an ornamented tunic." Whether one translates *ketonet passim* as "technicolor dream coat" à la Andrew Lloyd Webber, or as "ornamented tunic" in the more sober NJPS rendering, this article of clothing offers a physical prompt to hatred.

vv. 5–11 Joseph relates two sets of self-aggrandizing dreams that a prudent teenager, possibly an oxymoron, ought to keep to himself.

These dreams get much more textual space than the other reasons for the brothers' hatred, and so it is no surprise that when Joseph finds his brothers at Dothan they exclaim, a little more aggressively than the NJPS translation has it: "Here comes that dreamer!" In the original one can practically hear the brothers choking on their resentment:

> "Hinei ba'al ha-halamot ha-lazeh—bah"

Dreams play such a prominent role in the Joseph narrative that chapter 2 of this volume is devoted to them. For the purposes of unfolding Genesis 37, the reader observes that the dreams serve as the proverbial final straw, cementing the hatred narrated in the opening verses. Additionally the dreams establish Joseph not only as the object of his father's favoritism but as a person of exceptional ability. The young man's self-confidence can be detected in Joseph's first spoken words, "Hear this dream which I have dreamed."

The dreams are central. Yet each of these causes gets weighed in the rabbinic balance. What, for instance, was the nature

of the "bad reports"? Were these reports about all the brothers, or exclusively about the sons of the midwives? Midrash
imagined a variety of misdeeds, including the eating of limbs
from living animals, a dietary practice banned since the time
of Noah. Joseph's "shepherding" of the brothers has been read
ironically. But other commentators wonder whether or not the
brothers actually did anything wrong at all. Nearly everyone in
this story practices deception: Jacob, Joseph, the brothers, Mrs.
Potiphar, and Tamar.[17] Joseph bears derogatory tales, but the
text does not tell us what they are or whether they are true.

What does the description "son of his old age" (ben zekunim)
signify? Joseph is not the youngest son; Benjamin had been
born two chapters ago. As James Kugel comments, "If anything,
Benjamin should have been loved more than any of the older
brothers."[18] Rashi, playing on an Aramaic homonym, imagined that father and son looked alike. Just as likely, should one
travel down this route, is that Joseph looks like his mother,
Rachel, since their physical attractiveness is described in similar language.[19] Perhaps Jacob's favoritism stems partly from
this visible reminder of his beloved wife. The preceding verse
describes Joseph as both a youth (na'ar) and also as seventeen
years old. Kugel points to a tradition that these ancient interpreters equated "old age" and "wisdom," thus "son of his old
age" was understood as a comment on Joseph's wisdom, arguably quite limited in Genesis 37, but certainly evident in the
remainder of the story. Whatever "son of his old age" means,
it is given as the reason that "Now Israel loved Joseph best of
all his sons." This narrative declaration should not be skipped:
since we see signs of this favoritism right and left, this verse
seems an affirmation of what might be deduced anyway. But
the verse highlights the public nature of Jacob's feelings, in
turn a further cause of jealousy.

The "ornamented tunic," magnificently imagined by Thomas
Mann to be Rachel's tunic, is a visible reminder to the brothers of Joseph's status. Items of clothing often play an impor-

7

tant role in biblical stories.[20] The narrator further implies that Joseph handled this item of clothing indiscreetly, for it is clear that he appeared in Dothan before his brothers wearing that *ketonet passim* (Gen. 37:23), and that the brothers used this bloodied coat in Gen. 37:31–33 to deceive Jacob about Joseph's fate.[21] Once again Mann seems spot-on when he imagines the brethren shredding the coat in anger. Many commentators stress the poetic justice of Jacob being fooled by a garment as he fooled his own father, Isaac, into giving him the blessing intended for Esau's many years earlier. I would add that the brethren display passive-aggressive behavior here by asking Jacob to examine with his own eyes this garment, just as he had allowed Joseph to wear this sign of favoritism in plain sight of his brothers (Gen. 37:23). What *ketonet passim* actually means is open to doubt. The term appears again only in 2 Samuel 13, at the rape of Tamar by her half brother Amnon. In that chapter the *ketonet passim* signifies a costly or royal garment, and this is the meaning ascribed to the cloak by Speiser.[22] The text emphasizes sight and sound: directly after receiving the *ketonet passim*, the brothers *see* that Joseph is Jacob's favorite, and as a consequence, the text tells us, the brothers could not *speak* a peaceful word to him.

How Do I Hate Thee? Let Me Count the Ways

These causes for sibling hatred in Genesis 37 seem more than adequate. But as the great German Jewish literary scholar Erich Auerbach (1892–1957) noted, the Bible is "fraught with background."[23] How true this is in the case of Joseph! Long before Genesis 37 the brothers already have ample reason to despise Jacob's favorite. Readers who rush to censor the violence perpetrated on Joseph by his elder brothers, without question a terrible deed, should recall the suffering of Leah as the unloved wife and consider what effect this had on her *and her sons*, for Jacob's partiality toward Joseph stretches back before his birth, to his preference for Rachel over Leah, made explicit in the

Bible (Gen. 29:18, 29:30).[24] Evidence for this paternal favoritism continues when the birth of Joseph prompts Jacob to return to his homeland, although the Hebrew (*ka'asher*),[25] translated in NJPS as "after," leaves the degree of causality uncertain:

Va'yehi ka'asher yalda rachel yosef, . . .

After Rachel had Joseph, Jacob spoke to Laban. He said, "Send me on my way. I want to go back to my own home and country." (Gen. 30:25)

Consider this: imagine being one of the older siblings, suddenly asked to leave grandparents, familiar friends, school systems, and sports teams because of the arrival of the twelfth named child (eleven boys plus Dinah). Scholars who isolate the Joseph story as a completely independent unit from the rest of Genesis have much to learn from the rabbis who kept the biblical context constantly in mind. Jacob's early favoritism toward Joseph is displayed most egregiously when Jacob prepares to meet Esau. Fearing the worst, Jacob arrays his camp such that the most precious members (Rachel and Joseph) are placed in safest place. "And there was Esau, coming with his 400 men! So Jacob separated the children. He put them with Leah, Rachel and the two female servants. He put the servants and their children in front. He put Leah and her children next. And he put Rachel and Joseph last" (Gen. 33:1–3, 33:6).[26] These details in the story of Jacob and his wives, which precede the Joseph story, add considerable depth to two key themes in the Joseph story—Jacob's favoritism and the brothers' hatred. As *The Jewish Study Bible* puts it, "Joseph is caught between his doting father and his envious siblings."[27]

One must consider the sibling competition for privileged status, which also began before Genesis 37. The natural candidate is Reuben, the firstborn (*bekhor*), who according to Deut. 21:15–17 ought to receive a double portion as his birthright. But those familiar with the Bible recognize that this law will be

9

overturned again and again by God, and that primogeniture may not be the norm in ancient Israel.[28] Cain, after all, is Abel's older brother and takes the initiative to bring an offering, yet God accepts Abel's sacrifice instead. This sets a pattern that recurs with Ishmael and Isaac, and Esau and Jacob, as well as in the lesser-known cases of Manasseh and Ephraim, and Zerah and Peretz. Only in the first of these examples, Cain and Abel, does God intervene tangibly at the moment of supplanting, yet the reader emerges in each case with the sense that the result accords with God's wishes. The oldest son's status as *bekhor* turns out to be less than meets the eye—neither being the oldest nor being the youngest guarantees success in the Bible. But if God ultimately disposes, human agency plays a role in the disposition. Reuben contributes to his own displacement by sleeping with Jacob and Rachel's handmaid Bilhah (Gen. 35:22). 1 Chron. 5:1–2 recalls Reuben's scandalous act many centuries later as a reason for his demotion: "The sons of Reuben the first-born of Israel (He was the first-born; but when he defiled his father's bed, his birthright was given to the sons of Joseph son of Israel, so that he is not reckoned as first-born in the genealogy; though Judah became more powerful than his brothers and a leader came from him, yet the birthright belonged to Joseph.)"

Ironically two biblical texts referring explicitly to the competition between Joseph and Judah highlight their ultimate collaboration. 1 Chron. 5:1–2 insists that the birthright still belongs to Joseph, despite Judah's ultimate political triumph as leader of the nation, which Ezekiel 37 emphasizes. Reuben's moral failure (Gen. 35:22), recalled pointedly in Genesis 49 by Jacob, is followed by the reprimand to Simeon and Levi for their brutal slaughter of the town of Shechem in revenge for the rape of Dinah. (Dinah, though clearly the victim by modern standards, seems less the object of her brothers' sympathy than of their wounded pride.) Simeon and Levi get the last words in Genesis 34, but Jacob clearly disapproves of their actions, indicting their political judgment as risking the destruction of his entire family.[29] Since family rivalry has been a theme throughout Genesis, including the sororal competition between Leah and Rachel, we should not be surprised to find it in the next generation too. Thus the three oldest sons of Leah, jockeying for position, all show themselves unfit for responsible leadership, clearing the way for the fourth, Judah. But Judah is not the only dark horse. Yair Zakovitch notes that Joseph begins the story in a surprisingly disadvantageous starting point: "The storyteller does not explain how it is that the son of Jacob's favorite wife has been relegated to such a subordinate position, to serving the sons of concubines."[30] This status imbalance reflects the prehistory: sibling jockeying for power precedes Joseph's provocative behavior and continues in Canaan long after Joseph is erroneously presumed dead. But in both Judah's and Joseph's case there is an arch of triumph that bridges Genesis with later books.

Hatred of Joseph is central to Genesis 37–50, but other themes gain prominence by a glance backward. The burial of Isaac by Jacob and Esau (Gen. 35:28–29) offers a premonition that fraternal strife can give way to reconciliation—specifically it points toward the splendid burial of Jacob by his children. Gen. 35:22–26 offers a bland misdirection with its systematic listing of Jacob's sons by order of birth: neither the reversal of primogeniture nor Jacob's egregious favoritism is hinted at in this genealogy, unlike in Gen. 37:2. Genesis 36, which relates the genealogy of Esau, points both backward and forward to the difficulty of fraternal relations in Genesis—and reminds the reader that even the child not chosen has a story. The story of Joseph, from this perspective, culminates a passage from less-than-fraternal to more-than-fraternal relations begun with Cain and Abel in Genesis 4. The survival of Israel as a nation of slaves that preserves its identity for generations—the story of Exodus—depends on reaching the finish line of Genesis with some success. Joseph's dying words connect back to the very beginning of the Patriarchal-Matriarchal narrative: "God will surely take notice of you and bring you up from this land to the land which he promised on oath to Abraham, to Isaac and to Jacob" (Gen. 50:24).

Joseph Meets a Mysterious Stranger

Divine Providence and human agency seem at play again in his father's request to Joseph to go find his brothers.[31] This charge surprised many commentators, who, being parents, wondered at the former's obliviousness to family politics. Especially since we have just been told after Joseph's second dream that "his father kept the matter in mind" (Gen. 37:11), it is astonishing that Jacob sent Joseph off to his brothers—a significant distance—unaccompanied.[32] Jacob's instruction to "bring back word" about the brothers adds to our surprise, since Joseph's having brought back bad words concerning his brothers (at least some of them) has been cited as one cause of their hostility. Jacob's doubled use of the word for peace, *shalom*, applied to the brothers and to the flocks, will remind the reader that the brothers could not find a word of shalom where Joseph was concerned (Gen. 37:4). Finally the place that Jacob thinks his children are shepherding is none other than Shechem, the site of his daughter's rape and his sons' slaughter of the inhabitants. Even if every last male Shechemite was dead, as Gen. 34:25 states, the place ought to have struck Jacob as a site of excessive violence if not danger.

Joseph's one-word response, "Here I am" (*hineni*), is the same as Abraham's to God when the latter commands him to sacrifice his son Isaac (Gen. 22:1). Commentators ancient and modern have understood this one-word response as a loaded one. Midrash emphasized the vocalization of the letter *bet* preceding morning (*boker*), the very next thing Abraham does after uttering his (*hineni*), and parsed it as *early* morning, highlighting Abraham's zealotry to fulfill God's command. Rashi praised Abraham's response as signifying his spiritual readiness and obedience; Erich Auerbach focused on *"hineni"* as a literary device, noting that it cannot be a marker of location, as God knows where everyone is, but rather as an assertion of readiness: "I am prepared to do as you command."[33] Another dimension of this combination of call and response is that when Abraham responds to God he has been called to an exceptionally difficult task. With this precedent in mind, Joseph's call is fraught, particularly as the issuer of the command is not God but Jacob. Joseph knows what he must do. Joseph sets out, and when he reaches Shechem, "a man [comes] upon him wandering in the fields" (Gen. 37:15). This man redirects Joseph to Dothan, where the brothers are presumably tending the sheep. (Children's Bibles often picture the brothers being negligent in their duties.)

But why does this digression appear here at all? Could not Joseph have found the brothers easily and on his own? Who is this mysterious stranger who redirects a wandering Joseph toward his brothers? The first question may be answered by appealing to a major theme in the Joseph cycle. Events operate on both a human and a divine level, only the first of which is obvious to the characters in the drama. Nevertheless commentators are divided on the identity of the stranger and the nature of the intervention. Abraham ibn Ezra considered "the man" in Gen. 37:15 to be a human wayfarer. To Joseph's question regarding his brothers' whereabouts, ibn Ezra added the words, "if you know," as if to drive home the merely mortal status of this unnamed man. At the opposite end of the spectrum, Rashi stated categorically, "This refers to the angel Gabriel," on the slim basis of a description in Dan. 10:5 of Gabriel as "the man Gabriel" (*ha-ish*), the same word used in Gen. 37:17.

Rashi's association of "the man" with the angel Gabriel has midrashic roots. Still this seems like skating on thin ice. Perhaps Rashi's identification emerges from his sense of the mystical context of these verses. According to the text Jacob sends Joseph out from the Valley of Hebron (Gen. 37:14). But Hebron, in reality, is on the same hilly ridge as Bethlehem and Jerusalem. This slip, in Rashi's view, alludes to the spirit of Abraham, interred at Hebron, and to the promise made to the first patriarch that his family would both descend down to Egypt and return to the Land of Israel. Likewise when the mysterious stranger says, "they have gone from here" (Gen. 37:17), the Hebrew is peculiar. The stranger literally says, "they have gone from this." Rashi takes from this odd phraseology (*nasu mizeh*) hyperliterally, to mean that the brethren have lost the spirit of brotherhood, a gloss well supported by their actions in the next few verses.

Is this disagreement between ibn Ezra and Rashi merely technical, a reflection of ibn Ezra's predilection for a *peshat* analysis and for Rashi's preference for a balance between *peshat* and *derash*? Living in a pious Jewish community in northern France surrounded by equally pious Christians, Rashi felt God's presence as imminent. For Rashi God intervenes in human affairs directly, explicitly, and through divine messengers. Ibn Ezra, living in sophisticated and philosophical Spain and North Africa, stressed God's transcendent nature and experienced God's Providence accordingly.[34] Nachmanides effectively split the difference between the two, agreeing with ibn Ezra's view that the messenger is human, but stressing the role of the Divine Providence in sending him.[35] What transpires next illustrates the old adage "God works in mysterious ways."

Joseph in the Empty Pit

When the brothers see Joseph approaching them in his long-sleeved tunic they do not hesitate to condemn "that dreamer" to death, but the action that follows is quite confusing. Reuben plans on returning later to save him; Judah proposes selling Joseph. The brothers conspire (the narrator uses "they" to implicate them all), then throw him in a pit. Rashi moved to eliminate the seeming redundancy in the second half of the verse (i.e., if the pit was empty we already know "there was no water in it"), by positing snakes and scorpions as residents. Rashi's logic runs something like: "there was no *water* in it" so there must have been something else in the pit—snakes and scorpions certainly convey the brothers' fratricidal impulse.

Medieval and modern commentators alike have found Rashi's view of the well a bit fanciful. Nachmanides wrote, "In line with the simple meaning of the verse, it states that the pit was completely empty and void of water. . . . Such redundancies are all for the purpose of clarification and emphasis."[36] Once again more is at stake than whether this particular pit contained snakes, a few drops of water, or rose petals. Rashi's reading, which he culled from earlier midrashim, relies on a view of the Bible often associated with Rabbi Akiva, that every word and every letter of the text can yield a distinct teaching. Nothing can be superfluous, for the Torah presents the reader with a more than human text. Nachmanides, relying on an equally august tradition, which also affirms divine origins, presumes that the Torah speaks in human language. Just as human texts use redundancy, repetition and exaggeration to make a point, so does the Torah.

Who Sold Whom? Three Approaches to the Sale of Joseph

Confusion abounds in trying to unravel the respective roles played by the brothers, the Midianites, and the Ishmaelites in this sordid drama. Take a look at Gen. 37:25–28 in this curious, on-line, self-described Orthodox translation, which eliminates ambiguity, partly by failing to translate the Hebrew, and then in the vastly clearer NJPS translation, in which the narrative uncertainty of the original remains:

> And they sat down to eat *lechem*; and they lifted up their eyes and looked, and, *hinei*, a caravan of *Yishm'elim* was coming from Gil'ad with their *gemalim* bearing spices and balm and myrrh, going to carry it down to Mitzrayim. And Yehudah said unto his *achim*, What *betza* [profit, gain] is it if we kill *achinu* [our brother], and

conceal his *dahm*? Come, and let us sell him to the *Yishm'elim*, and let not *yadeinu* [our hands] be upon him; for he is *achinu* [our brother] and *besareinu* [our flesh]. And his *achim* agreed. Then there passed by *anashim Midyanim socharim* [men of Midyan, traders]; and they drew and lifted up Yosef out of the *bor*, and sold Yosef to the *Yishm'elim* for *esrim kesef*; and they took Yosef to Mitzrayim.[37]

Then they sat down to a meal. Looking up, they saw a caravan of Ishmaelites coming from Gilead, their camels bearing gum, balm, and ladanum to be taken to Egypt. Then Judah said to his brothers, "What do we gain by killing our brother and covering up his blood? Come, let us sell him to the Ishmaelites, but let us not do away with him ourselves. After all, he is our brother, our own flesh." His brothers agreed. When Midianite traders passed by, they pulled Joseph up out of the pit. They sold Joseph for twenty pieces of silver to the Ishmaelites, who brought Joseph to Egypt. (NJPS)

Later references to Joseph's sale keep the matter unclear, as Gen. 39:1 refers to the Egyptian Potiphar as having purchased Joseph from the Ishmaelites. Joseph himself adds to the textual problem, stating both that he was "stolen, stolen from the land of the Hebrews" (Gen 40:15), and also that the brothers refused to hear his entreaties (Gen. 42:2), which suggests that the sale proposed by Judah actually transpired. Joseph surely said something when he was thrown into the pit—but it is not recorded. That Joseph relates in prison that he was "stolen, stolen from the land of the Hebrews" to the Egyptian prisoners has been explained as reticence regarding the shameful circumstances of his enslavement. The exact sequence of events remains foggy.

Three basic approaches may clarify the action at the end of Genesis 37. The first, found in traditional commentators, assumes a coherent text that can be unraveled with sufficient ingenuity. Yet not all traditional commentators unravel these verses in the same way.[38] Rashi attempted to solve the problem by positing a number of sales, eventuating in Joseph's final sale from the Ishmaelites to the Midianites. But other commentators have held that Ishmaelite is a synonym for merchant—in other words there is only one group with whom the brothers negotiated. (Midianites and Medanites are both mentioned in this text, but this minor problem may be dismissed as a scribal error.) A larger problem is how either of these groups, assuming that there were two, conveyed Joseph to the Egyptians. And, whether one group or two was involved in the sale, the problems do not end here, because the subject involved in the sale the subject of verse 28, "they," is uncertain. Did the Midianites draw Joseph out of the pit, or did his brothers draw him out and sell him? Ultimately the brothers bear responsibility for their misdeed. But several major commentators, beginning with Rashbam, believed that the brothers did not sell him and that they believed that Joseph had been sold—or even slain by an evil beast, just as Jacob assumed.[39] Rashbam's argument rested on grammar—in his view, "they" in verse 28 could only be the Midianites. But this line of argument has moral implications too. As Nehama Leibowitz writes, "Joseph was sold by heathens to heathens."[40] As horrible as their act was, the better intentions of Reuben and Judah toward Joseph (to redeem and to sell, respectively) were not stymied by the other brothers, but by total strangers. The presumption of all these traditional Jewish sources, however, is that the text proceeds from one author and that with sufficient ingenuity the true story can be discovered.

A second approach, which prevailed in the secular academy for decades, may be found in the Documentary Hypothesis, which resolves many textual inconsistencies by identifying more than one author. In the case of Joseph, the Elohist (E), the Jahvist (J), and Priestly (P) sources all have a hand in the resulting narrative. Some find the confusion in the narrative easily resolvable by the premise that both J (with its focus on Judah) and E (with its focus on Reuben) played a role. Here is Speiser on Gen. 37:28:

The first part of the verse is manifestly from another source which knew nothing about the Ishmaelite traders. It speaks of Midianites who pulled the boy up from the pit, without being seen by the brothers, and then sold him into slavery. This is why Reuben was so surprised to find that Joseph was gone. The sale to the Ishmaelites, on the other hand, had been agreed upon by all the brothers, so that Reuben would have no reason to look for the boy in the pit, let alone be upset because he did not find him there. *This single verse alone provides as good a case as is for a constructive documentary analysis of the Pentateuch*; it goes a long way, moreover, to demonstrate that E is not just a supplement to J, but an independent and often conflicting source. [my emphasis][41]

A third approach can be found in Edward Greenstein's postmodern literary perspective. Greenstein takes no stand on whether the text proceeds from one or many authors. He writes that the complicated narrative in Genesis 37 (and elsewhere in the Bible) achieves an effect like a Faulkner novel, a Cubist painting, or an Akira Kurosawa movie, with the same story being narrated from different perspectives. Greenstein summarizes his conclusions as follows:

An equivocal reading of the sale of Joseph leads to the realization that, in the view of the narrative, it is not crucial to our understanding of the story whether the brothers sold Joseph to the Ishmaelites or whether the Midianites kidnapped him. It is important, rather, to perceive that the descent of Joseph to Egypt and his subsequent rise to power there reveal divine providence in history. This, of course, is the single most pervasive theme in the Bible. But in our text the theme is evinced not only by the action of the narrative but also, as I have tried to show, by the structural arrangement of the narrative. Somewhat simplified, one sequence of human action rivals the other, leaving only the divine manipulation of events clear and intelligible.[42]

Liturgical Reflections on a Terrible Deed

Whatever their measure of culpability, the brothers' regret over this terrible deed constitutes an important theme in the Joseph story, one that extends until Genesis 50.[43] The text implies that the brothers' guilt feelings begin immediately. Reuben, the presumptive leader, declares his angst dramatically: "The boy is gone! Now, what am I to do?" (Gen 37:30). No translation can quite capture the almost choked sound of this Hebrew clause, which features four words in a row starting with the first letter of the Hebrew alphabet—*aleph* (*aynenu/ani/ana/ani/ba*)—and ends with the monosyllabic "*ba*." Judah, the other brother who failed to take effective responsibility for averting this borderline fratricide, leaves immediately for the hinterlands of Canaan, what would become Philistine country, at the beginning of Genesis 38.

Recent scholarship pays much attention to reading communities as well as texts. The principal way Jews would experience the Joseph cycle was during the Torah reading, which takes up four full weeks—from late autumn until after Hanukkah. The Torah reading has long occupied an important place in the worship service. For the last two thousand years, more or less, congregants heard the Joseph story in conjunction with its *haftarot*.[44] While the choice of matching Torah and haftarah can be merely lexical, all four portions shed light on the Joseph story.[45] This effect may be heightened if the sermonizer (*darshan*) begins with a text in Ketuvim-Writings, proceeds to Neviim-Prophets and culminates in the Torah portion.[46] The prophetic passage for Va-yeshev invites auditors to focus on the shameful way Joseph found himself in Egypt: the sin for which Israel will not be forgiven is the sale of the righteous for silver and the needy for sandals (Amos 2:6). That one character in the Hebrew Bible alone, Joseph, gets awarded this appellation *righteous* probably drove this choice of haftarah. We know that early midrashic traditions imagined that the brethren purchased sandals with the proceeds of Joseph's sale.[47] Auditors of this haftarah may have considered Joseph's virtue especially noteworthy when hearing the prophet condemn, "father and son go to the same girl . . . on garments taken in pledge" (Amos 2:7), reminiscent of Judah and his two elder sons sleeping with Tamar. Even before the emergence of the rabbinic movement, *Jubilees* linked the sale of Joseph to the institution of the Day of Atonement (Yom Kippur).[48] The enormity of this transgression also informs "These I Recall" (*eleh azkarah*), recited during the additional service on the Day of Atonement until today.[49]

Not Telling Jacob

One dilemma remains after the sale of Joseph: how will the brothers break the news to Jacob? When the brethren return to Jacob, they allow a third party to bear Joseph's tunic, stained with goat's blood, and allow it, in Robert Alter's words, to do the lying for them. The theme of deception and revelation, critical to the whole Joseph cycle, and often involving clothing and physical appearance, is introduced when the brethren ask Jacob whether he recognizes the bloodied tunic (*haker-na*). Jacob does indeed recognize it (*va'yaker*) and exclaims in excruciating onomatopoeia: "*tarof toraf Yosef*," which Everett Fox's *The Five Books of Moses* translates, "Yosef is torn, torn-to-pieces!" (37:33).[50] The bloody cloak is a provocative yet empty symbol: it cannot avert a violent act that has already been committed, and Joseph will be lost to the family for many years.[51] The concluding verses of Genesis 37 detail Jacob's mourning for his favorite son. From this intense scene of grief, the rabbis derived several mourning habits and beliefs that became normative for Judaism, including the tearing of the mourner's garment (*keriyah*). If Jacob's refusal to be comforted for his remaining children and grandchildren spurs still more resentment about Jacob's favoritism, the narrator has chosen to conceal it. We are left only with a bereaved father, ten guilt-ridden men, and a hitherto insufferable seventeen-year-old boy who has learned a hard lesson about the limits of fraternal bonds. Genesis has thirteen chapters to rectify this tragic situation, which includes one of its central themes, well expressed by Jon D. Levenson:

> The story of Joseph in Genesis 37–50 is not only the longest and most intricate Israelite exemplar of the narrative of the death and resurrection of the beloved son, but also the most explicit. In it is concentrated almost every variation of the theme that first appeared in the little tale of Cain and Abel and has been growing and becoming more involved and more complex throughout the Book of Genesis. The story of Joseph thus not only concludes the book and links the Patriarchal narratives to those of the people Israel in Egypt for which they serve as archetypes; it is also the crescendo to the theme of the beloved son, which it presents in extraordinarily polished literary form. It is arguably the most sophisticated narrative in the Jewish or the Christian Bibles.[52]

The last verse in this chapter serves as a transition and a cliff-hanger to the story's resumption with our still young but chastened and enslaved hero. "The Midianites meanwhile, sold him to Egypt to Potiphar, a courtier of Pharaoh and his chief steward" (Gen. 37:36). Before the narrative resumes in chapter 39, however, let us pause to consider Joseph's dreams, the most prickly thorn in the side of the brothers, but also the vehicle of Joseph's eventual triumph.

I cannot nominate a better opening in literature than Genesis 37. We have a vivid picture of Joseph, doomed to tension with his brothers by what has come before the opening of the story. We have a father engaging in shameless favoritism, seemingly oblivious to his role in recapitulating his own fraternal conflict. We have Joseph's fateful quest for his brothers and brotherhood, and a violent response that reverberates in our liturgy until today (Christianity sees the brothers' acts against Joseph as foreshadowing the fate of Jesus). And, despite his culpability in fostering fraternal animosity, we feel Jacob's sincere mourning over the loss of his beloved son. But all is not lost.

2

Joseph the Dreamer

Any contemporary thinking about "dreams" with Joseph in mind is likely to have two sharply contrasting associations. On the one hand we have Andrew Lloyd Webber's blockbuster *Joseph and the Amazing Technicolor Dreamcoat*, reprised many times on the stage and likely in continual production somewhere in the world since its debut in 1968. This dreaming Joseph, known to many an American high school student, has been "Googled" by over two hundred million people at the time of this writing (see how many more since the publication date). If there is no arguing with success, a major theme in the biblical narrative, it would be difficult to imagine a more complete takeover of the Joseph story than that of the duo of Webber and Tim Rice. "Any Dream Will Do," often the opening and closing number of this musical, establishes one reference point. Here is the first stanza:

> I closed my eyes, drew back the curtain
> To see for certain what I thought I knew
> Far far away, someone was weeping
> But the world was sleeping
> Any dream will do.

One need not be a scholar of the Bible (or of musical theater) to recognize the spin on the original. "Dream" in this usage means something like "aspiration," and aspiration, of course, is part of Joseph's character. But the idea of that aspiration as adventitious, almost random, works far better as theater than as interpretation. Joseph's own dreams are aspirational but focused. He aims at being, at the very least, the centerpiece, the dominant member of his family. The brothers' sheaves bow down to Joseph's sheaf, but the sun, moon, and eleven stars bow down to him. The dreams of others, which Joseph has the sagacity and temerity to interpret, are means to an end—admirable to be sure—namely, Joseph's exaltation and rule over Egypt and salvation of all humankind against a highly improbable universal famine. Will any dream do? Hardly.

The other association educated people will have with dreams (especially if one mentally adds the key word "Jew") is with the father of psychoanalysis, Sigmund Freud. In his landmark book *Die Traumdeutung* (*The Interpretation of Dreams*), Freud takes Joseph's interpretation of Pharaoh's dreams as paradigmatic of symbolic "dream interpreting." As Freud writes:

> Most of the artificial dreams constructed by imaginative writers are designed for a symbolic interpretation of this sort: they reproduce the writer's thoughts under a disguise which is regarded as harmonizing with the recognized characters of dreams. . . . It is of course impossible to give instructions upon the method of arriving at a symbolic interpretation. Success must be a question of hitting on a clever idea, of direct intuition, and for that reason it was possible for dream-interpretation only by means of symbolism to be exalted into an artistic activity dependent on the possession of peculiar gifts.[1]

Freud returns to this dream, using it as a prime example of how a dream can contain various pieces of information, which the dreamer will dream more vividly over time. Freud takes the historian Flavius Josephus's expanded version of Pharaoh's dream as a good indication of how dreams work.[2]

Scholars agree that the remarkably learned Freud often paraded his classical Greco-Roman erudition and downplayed his knowledge of Jewish sources—and things Jewish generally.[3] Many collections of the master, including Peter Gay's *The Freud Reader*, abet Freud's self-censorship by excising the biblical and postbiblical references in Freud's work.[4] In a telling footnote Freud admitted that he naturally gravitated to the character of Joseph in order to make his point about dream interpreting. Even the stridently antireligious Freud, apparently, fell under the spell of a character who insisted that "interpretations belong to God."[5]

Ancient Dreams in Modern Perspectives: Oppenheim and Beyond

Whether Freud provided the key to understanding all dreams in all eras is a question best debated by scholars willing to devote their lives to the matter. A cursory glance suggests that many have. Although I am interested in what Freud's dream book has to say about the German Jewish world of the late nineteenth century, our interest is what dreams signify in the ancient Near East and the Bible. Whatever Freud discovered, ancient civilizations believed that dreams originated from the God or the gods; that is, from an external source, not from the subconscious of the dreamer. Adolph Leo Oppenheim (1904–74), a pioneer in ancient dream research, and like Freud and Auerbach, a refugee from the Nazis, divides biblical dreams into "message" and "symbolic" dreams, that is, the sort that Joseph interprets. Oppenheim writes: "Most of the 'symbolic' dreams of the Old Testament occur in a context which is typical. They are primarily meant to serve as a vehicle for the display of the piety and the sagacity of their god-inspired interpreter."[6]

To Israelites the Lord speaks in "message dreams" and not in dark speeches (Num. 12:8). Oppenheim infers that the great figures of Israel receive message dreams, while non-Israelites mainly receive symbolic dreams. Thus Joseph's case is unusual, if not unique. "It is immediately evident to Joseph as well as to his brothers (a) that the sheaves standing around his sheaf and making obeisance, or that the sun and the moon and the eleven stars showing their submission to him, forecast future events, and (b) that the sheaves and the stars "symbolize" the brothers, while the luminaries refer in the same way to his parents. Their reactions show this. The structure of the dream is very simple; it substitutes objects and phenomena in the sky for persons, taking even their social rank into consideration."[7]

This dream typology invites qualification. Bible scholar Scott Noegel explains that Oppenheim

> articulates no distinction between textual genres and it does not place the data into any historical contexts. Moreover, not every dream account fits neatly into one of the two categories. There are symbolic dreams that require no interpreters, and message dreams that do. There are prophetic message dreams and also prophetic symbolic dreams. If one also considers the significant conceptual overlap between dreams and visions, the problem of typology becomes even more acute. Moreover, there are serious problems with applying the word "symbolic" to cultures that likely did not understand language and dreams in symbolic terms in the same way that we might do today.[8]

Oppenheim distinguished different "types" of dreams more sharply than the ancients would have. Noegel also questions the preference of Israelites for "message" over "symbolic" dreams. How would one make that determination? Counting the number of "message" versus "symbolic" dreams? Judging which dreams are more important to the story line? God's direct speech may enjoy a status that a human interpretation does not, but in the case of Joseph and Daniel at least, the interpreters insist on giving God credit for their correct interpretations. Would Oppenheim's distinction be comprehensible to an ancient author?

Bible scholar Shaul Bar dissects the various biblical terms used for dreaming, analyzes the ancient Near East analogues, and provides illuminating readings of the biblical dream narratives. [9] Bar notes that "the ancients, unfamiliar with the byways of the human soul revealed by modern psychology, saw dreams as channels of communication between human beings and external sources. In sleep, they believed, messages were conveyed to the unconscious mind, messages often relating to the future and sometimes including clear and unambiguous announcements, advice, injunctions, or warnings."[10] Bar observes that these dreams come to the reader only indirectly, mediated by authors working in a genre widely used in the ancient world. That biblical dreams are less actual dreams liable to psychoanalysis than literary constructs should be granted; I doubt that even Freud would contend otherwise. Bar writes, "Biblical authors used dreams for their own purposes, fitting the details into the familiar paradigm."[11]

Two Other Dreams in the Hebrew Bible

Joseph contains dreams in Genesis 37, 40, 41, and 46, which we will consider soon. But two other dreams shed light on the Joseph story: Daniel's and Solomon's. (The pivotal verse Esther 6:1 turns on an insomniac nondream. "That night, sleep deserted the king, and he ordered the book of records, the annals to be brought; and it was read to the king.") Daniel and Joseph both find themselves in a precarious foreign court, before an unpredictable ruler. In place of the Egyptian "magicians and wisemen" in Joseph, we have "magicians, exorcists, sorcerers and Chaldeans" (Dan. 2:2). Both narratives display the Israelite contempt for professional dream interpreters (oneiromantics).[12] Nebuchadnezzar demands that the interpreters not only interpret, but tell him the content of the dream from the onset (Dan. 2:5, 2:9). The would-be interpreters call the reader's attention to the outlandishness of this demand: "none has ever asked such a thing from any magician, exorcist or Chaldean" (Dan 2:10). Likewise Nebuchadnezzar's explicit death threat, that failures will "be torn limb from limb" (Dan 2:5), is far more menacing than Pharaoh's. As for rewards, Nebuchadnezzar promises Daniel up front that he will receive great rewards if he succeeds in his challenging task. Pharaoh, by contrast, promises nothing to Joseph.

Daniel buys some time, wisely, for he receives a night vision revealing the mystery (*raza*; Dan. 2:19). He then praises the Lord in words that will become the central refrain of the *Kaddish* doxology: "Let the name of God be blessed forever and ever" (Dan 2:20).[13] Nebuchadnezzar strikes the reader as an exaggerated version of Pharaoh, and the challenge, to relate the dream and then interpret it, is an exaggerated version of Joseph's challenge. Daniel's response seems patterned on Joseph's. Daniel insists that no human power can do what he is about to do, but only someone who has been vouchsafed mysteries privy to God in heaven. Although the details of the dream differ greatly from the one Joseph interprets for Pharaoh, some lessons are the same: dreams belong to God, God chooses certain people to be trustworthy interpreters, God looks after the king's peace (at least those lucky enough to have a Hebrew interpreter on hand), and the favor of God assures the accuracy of the dream's interpretation. Daniel 2 and Dan. 7:1, in which the hero had his "dream and vision" "in bed" and afterward "wrote down the dream," presents an exaggerated version of Joseph as dreamer and dream interpreter. What seems clear is that whoever wrote Daniel had Joseph and his dreams in mind.[14]

Solomon's dream (1 Kings 3:4–15) has been categorized as a "message" dream. Recently invested as king, Solomon recalls the ancient Near East pattern focused mainly on rulers, though one assumes that commoners had their dreams too. Solomon receives the dream from the Lord directly, with no intermediary, at the shrine of Gibeah in Benjamin. God and Solomon converse, with Solomon modestly emphasizing his youth and the magnitude of following his father David. In response to God's offer to grant him what he wants, Solomon sagely requests "a listening heart." God grants him not only "a wise and discerning mind" (more than he asks), but also long life, riches, and glory (much more than he asks). Solomon is a king: in this sense he resembles Pharaoh and Nebuchadnezzar. Solomon is an Israelite: in that sense he resembles Joseph and Daniel. To which is he closer? It seems ethnicity trumps social standing. "Then Solomon awoke: it was a dream!"(1 Kings 3:15) recalls Pharaoh (Gen. 41:5, 41:7), but Solomon, in this scene, is modest, pious, and animated by his role as servant of the Lord.[15] If this comments on his gentile counterparts, it may be by way of polemical contrast. Solomon's posture seems like Daniel and Joseph, who see wisdom, discernment, and subservience to God as the tools most needed for a life well lived. Of course this spiritual kinship may not be coincidental, nor my comparison of Solomon and Joseph so forced. Some Bible scholars still believe that Joseph was composed not long after the era of Solomon,[16] and quite a few believe that Joseph and Solomon represent classical Wisdom figures.[17]

Jacob Dreams a Different Kind of Dream

Jacob experiences the only "message" dream in the Joseph cycle, as he prepares both to reunite with his long lost son, Joseph, and to lead his family down into Egypt. The great drama of this short passage has sometimes been obscured by the climax of the entire Joseph story in the preceding chapter, and by the lengthy genealogy that follows (Gen. 46:8–27). This genealogy, which retards the long-anticipated reunion of Jacob and Joseph, is considered by many a crude interpellation.[18] On first glance the placement of Jacob's theophany seems abrupt:

> So Israel set out with all that was his, and he came to Beer-sheba, where he offered sacrifices to the God of his father Isaac. God called to Israel in a vision by night: "Jacob! Jacob!" He answered, "Here." And He said, "I am God, the God of your father. Fear not to go down to Egypt, for I will make you there into a great

nation. I Myself will go down with you to Egypt, and I Myself will also bring you back; and Joseph's hand shall close your eyes. (Gen. 46:1–4)

Although this theophany stands out against the background of a general narrative, the narrator has woven this passage into its surroundings. Jacob's own utterance, "My son *Joseph* is still alive! I must go and see him before I die" (Gen. 45:28), immediately precedes the theophany, and God's reassurance to Jacob that "*Joseph's* hand shall close your eyes" (Gen. 46:4) creates a bracketing effect and creates a transition to Joseph's dominant role in Egypt even in family matters. (The firstborn would ordinarily perform the mitzvah of closing the deceased parent's eyes, but Joseph will take the leadership role even in this family matter.) To attribute verse 1 to biblical writer "P" because of its use of the name "Israel," and then to insist on verses 2–5 as proceeding from "J," is the sort of dissecting that skeptics of source criticism find circular, especially when paired with comments such as, "The isolated 'Israel' in v. 2 is an accidental carry-over from the preceding verse."[19] In other words this admits that for the source critical system to work here, verse 2, being J, should read "Jacob," not "Israel."[20] Finally the prominence of "going down" and "being brought up" seems to be deliberately placed within the greater narrative—the "going down" is about to transpire, and the divine promise could hardly be more relevant.[21] One should not overinterpret commonly used words such as "down" and "up," but in this case their use seems designed to signal a pivotal moment to the reader.[22]

The descent to Egypt likely prompts the divine reassurance "Fear not,"[23] also an admonition from God to Abraham and Isaac. Yet the description "God of his father Isaac" begs explanation. Nahum Sarna maintains the exclusion of Abraham here has to do with Isaac's sole construction of an altar at Beer-sheba; Rashi, on the pious grounds that one ought to honor the father more than the grandfather. One might reply: why not honor both? Nachmanides offers a complex response that finds the use of the name Jacob rather than Israel the greater dilemma. Nachmanides navigates early midrashim, the Aramaic translator Onkelos, Moses Maimonides' antiliteralism, and the secrets of the Kabbalah, the last of which Nachmanides clearly considered necessary for a full understanding of these night visions. Ultimately Nachmanides explains the name choice of "Jacob Jacob," rather than "Israel Israel," as reflecting the darkening context of Genesis 46. As Israel prepares to descend into Egyptian exile it is no time for the triumphant appellation "Israel."[24]

"Jacob's Fear": Three Levels of Anxiety

Similarly "so Israel set out with all that was his, and he came to Beer-sheba, where he offered sacrifices to the God of his father Isaac" (Gen. 46:1) invites the obvious question, why does the text not read, "God of his fathers, Abraham and Isaac? After all, as the first Israelite, and as one of the great characters of Scripture, one would expect Abraham to get top billing. However, Nehama Leibowitz notes that only Isaac is specifically prohibited from going down to Egypt (Gen. 26:2). Thus the first level of explanation for this verse is that Jacob fears violating a divine commandment enjoined on his father, Isaac—and already violated by his son Joseph. Leibowitz deepens this explanation by referring to the next set of verses, the core of this episode, telling him not to fear the descent into Egypt on pragmatic grounds. Second, as someone who spent twenty difficult years in exile in Padan-Aram, Jacob knows all too well the perils of being a stranger in a strange land. Jacob fears that leaving the ancestral homeland is a journey into powerlessness, which proves to be the case. Third, Jacob reasonably fears for his descendants' ability to maintain their identity as a minority. Naphtali Zvi Yehuda Berlin, a nineteenth-century commentator, read this situation as a modern parable of assimilation.[25] "Jacob was afraid that his seed would be absorbed by the Egyptian nation. Only in the land of Israel could the unique Jewish spark be preserved down the ages. It was on this score that the Almighty reassured him: 'Fear not, for I shall make of thee a great nation.' Our Sages interpreted the phrase 'great nation' to imply that the Jews would preserve their national identity, and not be absorbed into Egypt."[26]

A couple of features of this divine vision, the last in Genesis, also merit comment. As in Genesis 28 (the ladder to heaven) and Genesis 32 (Jacob's wrestling match), we have an action of Jacob, taken at night, involving stones, and connected to an appearance of God.[27] These night visions are not dreams and thus emphasize that Jacob's relationship with God differs from his sons' relationships with God—even his most talented. Genesis 46 begins with Jacob offering sacrifices to God at Beer-sheba, even today the most important city in the Negev. Jacob's appearance, as is often the case in the Joseph cycle, accompanies a ritual, a place, and a divine invocation particular to Israelites.

Joseph Dreams Himself

Joseph's brothers already disliked him mightily, and relating his two grandiose dreams to them transformed seething resentment into burning hatred. The rabbis were not privy to the information excavated by archaeologists, and therefore unaware of the roles played by dreams throughout the ancient world. But they knew well that the Bible's doubling of the dreams in the Joseph cycle pointed to their seriousness and reliability. The dreams and the reactions to them in Genesis 37 emphasize the theme of mastery, first over the agricultural world (the sheaves of wheat) and then over the cosmic world (the stars, sun, and moon). This corresponds to both the means (clever policies averting famine) and the ends (promotion to viziership) by which Joseph would become the brothers' ruler, which would force their literal genuflection. The root for "dream"

(*chet-lamed-mem*) appears eleven times in Gen. 37:1–11, distrib-
uted among the narrator, Joseph, and Jacob, a repetition won-
derfully picked up on later in the chapter (Gen. 37:19), when
Joseph approaches and the brothers say, "Here comes that
dreamer; we'll see what becomes of his dreams."[28] Unlike the
Egyptians (Gen. 40:8; 41:15), both Joseph and his brothers
clearly understand their import.

Joseph Interprets the Dreams of the Cupbearer and the Baker

At the end of Genesis 39 Potiphar places Joseph in the king's
prison, and this is the setting of Genesis 40, which has a dream
narrative at its core. Once again the phrase "And it came to pass
after all these things," as in Gen. 38:1 and Gen. 39:15, serves
nicely as a way of resuming the narrative without filling in
details regarding the specific nature of the offenses committed by the cupbearer and baker. Not coincidentally this beginning also opens the door to rabbinic speculation regarding the
nature of the unspecified "things"—matters of state according
to the rationalist ibn Ezra: flies in the wine and stone chips in
the bread according to Rashi. The ruler is twice described here
as the "king of Egypt" rather than Pharaoh, perhaps as a literary link to the twice-repeated description "Potiphar the Egyptian" in Genesis 39. The text moves ahead through the scene
setting (vv. 1–4) with usual biblical alacrity, employing the
single Hebrew letter *vav* (and/but) like a conveyer belt transporting us to the real substance of this chapter: the servants'
dreams.[29] In addition to establishing the narrative background
for the dreams, these verses confirm Joseph's subordinate but
trustworthy character.

One "dream theme" developed in Genesis 40–41 is whether
we are dealing with one dream or two dreams.[30] The language
of the text deliberately confuses the issue. "And they dreamed
a dream both of them, each man his dream, in one night, each
man according to the interpretation of his dream, the cup-

bearer and the baker of the king of Egypt, who were bound in the prison." (If you are a reader of Hebrew, go word by word here and observe the alternation in number between singular and plural.) After the breakneck pace of verses 1–4, the text noticeably slows as Joseph takes the initiative to inquire as to the nature of the royal prisoners' visible discomfort. Joseph's question "Why are you so sad-faced" (*p'naichem rah'im*) today? (Gen. 40:7) foreshadows the sorry-looking (*rah*) cows that will appear to Pharaoh (Gen. 41:1–4). The gumption of a Hebrew prisoner asking after Pharaoh's cupbearer's and baker's welfare is considerable. Both Nachmanides and Thomas Mann see this solicitude as indicative of Joseph's innately aristocratic, self-confidant nature. The former mordantly notes that had the baker been restored to favor, Joseph would have paid for his misinterpretation with his life. Ovadiah Sforno, a sixteenth-century CE Italian commentator familiar with the life of a courtier, sees Joseph's self-confidence as reflecting his determination to carry out his office successfully and with politesse.

The two Egyptians' responses to Joseph opens up the issue of whether the dreams themselves are inherently difficult to interpret, or whether the Egyptians simply lack the right man for the job. Joseph's response ("Do not interpretations belong to God? Tell it me, I pray you") continues to display a dual nature. Modern readers often read this statement as arrogant—as if Joseph were conveying to his listeners that he and God were functionally the same! But biblical religion found attributing actions to God and human activity highly compatible, and ancients authentically believed that dreams originate from without. Probably Joseph's reply was intended by the narrator to convey the notion of his piety. If so it further suggests that Joseph's rhetorical response to Mrs. Potiphar ("How then could I do this most wicked thing, and sin before God?" [Gen. 39:9]) was not just a matter of prudence, but of belief. Neither the Bible nor Judaism teaches that trust in God exempts one from making an effort on one's own. Hence the second part of Joseph's response: despite the presumptive difficulty of the task ("We have dreamed a dream and there is none that can interpret it" [Gen. 41:8]), Joseph steps up to the plate and asks for a swing at the troublesome dream(s). Note that Joseph has no training as an interpreter of other people's dreams. Ancient Israel developed no caste of dream interpreters, and Deut. 17:9–12 specifically prohibits its development. With God on your side, professional credentials pale in importance.

Since the specifics of these dreams are critical to their meaning, let us place them side by side:

[The cupbearer:] "In my dream, behold, a vine was before me; and in the vine were three branches; and as it was budding, its blossoms shot forth, and clusters thereof brought forth ripe grapes, and Pharaoh's cup was in my hand; and I took the grapes, and pressed them into Pharaoh's cup, and I gave the cup unto Pharaoh's hand." (Gen. 40:9–11)

[The baker:] "I also saw in my dream, and behold, three baskets of white bread were on my head; and in the uppermost basket there was of all manner of baked food for pharaoh; and the birds did eat them out of the basket upon my head." (Gen. 40:16–19)

Can one separate the dreamer and the dream? Not here. Rabbi Samson Raphael Hirsch (1808–88) emphasizes that Joseph had paid careful attention to the actions and personalities of the two men. The details of the two dreams, in Hirsch's view, confirmed Joseph's evaluation and gave him the confidence that he understood the dreams' significance. Even before Hirsch, of course, Jewish commentators had probed the wording of these dreams carefully and many found that Joseph's predictions were less prophetic foresight than shrewd text analysis. For the "three branches = three days," Nachmanides called attention to the words "shot forth," suggesting a short duration of time (in other words not three months or three years). Benno Jacob (1862–1945) went further, suggesting that the date of Pharaoh's birthday, a likely time for Pharaoh to act, would surely be common knowledge in a royal prison. Benno Jacob also stressed that the details of the cupbearer's dream suggest great care on his part and also the personal handing over to Pharaoh of the wine. The baker, on the contrary, leaves the bread in plain sight of ravenous birds, which devour it, seemingly without any intervention on the baker's part. Indeed, unlike the labor of the cupbearer, which is detailed, the baker's bread seems to have magically appeared. Finally Pharaoh receives the cup directly from the cupbearer, while Pharaoh appears nowhere in the baker's dream. Thus, although a surface reading of the dreams make them appear as one, as the baker (incorrectly) assumed when he asked Joseph for an interpretation, a wiser reading of the dreams shows them to be two—indeed diametrically opposite.[31]

A further note on characterization implied in this chapter: the cupbearer is always mentioned first, and it is he who takes the bold step of asking Joseph for an interpretation. The baker follows suit and asks Joseph to interpret his dream when he sees that Joseph's interpretation is *true*, according to Rashbam's reading; or, alternatively, when the baker falsely concludes that the outcome of his own dream will be *favorable*—for the Hebrew (*ki tov patar*) may be rendered either way. The contrast in character between the cupbearer and the baker suggested by the content of the dreams thus gains support from the surrounding narrative. The baker, on closer inspection, seems like the sort who would let stone chips fall into his bread, though one may reasonably question whether that offense deserves the death penalty. Joseph's enigmatic response, "Pharaoh will lift up your head," could hardly be more ironic: for the cupbearer it means elevation; for the baker, beheading or impaling.[32]

Joseph Is Left to Languish

The short interchange between Joseph and the cupbearer separating the two dreams also deserves scrutiny. Reasonably, but firmly, Joseph asks the cupbearer to remember him and mention him to Pharaoh when things take a good turn. The emphatic Hebrew verb "to remember" (*zakhar*) is used twice in this request (*zakhartani*) and (*hizkhartani*)—first in the simple and then in the causative, or *hifil*, form. Remembrance is a major theme in the Hebrew Bible, used about 169 times, and denotes something more active and activist than the English word. In any event the last verse of the chapter (Gen. 40:23) tells us pointedly, "Yet the chief cupbearer did not remember Joseph, but forgot him." Not only are we given a view into the cupbearer's lack of gratitude, but we are also reminded that the solution to Joseph's problem, ultimately, lies with God. We are less inclined than Rashi to blame Joseph for putting his confidence in the cupbearer; we hope that doing such a good turn would bring some measure of gratitude. On the other hand perhaps the cynicism of Abraham ibn Ezra, who commented that the cupbearer did remember Joseph (possibly indicated by Gen. 41:9–13), but could not be bothered to help him, is truer to reality. In the master narrative it is clearly God who stage manages events such that the cupbearer will have cause at a critical juncture to live up to his obligation to the imprisoned Joseph.

Joseph's request for intervention grants us insight into his still smoldering resentment over the events in Genesis 37. He tells the cupbearer that he was "stolen, indeed stolen" (*gunav gunavti*) from the land of the Hebrews (Gen. 40:15). Was Joseph too humiliated to tell of his brothers' intended sale to the Ishmaelites? Was the only reality he remembered from that traumatic event being hoisted out of the pit by the Midianites? We cannot know, because the end of Genesis 37 is such an ambiguous account. The likelihood that Joseph understood the events in Pharaoh's jail as a recapitulation of the events in Genesis 37 may lie in one word, uttered by Joseph to the cupbearer: "I have done nothing that they should put me into this *pit (ba'bor)*— the very same word used in Gen. 37:24. Any English rendering that fails to take the Hebrew *"ba'bor"* literally will cause the reader to fail to make this connection. (Even splitting the difference between jail and pit, "dungeon," in the NJPS translation, runs this risk.) The outcomes of the dreams, needless to say, are exactly as Joseph foretold:

> On the third day—his birthday—Pharaoh made a banquet for all his officials, and he singled out his chief cupbearer and his chief baker from among his officials. He restored the chief cupbearer to his cupbearing, and he placed the cup in Pharaoh's hand; but the chief baker he impaled—just as Joseph had interpreted to them. (Gen. 40:20–22)[33]

On the third day—three being a recurring number in the Joseph story—Pharaoh throws a birthday bash (*mishteh*; Gen. 41:20). Since this is the same word used in Esther when another gentile monarch (Ahashuerus) initiates the nearly disastrous sequence of events that ends with Haman being hanged high in place of Mordechai, one can imagine the biblical author offering a little sermon against licentious non-Jews.[34] If that is a stretch, one would have to be rather obtuse not to catch the satire on royal power implied here—a birthday hanging is certainly not my idea of a good time. In any event the cupbearer is restored to his former position. The baker, if Joseph's interpretation is to be taken literally, is beheaded and then hanged. The seeming impossibility of hanging a headless man leads Sarna to suggest that the Hebrew "*talah*," in this case at least, probably means impaling, a common ancient Near Eastern punishment. Sarna, always a trusty guide, calls this a "grim play on words" with the biblical author juxtaposing lifting up one's head (to show favor) and lifting one's head off one's shoulders (decapitation).

The cupbearer's return to favor concludes this chapter and also the first Torah portion of the Joseph story (Va-yeshev). Now in his late twenties rather than his late teens, Joseph must wait two full years for his redemption.

Joseph as Dream Interpreter in Pharaoh's Court

Chapter 41 marks the beginning of the weekly portion in the traditional Jewish division of the Bible. Since this chapter will see Joseph's elevation from prison to power, the division is well chosen. The Torah portion (Mikkets) begins, "And it came to pass at the end of two full years, that Pharaoh dreamed; and, behold, he stood by the river [Nile]." The Bible employs the proper title, Pharaoh, rather than "king of Egypt" (Gen. 40:1), since the royal court itself, rather than the transition from Potiphar's house to prison, is now the focus. The time lag allows us to ponder the changes in Joseph's life during these "two full years." Did Joseph use these two years to regret his boastfulness? Did these two years of imprisonment further embitter him toward his brothers? We are not told. Here is another example of Auerbach's "fraught with background" designation. Sometimes biblical actions are only graspable on the basis of our prior knowledge of that character. Abraham's willingness to sacrifice Isaac (Genesis 22) strikes the reader as plausible only because we have witnessed the relationship that began years earlier with a command to leave country, birthplace and family (Genesis 12). Another kind of background is supplied by our common humanity: we imagine how Joseph had time in prison to meditate on his fate; we imagine how often Jacob "replayed" his fateful decision to send Joseph in search of his brothers, how often the brothers regretted their actions, and so on. But these remain background reflections, rarely narrated.

Pharaoh's dream takes place at the banks of the Nile, the lifeline of the nation. The two pairs of seven cattle and the two pairs of seven cornstalks clearly point in an ominous direction: both times the dream ends badly. Whether the order of cattle to corn signifies plowing to reaping (the natural sequence of the agricultural season) or simply an increasing level of dire necessity (hamburgers are a luxury; bread is a necessity) is uncertain. But no reader can be surprised that when Pharaoh wakes up in verse eight "his soul was troubled." Joseph—and the reader—know more than the other characters in the story. As in chapters 37 and 40, the dreams are doubled, signifying their authenticity and seriousness—as the brothers realized in Genesis 37 and as Joseph realized in Gen. 41:32. This is also the third time that a specific number plays a role in these dream sequences. In the case of the cupbearer and baker, the number three recurs; here, the number seven (seven good cows, seven bad cows, seven good ears of grain, seven bad ears of grain). Joseph, in other words, possesses insider information.

Pharaoh's reaction may reflect more of the ethnocentric satire we saw in chapter 40: All the magicians and all the wise men of Egypt cannot interpret his dream. Considering that dream interpretation was a highly specialized and skilled profession, this is an admission of defeat. Indeed the fact that Pharaoh calls first for magicians (*hartumim*) and secondly for wise men (*hakhamim*) may indicate his limitations as a ruler. Perhaps, as some sources intimated, the "specialists" understand Pharaoh's ominous dream without being able to either confront their master or come up with some kind of program to deal with the impending disaster. There is some support for that position in the seemingly extraneous last word of the verse 8: "But there was none that could interpret them unto Pharaoh." A hyperliteral reading suggests that they did understand, but were afraid to tell the boss. On the other hand other sources note the alteration of number in the verse, "And Pharaoh told them his *dream* (8a—singular); but there was none that could interpret *them* (8b—plural) unto Pharaoh." Abravanel thinks that Pharaoh, but not the magicians, realized it was one dream.[35] Sure enough in Gen. 41:15 Pharaoh again employs the singular when he tells Joseph that he has dreamed a dream. (To be fair to the Egyptian magicians, however, it should be noted that Pharaoh did wake up in between the dreams.)

Pharaoh's dreams become a matter of national concern. The "forgetful" cupbearer thus finds his memory jogged by possible advantage and mentions Joseph but hedges his bet by describing him as a "young man, a Hebrew, a servant"(Gen. 41:12). In other words, the cupbearer implies, do not be too surprised if the fellow before you is an unprepossessing, scraggly foreigner. Rashi reacts to this characterization of Joseph with anger: "Cursed be the wicked, because even their favors are incomplete. He recalled Joseph in the most disparaging term: a young man (ignorant and unfit for distinction); a Hebrew (a foreigner who does not understand our language); a servant (it is written in the laws of Egypt that a servant can neither be ruler nor wear the raiment of a noble)."[36]

The cows may be eating reed grass, Pharaoh may be grasping at straws, but God has directed his hand to the right man. Joseph is brought, this time for good, "out of the dungeon" (*min-ha'bor*). Three steps have brought Joseph down: down to the pit, down to the house of Potiphar in Egypt, down to the royal jail. Now one dramatic step brings him back up. The intensive verb form is employed as Joseph hastily shaves and changes his clothes—clothes serving in this story as a sign of elevation (Jacob's gift of the long-sleeved garment), degradation (the stripping that gift off), and now elevation again. A variety of interpretations have been offered for Joseph's preparations for meeting Pharaoh. One may stress his self-respecting nature: he simply did not want to appear before Pharaoh disheveled. One may stress Joseph's awareness that this is his big chance: he wants to look his best for what is to come. Without argument the three-fold verbal form in Gen. 41:14 reveals Joseph's sense of self-possession, as does his response to Pharaoh's dream: "it is not in me; God will give Pharaoh an answer of peace." Yet even more strikingly than with the cupbearer and baker, Joseph's assertion of God's providence does not minimize his own actions. After Pharaoh's somewhat histrionic retelling (Gen. 41:17–25), Joseph provides the interpretation, starting with the critical piece of information, "The dream of the Pharaoh is one." Joseph concludes his dream interpretation with the explanation of why the dream was doubled: one, because it came "certified" from God, and two, because God will bring the dream about right away.

Talmudic Dreams: Joseph as Text and Subtext

Joseph provides text and subtext to the Talmud's longest discussion of dreaming. Appearing near the end of tractate "Blessings" (*Berachot*), the Sages consider the possibility that dreams originate from external forces, but also the modern view that dreams represent the subconscious working out of the individual's own repressed desires. "Blessings" deals primarily with the forms and observances surrounding statutory prayers, incidental prayers, and the phenomenology of praying generally. "Blessings" deals with many familiar topics, including rules concerning the recitation of the *Shma* and the *Amidah*, special holiday blessings, Grace after Meals, and so on. "Blessings" constitutes the first tractate in collected volumes of Talmud, although one does not learn Talmud from beginning to end.[37]

Rabbi Hama ben Hanina asks: Why did Joseph die before his brothers? Rabbi Hama explains Joseph's "early" demise as the consequence of one who exercised power. He hangs his conclusion on Joseph's death narrative in Gen. 50:24–25, when he makes his older brothers swear that will bring his bones up to Canaan for reburial, and on the word order in Exod. 1:6, which confirms this sequence: "And Joseph died, [read: then] and all his brethren, and all that generation."[38]

Prompted by Rabbi Hama ben Hanina's mention of Joseph, the Talmud enters into a lengthy digression on dreams. Anyone familiar with the associative logic of the Talmud will not find this surprising, especially as Joseph is arguably the first biblical character to receive a symbolic dream.[39] The Talmud enumerates three matters that require supplicating God, and three matters that God proclaims without being asked. The first set of three: a good king, a good year, and a good dream. And the second triplet: famine, plenty, and a good leader.

Neither set of threes mentions Joseph or cites proof texts from the Joseph cycle. But the Talmud patently has Joseph in mind—from the topics discussed, from the prominence of Joseph in this talmudic chapter overall, and even from the prominence of the number three in a discussion of dreams, since Joseph had three sets of doubled dreams.[40] The relationships of dreams, fasts, leadership, and prophecy occupy the Talmud in several more give-and-takes before returning to Joseph as a model of dream fulfillment. Israeli polymath Adin Steinsaltz translates:

> On a similar note, Rabbi Berakhya said: Even though part of a dream is fulfilled, all of it is not fulfilled. From where do we derive this? From the story of Joseph's dream, as it is written: *"and he said: 'Behold, I have dreamed a dream and behold the sun and the moon and the eleven stars bowed down to me'."* (Genesis 37:9) Even this dream that was ultimately fulfilled contained an element that was not fulfilled. From where do we derive this? From the story of Joseph's dream, as it is written: *"And he said, 'Behold, I have dreamed yet a dream: and behold, the sum and the moon and eleven stars bowed down to me'."* According to the interpretation of the dream, the moon symbolizes Joseph's mother. Even this dream that was ultimately fulfilled contained an element that was not fulfilled.

One can only applaud the Talmud's bluntness about a textual problem that all proffered solutions fall short of answering: Joseph's mother is dead—she cannot bow down to him in Egypt. Rabbi Berakhyah's view that the entirety of a dream cannot be fulfilled goes beyond the view that every dream has a bit of nonsense in it—and suggests something generically human. Dream fulfillment involves the passage of time. By the time the brothers bow down to Joseph Rachel is long dead, and Joseph is burdened by a multitude of responsibilities he did not have as seventeen-year-old. Joseph affirms that his dreams have been fulfilled in conformity to God's plan. One may sense fatalism on Joseph's part, maybe a lit-

43

tle "I told you so," maybe even a little Schadenfreude. But I do not know of any reader who imagined Joseph as simply delighted—too much water had flowed under the bridge. Do dreams have an expiration date? How long should one wait for the fulfillment of one's dreams? The Talmud states: twenty-two years, which Rabbi Levi calculates on the basis of Joseph's case: seventeen in Genesis 37, plus thirteen years from seventeen to thirty (the age he stood before Pharaoh) plus seven years of plenty plus two years of famine, which equals twenty-two years total.

The Talmud continues its exposition of the power of Joseph's dreams. In the case of an unclear dream, one may nudge its outcome favorably by invoking biblical figures. First among these figures comes Joseph, whose good dreams may strengthen and reinforce one's own good dreams. Joseph's merit has power to mitigate bad dreams too. The Talmud advises that when one comes into a city and fears the evil eye, one should grasp the thumbs of the opposite hands into each other, and proclaim oneself the descendant of Joseph, over whom the evil eye has no power. An anonymous Sage suggests reciting this verse: "Joseph is a fruitful vine, a fruitful vine by a fountain" (Gen. 49:22). A second opinion connects this prophylactic measure to a slightly earlier verse from Jacob's blessing: "And let them grow into a multitude [like fish]." Often the Talmud uses a biblical verse as a formal proof text, with only tenuous substantive relevance. But that is not the case here. The Talmud seems to draw on Joseph's remarkable policies which, in truth, were what turned Pharaoh's dream of feast and famine to the good. The passage, which commences with "one who enters a city and fears the evil eye," surely has Joseph's chastity with Mrs. Potiphar in mind. When Rabbi Yosi ben Hanina asserts that the evil eye has no dominion over the sons of Joseph, he might be reflecting on the physical gesture that accompanies the recitation of this verse, suggesting Jacob's cross handed blessing of Ephraim and Manasseh, from which Rabbi Jose draws his proof text. The blessing of Joseph in Genesis 49 has undoubted power and so perfectly fits the scenario imagined by the Sages.

Joseph's pragmatic use of Pharaoh's dream naturally raises another question: does the dream follow the interpreter. Do "all dreams follow the mouth"? Rabbi Elazar affirms that that is the case. With the caveat that this is only true when the interpretation follows the dream plausibly, the Sages accept this view. But what about the unfortunate baker in Genesis 40—how did he know the cupbearer's dream and Joseph's interpretation was plausible? How did he know that Joseph's interpretation of the wine cupbearer's dream was correct?

The Sages also invoke the Joseph story in response to a critical question: which dreams get fulfilled? Rabbi Johannon says three kinds of dreams are fulfilled: an early morning dream, a dream that a friend has about one, and a dream that is interpreted in the midst of a dream. The Talmud continues, "Some also add, a dream which is repeated twice, as it says, *and for that dream was doubled unto Pharaoh twice*" (Gen. 41:32). Genesis 37–50 reverberates throughout this chapter of "Blessings," as do citations to Daniel, Esther, and the dream of Solomon in 1 Kings 3:4–15, all of which reflect Joseph's model.

What does this talmudic discussion tell us about Joseph the dreamer? First, the discussion of dreams in "Blessings" offers a subtle, deeply psychological view that questions the malleability of dreams while affirming that both dreamer and interpreter play a role in determining ultimate outcome. The positions of the Sages are ambivalent. Some dismiss dreams as inconsequential; others think dreams need to be dealt with to assure the best possible outcome. Second, the Talmud weaves the story of Joseph, the text of Joseph (exact words and phrases, not just overall story), into the experiences and teachings of the Sages. In a striking illustration of "intertextuality," Joseph provides both a text and a subtext for the Talmud's longest sustained discussion of dreams.[41]

Joseph's Dreams as Characterization

Dreams form a prominent part of the Joseph cycle. Yet we might ask, what does this tell us about Joseph? To Josephus this ability amounts to additional proof of Joseph's extraordinary skill set. To simplify the talmudic discussion, the Sages took Joseph as an embodiment of the power of dreams and their interpreters.[42] Steinsaltz acknowledges the "strange and inexplicable" elements of Joseph's character and ties them to the biblical description of Joseph as dreamer (ba'al halamot). For Steinsaltz Joseph is not a prophet yet is determined to see his dreams through to their fulfillment:

> Joseph did not try to convert the good years into anything else, or pretend that the difficult years would soon be over. He kept to the scheme of seven consecutive years and preserved what he could—relying completely on his own experience of dealing with dreams: that is, how to live out the dream and not struggle against it, to be receptive to its inevitability and yet come to grips with the real problems it imposes.[43]

Fortunately Joseph possessed the confidence and the patience to lead his childhood dreams to their conclusion. But the burden of possessing a dream so long delayed remained with Joseph, Steinsaltz suggests; it shaped his character, and not altogether positively.[44] Viewed from the perspective of Genesis 37, Joseph's dreams provoke the brothers more than anything else. Viewed from the continuation of the story, Joseph's abilities at dream interpretation propel him to the heights of power. His own dreams are impressive; they are not awesome like those of his father, Jacob, though they clearly inspired the author of Daniel and informed the Sages. Does God feed Joseph his interpretations, are they the product of his acute intelligence, or is this dichotomy too modern? Joseph tells the cupbearer and the baker, "Surely *God* can interpret" (Gen. 40:8) and "*God* will see to Pharaoh's welfare" (Gen. 41:16), but continues the first utterance, "tell me [your dreams]," and prefaces the second utterance, "Not I," before boldly reorganizing Egypt. Joseph remains an elusive hero and cryptic character. Before returning to Joseph, however, we meet two rougher and more direct figures, Tamar and Judah.

3

Tamar, a Difficult Hero

Readers familiar with Joseph mainly through sermons and popular culture may not be attuned to the interruption following
the sale of Joseph, so a brief summary of Genesis 38 seems in
order. At the beginning of this chapter, Judah departs from
his brothers and begins a new life on the outskirts of Judaean
territory in Keziv. In five verses we are told that Judah marries the daughter of Shua[1] and that this anonymous woman
gives birth to three sons: Er, Onan, and Shela.[2] This quick-
paced action indicates that we are not yet at the main focus
of the story. Judah chooses Tamar (we learn nothing about
her yet save her name) as a wife for his eldest son. Er, having done something to anger the Lord, is put to death, leaving Tamar a widow. Judah's second son Onan also dies, before
he can fulfill his levirate obligations; the Lord slays him too,
once again leaving Tamar a widow (more about levirate law
later in this chapter). Although the epithet "Judah's daughter-
in-law" is now used explicitly (Gen. 38:11), Judah is reticent
to marry his remaining son to this black widow. Judah promises Shelah to Tamar, but it becomes clear to her that Judah
intends to renege. Thus far Tamar has neither acted nor spoken. But now Tamar takes matters into her own hands. She
disguises herself as a prostitute at the Petach-Eynayim cross-
road on the way to Timnah (Gen. 38:14), negotiates a price,
and has sex with Judah; then she becomes pregnant. When

Judah is told that Tamar is expecting he orders that she be burned—a brutal way of removing an inconvenient woman.[3] Tamar, however, had wisely taken Judah's personal belongings as a pledge for future payment. She reveals—indirectly and ingeniously—that she is pregnant with Judah's son. Judah admits that he has treated Tamar unfairly; she is exonerated and gives birth to healthy twins, Peretz and Zerach. These are the rough outlines of an extraordinary story that appears, on first glance, as an interruption to the Joseph story. As usual the matter is not that simple.

Five points will receive particular attention. First, reactions to this story display a curious dividing line between Christian and Jewish interpreters. Martin Luther's view, refracted in much religious and academic scholarship, considers this incident shameful and one that, arguably, does not belong in the Bible. This attitude is contradicted by the entirety of Jewish tradition, beginning with the dictum that the story of Judah and Tamar deserves to be taught and explicated in synagogue.

A second consideration arises from the view that one can find Tamar and Judah morally justified, but it is still an awkward literary intrusion. Older scholars saw Genesis 38 as a clumsy interruption, but beginning with Robert Alter, scholars have argued forcefully for the artistic sensibility of the placement of Genesis 38 in Joseph, using themes, Leitwörter (key words), and the benefit of dramatic retardation of the plot. Many of Alter's observations were grounded in midrashim. Thomas Mann suggested that Tamar interpolates herself into the Joseph story, and that Joseph is itself an interpolation into Genesis!

Third, we will deal with the institution of levirate marriage, a brother's obligation to marry a deceased brother's wife (*yibbum*). Medieval scholars focused on law as well as narrative, and Genesis 38 offers a case where law and narrative may be fruitfully juxtaposed. Genesis contains relatively few commandments. Despite the injunction to be fertile and multiply, the basis of the rabbinic "laws of the children of Noah"

(Genesis 9), the decree of circumcision, the prohibition on eating the sciatica nerve, and so on, there are far more mitzvot in the weekly portion Mishpatim in Exodus than in all Genesis combined.

Fourth, the character of Tamar remains a delightful mystery. She succeeds, but the motives and means of her success are eyebrow raising, to say the least. Since she is the first of several female characters discussed in this biblical book, we explore her characterization at some length. The Bible displays an interesting technique with Tamar, juxtaposing her silence (Gen. 38:1–12) with her assertiveness in the verses that follow. But what does God think of her? The reader, typically, is not told directly, but Tamar wins Judah's admission of paternity, gives birth to twins, and becomes the font of the genealogy of Judahite line, continued in Ruth 4, and which culminates with the birth of David. This seems akin to a divine thumbs-up.[4]

Finally, we assess the rehabilitation of Judah, who will become a major character in this story, set apart from the brothers as a collective. Judah, the fourth-born son of Leah (her youngest, not counting the sons of Zilpah her handmaid) will emerge as the leader in Genesis 42–44, but signs of his distinction are obvious early on, from his plan to sell Joseph rather than kill him (Gen. 37:26–27), to his willingness to strike out on his own in Genesis 38.

Interpretive Dividing Lines:
Christian Author, Jewish Book?

Thomas Mann's *Joseph and His Brothers*, arguably the greatest biblically inspired novel, occupied Mann for nearly two decades. Mann built his "pyramid" of a novel with ancient Near Eastern texts, biblical scholarship, and copious rabbinic materials. His artistry was also fueled by his own political voyage from right to left, from antisemitism to philosemitism, from monarchism to republicanism. According to his correspondence, Mann's progress on *Joseph the Provider* had been impeded by the lack of a female lead. Mann's artistic breakthrough came from a rereading of Genesis 38, specifically with his rediscovery of Tamar:

> Her name was Tamar. We look around our audience and see a light of recognition on only a very few scattered faces. Apparently the vast majority of those who have gathered here to learn the precise circumstances of this story do not recall, are not even aware of some of its basic facts. We ought to take exception to this— that is, if such general ignorance were not just what the narrator wanted and can only be of use to him by increasing the value of his work. So you really no longer know, have never known as best you recall, who Tamar was? A Canaanite woman, to begin with, a child of the land and nothing more; then, however, the wife of the son of Jacob's son Judah, his fourth son, the man of blessing's granddaughter-in-law, so to speak; above all, however, she was his admirer, his student in matters of the world and of God; who hung on his words and gazed up into his solemn countenance with such devotion that the heart of the bereaved old man opened up to her entirely—and he was even a little in love with her.[5]

Given the freedom of a novelist, Mann cut through the seemingly inexplicable motivation of Tamar to bear a child from Judah's seed with a stunning invention: Tamar had sat at the feet of Jacob and was swept away by his tales of the family's spiritual greatness and messianic destiny. Long before formal conversion entered Judaism (biblically there was no such thing: not even the book of Ruth qualifies on this score), Tamar became a true believer. And she was a determined one. In no way a pious man, Mann's admiration for Tamar turned less on her theology than on her sheer grit in pushing into the biblical story. Mann's reading displays his customary skill, but with a catch. Mann immersed himself in academic German Bible scholarship but completely rejected its distaste for Tamar. Mann, like most German Protestants, grew up reading Martin Luther's Bible (a picture of the Mann family Bible can be found in his many biographies) but broke from the reformer's judgment.

Luther himself minced no words about Genesis 38: "Since this chapter embraces nothing except the account of Judah's production of children and the departure from his brothers, and besides this, the account of the most disgraceful incest with his daughter-in law Tamar, a question recurs: Why did God and the Holy Spirit want to have these shameful and abominable matters written and preserved and read in Church?" Were Luther's the sole disparagement of Genesis 38, Mann's independence would not be so striking. But Luther's attitude echoed throughout nineteenth-century Bible scholarship, a preeminently German-language, Protestant enterprise. It should not surprise that judgments as acquired by children, students, and seminarians were imported into the university. Gerhard von Rad's judgment may stand for several others: "It is certain that she [Tamar] did something quite unusual and even repulsive for the ideas of her times."[6]

A striking contrast to this erstwhile Protestant (male?) disdain for Tamar can be found in an important dictum in Mishnah Megillah 4:10 regarding which passages are appropriate to hear and expound in synagogue:

> The story of Reuben is read but not explained; the episode of Tamar is read and interpreted; the first story of the Golden Calf is read and translated, and the second account is read but not interpreted; the Priestly benediction and the narrative of David and that of Amnon are neither read nor translated. They may not conclude with the Chariot chapter as a reading from the Prophets; but Rabbi Yehudah permits it. Rabbi Eliezer says, They do not read the chapter "Cause Jerusalem to know" as the concluding reading from the Prophets.

The Talmud (BT, Megillah 25a–b) teases out and formalizes via mnemonics the logic of this Mishnah. The Sages note a number of places where one might think that reading and expounding certain verses would be objectionable but are not, and they then explain the cases at hand. Out of respect for Reuben and Jacob, the incident from Gen. 35:22 is read but not explained. The rape of the Bible's other Tamar (2 Samuel 13) makes both father and half brother look bad (and shames the victim too). The Sages also did not approve of expounding the passage in Ezek. 16:3: "thy father was an Amorite and thy mother was a Hittite." All these passages selected by the Mishnah deal with respecting the honor of the people involved, demonstrating a moral lesson, or, as in the case of Ezekiel, showing discretion out of respect for the people of Israel. Since Judah confessed to his error sincerely, this is a sign of his righteousness, so the story of Judah and Tamar (Gen. 38:13–30) is both read and explained—"obviously," as the opening word of the discussion adumbrates.

Later ages agreed that Tamar's situation bears scrutiny. Although neither Philo nor Josephus dwelt on this episode, Midrash and Talmud reference Tamar's story positively, as did the medieval commentators. What accounts for this basic disparity between Christian and Jewish attitudes? No one answer suffices. But a few cultural factors may explain the divide between Luther and the Mishnah, between Jewish and Protestant readers generally (though, again, not Mann). Jews ascribed a great deal of importance to genealogy, and Tamar's ploy worked: she gives birth to two sons at the end of the chapter. Both sons, moreover, were considered by the rabbis righteous, unlike the earlier twins Jacob and Esau. The textual basis for this moral distinction is letter thin: the rabbis based it on the full spelling of the word twins here in Gen. 38:28, versus the "defective" spelling of twins in the earlier case (Gen. 25:24), where a letter has gone missing.[7] Here is one version of the contrast with Esau and Jacob:

> In the case of the further one (Peretz and Shelah) the period was abridged, whereas with (Tamar) it was complete. Below, te'omim

(twins) is written [with a *vav*], for Perez and Serah were both righteous, whereas here it is written defectively [without a *vav*], because of Jacob and Esau, one was righteous, while the other was wicked.[8]

Since *"vavim"* and *"yudim"* often serve as pronunciation aids in the Bible such variation is neither unusual nor conclusive.[9] One may suspect that the Sages' positive judgment on Tamar's progeny in this case is really the moralisitic horse that drags the exegetical cart; as so often in Midrash, the problem seems more imaginary than real. I would contend that however one spells "twins" in Hebrew, the commentary comparing these two birth narratives reflects the importance of family and fictive kinship in Jewish Bible reading. Typically Luther skips ahead to acknowledge that way down the road David comes from all this messing about, while the Jewish exegetes dwelled on the intermediate stages of this genealogy with greater affection.

Attitudes toward sexuality also come into play here. While the rabbis disapproved of fathers-in-law sleeping with daughters-in-law, motivation matters, and, as Rashi wrote, "Tamar acted out of pure motives." Tamar wanted to fulfill the levirate law, with its intent that the child of her union with Judah will somehow be reckoned to Er, her first deceased husband. Moreover the rabbis approved of Tamar's reluctance to shame Judah publicly. Rashi, relying on BT, Sotah 10b, relates that it is far better for a person to risk death—as Tamar did—than shame someone publicly. This Talmudic passage cites Tamar as a model of restraint regarding public shaming (*ona'ah*) in a way reminiscent of the rabbinic treatment of Hannah (1 Samuel 1–2), cited as a model for proper recitation of prayer.[10] Both women stand falsely accused: Tamar of lewdness; Hannah of drunkenness. Both women demonstrate proper comportment and wind up birthing important sons. In the rabbis' calculus, what Tamar did, however unconventional, had justification. Would it be irrelevant to note that medieval Christianity placed so much emphasis on sexual transgression as implicated in the first act of human disobedience that commentators were blinded to Tamar's justification? Would it be irrelevant to note that Luther was an Augustinian monk before he saw the light of Protestantism and advocated clerical marriage? Do such predilections influence one's reading of the biblical characters? I think so.

Genesis 38 seems to be one of those chapters (along with much more celebrated examples, such as the expulsion from Eden and the binding of Isaac, whose readings still reflect Jewish and Christian perspectives from earlier eras. (The exegetical traditions regarding Tamar contradict a frequently broached claim that the Christian Scriptures represents a jump forward in female equality from the Hebrew Bible. This claim, once popular among second-generation feminists, had an unpleasant underside, transferring the supersessionist orientation of Christianity toward Judaism generally to the specific realm of gender egalitarianism. However egalitarian the Gospels may be, and the mention of Tamar in the New Testament genealogy of David (Matt. 1:3) certainly constitutes positive inclusion, the Church Fathers seem no more progressive than the rabbis—and the same may be said of Greco-Roman society, the background for both emergent Christianity and Judaism, all of which validated patriarchies. The best-known intertestamental writers—of *Jubilees* and the Dead Sea Scrolls, Philo, and Josephus, did not have a great interest in Genesis 38, so it is not possible to say much about attitudes about Tamar in the period before the roughly contemporaneous canonizations of the Mishnah and the New Testament. Going forward Tamar has generally received approbation in Jewish sources—medieval and modern. Did Mann know of this rabbinic countertradition? That's another story, but yes, he did.[11])

Interpolations: Putting Tamar in Her Place

One can, of course, find the tale of Tamar and Judah morally justified, but still a literary interjection.[12] For E. A. Speiser, a representative of the "Pennsylvania school," which thoroughly mined ancient Near Eastern analogues and believed deeply in the historicity and antiquity of traditions, the presence of Genesis 38 may be attributed entirely to the desire to preserve ancient Judahite traditions.[13] Speiser considered the Joseph narrative to comprise J, E, and P sources. Genesis 38, in his view, came from the J source and had little to do with what came before or after. But Robert Alter's celebrated *The Art of Biblical Narrative* began with an argument for the redactional artistry of whoever inserted Genesis 38 in its current location.[14] Alter's consistent position remains that whatever the original components of biblical narrative (J, E, P, D, preexisting oral sources, etc.) the interpreter is best served by focusing on the final product. Not only has that final product—called the redacted or traditional, or masoretic, text—been inarguably the text that mattered to subsequent generations of Jews, but overhasty forays into the determination of what is J, E, P, or D also leads the interpreters away from the text at hand. (In his commentary *The Five Books of Moses*, Alter terms this the cardinal sin of "explanation" versus "interpretation.")[15]

Observing the text we actually have, Alter noted a series of themes and lexemes connecting Genesis 38 with what comes before and after. Among the connecting themes, Alter explicates the use of clothing, which is used in Genesis 37 first as a marker of Jacob's favoritism and Joseph's grandiosity and then as an object of violence and deception (the same tunic, now blood soaked). The "long-sleeved garment" or "coat of many colors" (nobody knows exactly what *"ketonet passim"* means) gets prime billing. The Bible continues the clothing theme in Genesis 39, where Potiphar's wife offers Joseph's tunic as evidence of his attempted rape, a bogus charge. Here, in Genesis 38, the self-veiling of Tamar as a prostitute plays an essential role, enticing Judah to sexual congress. In fact the theme of sexual aggression and sexual restraint, propriety and impropriety, revelation and concealment, tie chapters

38 and 39 together. Alter offers a set of words used in identical or similar instances in Genesis 37–39 to argue that there was careful editing of Genesis—and that the narrative of Genesis 38 coheres with the surrounding chapters. Most famously Alter observes the verbal combination *haker-na* (do you recognize) and *va-yaker* (and he recognized) used in that order at the climactic moments of both Genesis 37 and 38 as clearly intentional, not coincidental. Likewise, as Judah "goes down" from his brothers in Gen. 38:1, Joseph is "brought down" to Egypt in Gen. 39:1. Jacob ostentatiously "refuses consolation" for the loss of Joseph (Gen. 37:35), while Judah "seeks consolation" for the death of Bat-Shua (Gen. 38:12).

Alter took some of these connection clues from midrash, as David Berger noted when Alter first published his analysis of Genesis 38. Berger, like Alter, accepts that these connections count for a great deal. More skeptical, James Kugel sees Alter's attempt as apologetics, "literary criticism lite."[16] Kugel finds that Alter attempts to rescue the biblical text as a literary masterpiece, a source of moral teachings consonant with our own, the product of a coherent author, and more. The specifics of Alter's case do not impress Kugel much. The use of a theme word like "remember" or "descended" in Kugel's view proves little, given the frequency of those verbs and the limited vocabulary of biblical Hebrew. The homonymic (sound-alike) wordplay often used by other "new literary practitioners" strikes Kugel as far-fetched or inconclusive, especially when readers ignore differences between the letters *aleph* and *ayin* or *heh* and *chet* to make their point. Alter and Kugel are both scholarly giants, and besides that, both are male, white, Jewish, and from the same generation. Observing their considerable disagreements—methodological and aesthetic—offers a fascinating reflection on the limits of humanistic discourse to provide conclusive answers, or to put it more positively, testimony to the ability of honest observers to see things differently.

Less committed to getting the "right" answer, but every bit

as attuned to this chapter's anomalous position in the Joseph story, Mann offers this useful insight:

> Did Tamar, this child of the land, a simple Bal-worshipping farmer's daughter living in an episode within an episode, have any idea of this fact? Our answer is: She definitely did. The proof is found in her own behavior—simultaneously shocking and glorious, but based in profound seriousness. It is not without good reason that we have repeatedly and with a certain obstinacy used the word "interpolation." It is the watchword of the hour. It was Tamar's watchword as well. She wanted to interpolate herself—and did so with astonishing determination—into the grand story, into the vast play of events, about which she had learned by way of Jacob's instructions, and she was not to be left out of it at any price. Did not the word seduction come to mind just now? It had its reasons. It is, likewise a watchword. For it was by means of seduction that Tamar interpolated herself into that grand story of which our story is but an interpolation; she played the fascinating seductress, the harlot by the road, in order not to be left out, ruthlessly debasing herself in order to be raised up.[17]

Mann suggested that Tamar, having learned from Jacob that Judah was the one destined to sire the savior Shiloh (49:10), had no intention of being left in the historical dustbin. She consciously pushes herself into the Joseph story in Genesis 38. Mann, great reader that he was, recognized that the Joseph story is itself an interpolation into the Patriarchal narratives, into Genesis! Having created the heavens and the earth in six days (thirty-one verses), surely God did not need the thirteen chapters of Joseph to get Israel down to Egypt in order to be redeemed. Mann noted—I think justifiably—a true link between Tamar's actions and those of Joseph—or better, between their creators.

The Mystery of Levirate Marriage Law, Narrated

Medieval scholars focused on law as well as narrative. It is well known, at least among professional Bible scholars, that biblical narratives often contradict biblical laws. This is true not only for pre-Sinaitic events, which might be predicted, but even for post-Sinaitic ones. In a few cases this variance is presented as something bordering on explicit revision. The daughters of Zelophachad (Numbers 26–27), for instance, appeal to Moses to keep their father's name and estate alive even without the presence of a male issue. Moses brings their request to God, and God confirms their request—in contradiction to male-only inheritance laws elsewhere—presumably ordained by God too. More often the revision is less explicit, often accomplished by means of inner biblical exegesis.[18] Biblical texts repeatedly extend, qualify, and revise earlier biblical texts. The biblical law of levirate marriage (*yibbum*) seems fairly clear-cut:

> When brothers dwell together and one of them dies and leaves no son, the wife of the deceased shall not be married to a stranger, outside the family. Her husband's brother shall unite with her: he shall take her as his wife and perform the levir's duty. The first son that she bears shall be accounted to the dead brother that his name may not be blotted out in Israel. But if the man does not want to marry his brother's widow, his brother's widow shall declare:
>
> "My husband's brother refuses to establish a name in Israel for his brother; he will not perform the duty of a levir." The elders of the town shall then summon him and talk to him. If he insists, saying "I do not want to marry her," the brother's widow shall go up to him in the presence of the elders, pull the sandal off his foot, spit in his face, and make this declaration: "Thus shall be done to the man who will not build up his brother's house!" And he shall go in Israel by the name of the family of the unsandaled one [*halitzah*]. (Deut. 25:1–5)

Yet the two narratives presenting levirate marriages, that of Tamar and that of Ruth, both deviate from Deuteronomy![19]

Let us focus only on Genesis 38. On the face of it, it was up to Onan and then Shelah to declare their refusal in upholding the name of Er and submit to the humiliating *halitzah* ceremony. As Onan did not do this, there was no opportunity to engage in the sort of public shaming that Deuteronomy clearly intends for the brother unwilling to preserve his deceased brother's name. Although this took place in the Sorek Valley (outside Judah), "when brothers dwell together," certainly applies. We are told that God killed Er, but no cause is specified. We are told God killed Onan; the reason given is that he engaged in coitus interruptus with the intent of foiling the intent of this levirate injunction. But the nature of Er's sin could not be identical, midrashic cogitations to the contrary, for despite the double use of the often-revealing conjunction *gam* (also) in the verse describing their deaths, and the statement that God condemned both of them, Er (as firstborn) had no levirate obligation to fulfill. Their motives had to differ! Rashi (Gen. 38:7) employs midrash to explain that Er refused to impregnate Tamar because he did not wish to ruin her figure. This Rashi is reminiscent of his famous explication of the empty, waterless pit in Gen. 37:24 that we read about in chapter 2. The "seeming" redundancy of a waterless pit suggested "snakes and scorpions" to Rashi. Although readers such as Josipovici have found Rashi's reading utterly far-fetched, at the least the image of snakes and scorpions conveys the brothers' authentically homicidal intent. Similarly here Er's ostensible desire to preserve Tamar's figure relates thematically to the theme of improper sex (i.e., withholding seed), explicitly given as the reason for Onan's death, and as a way to do something with that little word *gam* (also).

Tamar's narrative, then, departs from the strictures of Deuteronomy 25. How do we explain this? Let us look at two explanations, one modern and one medieval. Calum Carmichael has argued that many deuteronomic laws emerged precisely as responses to narrative breaches of established custom. (Most contemporary scholars agree that commandments of the Torah were not intended to be a comprehensive law code for ancient Israel.) In Carmichael's judgment:

The entire law is inspired by the Deuteronomist's reflection upon the Tamar tradition. The problem which stands out in regard to the fulfillment of the levirate custom in that story is Judah's failure to ensure that his third son, Shelah, goes into Tamar. But this problem is essentially the same one that arose because of the second son's refusal, which was hidden from his father, to do his duty by his dead brother's widow. Stripping the story of its idiosyncratic features, the Deuteronomist is presented with the problem that lies before us in his levirate law: what to do in the absence of the enforcing authority of a father when a son refuses to act on behalf of his dead brother.[20]

Carmichael's view that the deuteronomic law presumes a patriarch enforcing levirate law seems reasonable, as does his explanation of the sexual shaming elements of the unsandaling (*halitzah*) ceremony. Carmichael concludes that some deuteronomic legislation emerged from reflection on the women in Genesis. Notably Carmichael rejects the idea that two chapters considered interpolations into the Joseph story—Genesis 38 and Genesis 49—do not belong. He finds the behavior of Judah in Genesis 37 and 38 specifically censored in Jacob's valediction over Judah in Genesis 49. Of course medieval exegetes were not inclined to interrogate the interaction of the various parts of Torah in this way. The five books of Moses were assumed by medieval rabbis to come from the same source and at the same time, although anomalies in the text were noted with considerable freedom. Still one should not gloss over this fundamental difference, or assume that traditional commentary labored under a handicap. Rather different issues excited the imagination. In the case of levirate marriage, the meaning rather than the composition of the traditions seemed of greatest interest. Nachmanides has this to say about levirate marriage:

The subject is indeed one of the great secrets of the Torah, concerning human reproduction, and it is evident to those observers who *"have eyes to see, and ears to hear."* The ancient wise men who were prior to the Torah knew of the great benefit in marrying a childless dead brother's wife, and that it was proper for the brother to take precedence in the matter, and upon his failure to do so, his next of kin would come after him, for any kinsman who was related to him, who would inherit his legacy, would a derive a benefit from such a marriage. And it was customary for the dead man's wife to be wed by the brother or father or the next of kin in the family. We do not know whether this was an ancient custom preceding Judah's. . . . They say that Judah was the one who inaugurated the commandment of marrying a childless person's widow, for since he had received the secret from his ancestors he was quick to fulfill it.[21]

Nachmanides, unlike Rashi, did not think the name of the deceased needed to be (literally) bestowed on the firstborn child of the levir. A minor note in 1 Chron. 4:21 listing Er as Shelah's eldest child supports Rashi's view. But Nachmanides notes that Boaz and Ruth's child is not called Mahlon, but Oved, a completely different name.[22] Nachmanides implies that in some mystical manner the soul of the deceased was reincarnated by this practice, and that it may be Judah who raised this mystical custom to the level of commandment, as suggested in Midrash Rabbah Genesis 85:5. (Thomas Mann, by contrast, imagined Judah complaining to Jacob that the latter had just fabricated levirate marriage out of his intoxication with Tamar.) Curiously, although the levirate law seems restricted to preserving the lines of males, it is worth noting that David's daughter, Absalom's sister, also named Tamar, does not wholly disappear after she is raped by Amnon. Absalom names his own daughter after his sister Tamar, and the narrator adds this note: "she was a beautiful woman" (2 Sam. 14:27b), as was her unfortunate aunt (2 Sam. 1:13). Finally one may admire the Chronicler's picayune "fix." 1 Chron. 4:21 makes Tamar and Shelah the parents of Er, indicating that they did ultimately fulfill the levirate law according to Deuteronomy 25. These examples suggest that the biblical period might have had a view of the soul's eternality that was assumed rather than stated dogmatically. That the Bible does affirm some kind of life after death, contrary to the assertions of much scholarship, seems to undergird Nachmanides' kabbalistic reading and has recently won some adherents in the secular academy.[23]

Portrait of a Biblical Hero

By this point even the readers who "no longer know, have never known as best you recall, who Tamar was" have come to some conclusions about her character. But more remains to be said, beginning, as is fitting for any biblical character, with one's name. Tamar does not get a formal naming speech (no woman in Tanakh does after Eve, though some, such as Sarai/Sarah, are renamed), but she does get a name, noteworthy enough in a text with about 115 named women and over one thousand named men. We are not told who named Tamar; this absence, in addition to highlighting her independent nature, also eliminates the perennial question of whether the naming reflects on the namer or the named, or both. Absent a namer Tamar presumably signifies something about the named. Tikvah Frymer-Kensky expounds Tamar's name beautifully:

> Tamar is the date palm tree, a tree that can bear copious and precious fruit. But the fertility of the date palm is not assured; it must be pollinated by direct human action. The name Tamar hints that this new daughter-in-law has the potential to bear, but her fertility will be endangered. The plot will determine whether she disappears (as did Tamar the daughter of David) or becomes the ancestress of a precious hero.[24]

As much as any woman in the Bible, Tamar is her own woman. She may be a Canaanite, but she "belonged" to no tribe until she chose one. Although Targum Onkelos, Rashi, Rashbam, Nachmanides, Gersonides, and even the eighteenth-

century enlightener Moses Mendelssohn gloss *"k'nani"* (Canaanite) as synonym for merchant, I think we can dismiss this
euphemistic suggestion (although Canaanite sometimes does
indeed mean merchant in the Bible). Here the commentators'
motive to make Tamar an Israelite, a merchant's daughter, is
obvious: it avoids the embarrassment of subsequent ages that
Judah was a willing intermarrier who married his kids exog-
amously after Abraham his great-grandfather had established
the precedent of marrying within the clan (Genesis 24). But
this argument pales in the face of weightier ones. The entire
narrative tension of this tale turns on Tamar being a foreigner,
as do the pointed reference backward to Tamar in Ruth 4.
Even Rebecca, while of the same clan as Isaac, is distant geo-
graphically and strikes readers as independent of her immediate family. More broadly the theme of striving, courageous,
non-Israelite women throwing in their lot with Israel (Zipporah, Rahab, Jael, Abigail, Ruth, Elisha's Shunamite hostess)
resounds so powerfully in the Bible that it makes little sense
to try to read the formidable Tamar out of this tradition.

What does God think? The reader is not told, but Tamar
gives birth to twins, a genealogy of Judahite line continued in
Ruth 4 with the ultimate birth of David. That the Lord can
make Davidic fruit of such seed surely constitutes part of the
point of this tale. In more humanistic terms, I think making Tamar Canaanite adds moral heft. Most eloquent on this
theme is Benno Jacob, a Reform rabbi from Dortmund, Germany, forced to flee the Nazis with his commentaries still in
manuscript. Jacob, one of the great modern Jewish commentators, saw the story of Tamar as a direct rebuke to the rac-
ism ascendant in his lifetime. "Tamar has been described as a
woman who wants a child at any price, disregards custom and
law, even commits incest and risks life and honor [to achieve]
her purpose. Actually this story, often regarded as objectionable, is the crown of the book of Genesis and Tamar one of its
most admirable women."[25]

Tamar represents a true original, yet she stands within the uppity, non-Israelite tradition of biblical women. Sarah and Rebecca, among the matriarchs, both display this tendency, perhaps Rebecca a bit more dramatically, since she is of the Abrahamic clan, but has lived with her father and brother (Nahor and Lavan) on the other side of the fertile crescent. Her decisive willingness to depart (the one-word Hebrew response *"eilech"* is usually rendered "I will go"). Rebecca's decisiveness of character can be inferred from several texts: she attended to the unknown, nameless servant representing Abraham in Genesis 24 (presumably the faithful Eliezer) with enormous energy, watering his thirsty camels; she may have been impressed by Eliezer's determination to bring her back as Isaac's bride; she may have found her patriarchal circle oppressive.

Lavan treats Jacob instrumentally; his daughters Leah and Rachel too. (Rebecca certainly responded positively to her sighting of Isaac, and veiled herself in preparation for marriage. Rebecca and Leah's act of veiling dramatically highlights Tamar's.) As Rebecca precedes Tamar, Tamar precedes Ruth, explicitly so. Ruth 4:12 reads, "And may your house be like the house of Perez whom Tamar bore to Judah." Of course the townspeople's prediction proves prophetic: Ruth will continue the procreative circuit that leads to the birth of David. In Ruth that last line may be an addition to the original text, which ends at verse 17 with the "father of David." I would say the additional pericope that concludes Ruth 4:18–22 makes didactic what a careful reader already understands. Ruth, like Tamar, constitutes a critical link in the generational chain. (Nor should this be read as a reduction of womanhood to procreation; these two non-Israelites merit their status as extraordinary moral agents, not as walking wombs.) Both Tamar and Ruth began life as non-Israelites, both had unfruitful prior marriages, both dramatically and unexpectedly join their fates to those of the people Israel. One final thought: representing a tradition and also being truly original have often seemed at odds since the

Renaissance. But I think this view was very different in the ancient world, and in the Bible. Ruth and Tamar are originals. How is this accomplished?

Genesis 38 juxtaposes Tamar's silence (vv. 1–12) and her astonishing assertiveness afterward; Alter noted this as a typically effective acceleration/retardation technique. I would add this mirrors the theme of salvation coming out of nowhere, with drama. Tamar's bargaining with Judah at the crossroads has received lavish attention, beginning with Alter's recreation of the bargaining between the two as highly reminiscent of a Middle Eastern bazaar. Does Tamar sense that a goods-for-service trade won't be enough? That she will need something more personal to win her case? Although Judah suggested selling Joseph for thirty shekels in Genesis 37, he was eager to acquit his debt to the woman he wrongfully took for a prostitute in Genesis 38.[26] The variation on the use of two terms (*zonah*/harlot versus *kedesha*/prostitute) has also been noted sufficiently. Some consider this a clever way to highlight Judah's desire to sanitize his actions, or at least, Judah's friend Hirah's way of making a better impression on the inhabitants of Timnah. (Asking "where's your sacred prostitute" is certainly less obnoxious than "where's your town whore?") But others are not sure we should read literary artifice into this dual usage. The Bible acknowledges at many places that Israelite usage varies and, if the context calls for it, uses language that is not religiously appropriate or even Israelite.[27]

However one parses Tamar's demand, it proves to be insightful. That Tamar situates herself at *petach eynayim* ("crossroads," but more literally "an opening of the eyes") has struck modern commentators as delightfully ironic—their sexual congress will open Judah's closed eyes to his levirate obligations. Judah does not recognize his daughter-in-law, and Tamar really does sit at a crossroads in her life. Midrash observed, with mock astonishment, that the phrase *"petach eynayim"* was mentioned in no other place in the Bible; to my mind that's more or less rabbinic idiom for acknowledging the irony of this meeting.[28] The biblical line "And he knew her not again," it seems to me, was well captured by Harold Bloom's observation that neither Judah nor Tamar would want a repeat performance, although *The Torah: A Women's Commentary* observes that Tamar, in this narrative, is denied the status of wife.[29] "At any rate, his [Judah's] response thus limits Tamar's success: she becomes a mother of twins but remains without a (sexual) partner."[30] Vanessa Ochs lucidly captures the price Tamar must pay to overcome the disability of being a foreigner and a woman:

> Here is the problem that I had: if Tamar truly had no other choice but to sleep with her father-in-law in order to move on with her life, what kind of a lesson does that teach? That desperate oppressed women ought to debase themselves and engage in trickery? However much Tamar's story intrigued me, I struggled with the disguise she had to endure, the degredation. While she may have "won" in the end, there was the price of that disguise. Once again, I found myself outside the biblical story.[31]

Ochs pressed on to note that Tamar let her disguise down in the end: she endured and emerged a survivor. I have already noted that the twins Tamar bore create a connection to Rebecca's twins in Gen. 25:21–26, though here the midwife attempts to resolve the uterine dispute of seniority at birth unsuccessfully; Peretz pushes past the scarlet-corded Zerah. As always with biblical type scenes, the variations demand attention. In Rebecca's case an anonymous "they" pronounce the names Esau and Jacob, while in the book of Ruth the townswomen swoop in and declare, "A son has been born to Naomi" (Ruth 4:17). There is nothing unusual in women doing the baby naming, and Ilana Pardes has wisely cautioned against both underreading and overreading the significance of these naming speeches.[32] In the case of Genesis 38, though, the wordplay focusing on the breaching of Peretz ("breaching" or "breaking into") seems a little piece of narrative sleight of hand, for Tamar has also broken into the story of Israel, decisively so, as Mann recognized. Mann adored Tamar and projected that sentiment onto Jacob. Tamar has won an impressive set of admirers, including Thomas Mann, Benno Jacob, and Harold Bloom.

Bloom's *The Book of J* gained fame for its supposition that J might be a woman, and Bloom accorded Tamar top billing.[33] Bloom sees Tamar as something of a female opposite to Jacob. *The Book of J* represents the thinly veiled transposition of Bloom's value system—agonistic strife, freedom from influence, vitalism, human autonomy—onto a biblical source. Great individuals though they are, Jacob and Joseph and Tamar see themselves as also working through God's will; the famous renaming of Jacob as Israel, "who has striven with God and man and prevailed" (Gen. 32:29), means winning an enduring relationship with God for himself and his progeny: independence from God is simply unimaginable in the biblical worldview. Job's "let me die" speech (3:3) may be the exception, but of course that utterance acknowledges that there can be no human life without God. These qualifications aside, Bloom captures Tamar's heroic goal ("more life") and recognizes that a character accorded little textual space can still rank as major one:

> Of all J's heroines, Tamar is the most vivid, and the most revelatory of J's identity, both as a woman and as a literary ironist of high civilization and intense sophistication. . . . Indomitable, she does not accept defeat, whether from Er, Onan or Judah. Her will becomes the will of Yahweh, and ten generations later leads to David, of all humans the most-favored by Yahweh. Pragmatically Tamar is a prophetess, and she usurps the future beyond any prophet's achievement. She is single-minded, fearless, and totally self-confident, and she has absolute insight into Judah. Most crucially, she knows that she is the future, and she sets aside societal and male-imposed conventions in order to arrive at her truth, which will turn out to be Yahweh's truth, or David.[34]

Judah Begins His Rehabilitation

As tempting as it is to leave this chapter with Tamar, Genesis 38 has also been seen as the beginning of Judah's moral rehabilitation. In Genesis 37 Judah had proposed the sale of Joseph, intending to save his life, though hardly qualifying as a profile in courage. Now Judah holds another life in hand. Although Tamar holds his seal, cord, and staff as pledge, Judah, presumably, could have denied his ownership and consigned her to the flames. He says: "Take her out and burn her," a particularly brutal punishment, indicated by the two words in Hebrew (*hotziuhah v'tisaref*), as Alter rightly noted. Burning was not among the normative capital punishments in Israel, and traditional commentators wondered how Judah could demand this punishment. The answer of Nachmanides, that as tribal chief, Judah had extrajudicial powers, seems as good as any. Of course Judah decides to fess up to his culpability (Gen. 38:26), although commentators debated whether the admission is one of paternity (Rashi: "She is right; the child is from me"), or simply that Tamar's had the better case (the majority view: "She is more in the right than I am"). One may also question the Talmud's conviction that Tamar would have faced death rather than shame Judah publicly. This pietistic reading seems to underestimate Tamar's willingness to play the cards that she holds. In any event these words (*tzadkah m'meni*) will be Judah's last until Genesis 42. Given Judah's later eloquence, it is not surprising that midrash imagines a pious reading here as well:

> With your permission, my brothers, I proclaim here and now that each human being is treated measure for measure, be it for good or for bad, and happy is the person who recognizes his sin. It is because I dipped Joseph's coat in the blood of a goat and brought it to my father, saying: "Please identify it. Is it your son's shirt or not?" that I must now identify before this tribunal to whom seal, cord and staff belong. . . . So, I acknowledge that Tamar is

innocent. She is pregnant from me not because she yielded to any illicit passion but because I did not give her my son Shelah.[35]

Interruption, interpolation, interlude: however one judges the story of Tamar and Judah, they are not the only characters who emerge forever changed: the reader returns to a chastened, wiser, and more mature Joseph, making the most of his service to the Egyptian Potiphar. Meanwhile, however, we have been introduced to Tamar, a truly remarkable figure, whose characterization uses every "trick" in the book: a well-assigned name; a pointed narrative contrast between silence and activity; a rich web of associations with other biblical women; a dramatic climax and a fruitful denouement. And the source critics are probably right too: the presence of Judah, although he is just starting his path to family leadership, probably played a key role in this story's inclusion into the Joseph cycle, and so, into Genesis.

4

Potiphar's Wife Vilified
and Redeemed

The attempted seduction of Joseph by Potiphar's wife in Genesis 39 utterly fascinated later interpreters, Jewish, Christian, and Muslim alike.[1] But it is not the only example of female sexual assertiveness in the Bible. When the daughters of Lot thought that he was the last man alive they got their father drunk and slept with him, for strictly procreative motives.[2] Tamar enticed Judah, but she too, as we saw in the previous chapter, had exemplary motives. Bathsheba might have been more modest while bathing on the roof, as Leonard Cohen's "Hallelujah" puts it, but David was the king, and his summons could not be ignored. Even the strange (or forbidden) woman in Proverbs 7 can be warded off by Wisdom. And Ruth's actions with Boaz, of course, are wholly praiseworthy. These examples highlight Mrs. Potiphar as an exception—she seems animated purely by lust, but her motives receive scant explanation. In fact this episode occupies a mere ten verses and even then seems secondary to the theme of Joseph's meteoric rise:

> When Joseph was taken down to Egypt, a certain Egyptian, Potiphar, a courtier of Pharaoh and his chief cupbearer, bought him from the Ishmaelites who had brought him there. The Lord was with Joseph, and he was a successful man; and he stayed in the house of his Egyptian master. And when his master saw that the Lord was with him and that the Lord lent success to everything

he undertook, he took a liking to Joseph. He made him his personal attendant and put him in charge of his household, placing in his hands all that he owned. And from the time that the Egyptian put him in charge of his household and of all that he owned, the Lord blessed his house for Joseph's sake, so that the blessing of the Lord was upon everything that he owned, in the house and outside. He left all that he had in Joseph's hands and, with him there, he paid attention to nothing save the food that he ate. Now Joseph was well built and handsome.

After a time, his master's wife cast her eyes upon Joseph and said, "Lie with me." But he refused. He said to his master's wife, "Look, with me here, my master gives no thought to anything in this house, and all that he owns he has placed in my hands. He wields no more authority in this house than I, and he has withheld nothing from me except yourself, since you are his wife. How then could I do this most wicked thing, and sin before God?" And much as she coaxed Joseph day after day, he did not yield to her request to lie beside her, to be with her.

The narrator begins the scene abruptly, with Mrs. Potiphar's imperative, "Lie with me" (only two words in Hebrew). Most readers find this abruptness troubling and agree with Thomas Mann's observation: "To be frank, we are dismayed at the grudging brevity of an account that does so little justice to life's bitter and exacting particularity as our source does here."[3] Living in our hypersexualized and hypercommoditized society, American readers may not share Mann's mock astonishment. The text describes Potiphar's talented head of household as:

Va'yehi Yosef y'fei to'ar v'ifei mareh "Now Joseph was well built and handsome" (Gen. 39:6b), like his mother Rachel (Gen. 29:17).

In both cases the narrative deploys this physical description for greatest effect. In Rachel's case this occurs at the well in distant Paddan-Aram, when Jacob and the reader both set eyes on her. In the Joseph story the description precedes Mrs. Potiphar's advances. In both, physical description, rarely supplied by the Bible, signifies desirability, although ensuing outcomes could hardly differ more. An eleventh-century Islamic historian portrayed Joseph's charms as unlimited:

> Yusuf was light skinned. He had a beautiful face, curly hair and large eyes. He was of medium build, his arms and legs were muscular, his stomach "hungry" or flat. He had a hooked nose, and a small navel. The black mole on his right cheek was an ornament to his face, and between his eyes was a spot white as the full moon. His eyelashes were like the feathers of an eagle, and when he smiled the light flashed from his teeth. When Yusuf spoke rays of light beamed from between his lips.[4]

Do Joseph's looks fully explain Madam Potiphar's actions? Surely there were other handsome servants in Potiphar's house, and though Joseph served more as a major domo than as a pool boy, his ethnic status makes him particularly vulnerable. She is Potiphar's wife, the household's mistress, and thus Joseph's ethnic, social, and economic superior, although Joseph's allure destabilizes their respective status.[5] One midrash imagines a narcissistic Joseph who curls his hair and pencils his eyes. This, in turn, provokes the predatory she-bear; his behavior invites female aggressiveness.[6] The physical description of Joseph's good looks directly precedes Mrs. Potiphar's first seduction attempt, but juxtaposition is only that—the biblical text stops short of saying that Joseph's good looks caused her response, only that she "cast an eye on him." Far more textual space is devoted to her presentation of events to the other household servants and to Potiphar than to her motives. In this case the attitude of the other servants receives no attention at all—since Joseph has proven capable of provoking both jealousy (his brothers) and admiration (the cupbearer and the baker) we are left in a no man's land on this subject. How did Egyptians feel about a Hebrew rising to dominance? Mrs. Potiphar's speech assumes resentment (39:14–15), but she has been proven wrong, and in any case she is clearly engaged in self-exculpation.

Let us stipulate that the lack of explicated motive stems from the Bible's terse style, which hurries through issues considered peripheral. Joseph's behavior, his sexual continence in particular, not Mrs. Potiphar's lust, concerns Scripture. Even Potiphar is called by name only once in this chapter (Gen. 39:1).[7] Support for this viewpoint may be found in the fact that the biblical author denies her a proper name—often a signal of where the Bible intends the focus *not* to be paid.[8] For all the enormous attention this incident drew from subsequent interpreters, the interlude serves mainly as a vehicle to propel Joseph back into jail as a preliminary to his exaltation before Pharaoh. Joseph's inevitable success despite all impediments may be the lesson that mattered most to the author.

The lack of explicated motive of Mrs. Potiphar might also derive partly from the author's assumption of the audience's familiarity with the "Tale of Two Brothers," a thirteenth-century BCE Egyptian tale of attempted seduction, vengeance, and violence. In this story the sexually attractive younger brother, falsely suspected of adultery with the older brother's wife, cuts off his own phallus to prove his innocence. Rather than the story ending with imprisonment and success as in Genesis, the younger brother dies, and the older brother exacts vengeance on the lying wife.[9] Although there is no hard proof of biblical indebtedness, unlike, let us say, the flood story,[10] the theme of the desperate housewife was a familiar one in the ancient world.[11] Perhaps the author of Joseph took familiarity with the theme for granted, making it unnecessary to detail Mrs. Potiphar's character.[12] Like "boy meets girl at well" or "prophet meets God in the wilderness," the type scene relieves the author of the burden of excessive narration.[13] These practical concessions, however, have little bearing on later commentators, who asked hard questions about Mrs. Potiphar and Joseph.

Mrs. Potiphar's Motives Reconsidered

Subsequent readers wanted to know what motivated the woman whom medieval Muslim writers first named Zulaika—a name that stuck, and found its way into late medieval Jewish midrash.[14] In the Qur'an Mrs. Potiphar assembled the ladies of her court to view Joseph—overwhelmed with Joseph's beauty they slash their hands with knives while peeling oranges. This tradition: "the ladies of the court," or "the ladies of the city," as some sources have it, goes back very far, and in the view of the Orientalist Eduard Meyer lies behind the Mrs. Potiphar narrative. In the Qur'an the irresistibility of Joseph mitigates Mrs. Potiphar's sin.[15] Exculpating Mrs. Potiphar on other grounds, Rashi cites a midrash that an astrological impulse made her approach Joseph; she mistakenly thought that the signs foretold that she (and not her daughter) was destined to bear his children. Was Asenath Mrs. Potiphar's daughter? Or was Asenath the daughter of Dinah, who eventually married Job in the majority of midrashic fables? Some held that Asenath was something like Mrs. Potiphar's foundling daughter, splitting the difference between these two traditions:

> Dinah went forth to see those girls who were making merry; and Shechem seized her, and he slept with her, and she conceived and bore Asenath. The sons of Israel said that she (the child) should be killed, for they said that now people would say in all the land that there was an immoral daughter in the tents of Jacob. What did Jacob do? He wrote the holy name upon a golden plate, and suspended it about her neck and sent her away. She went her way. Michael the angel descended and took her, and brought her down to Egypt to the house of Potiphera; because Asenath was destined to become the wife of Joseph.[16]

Rashi seems to exonerate Mrs. Potiphar yet a few verses later condemns the sinfulness of her proposal, even by Egyptian standards. Rashi comments that "incest and adultery were forbidden to the children of Noah," the rules incumbent on all humanity. Even as Joseph's social superior, Mrs. Potiphar had no right to demand sexual favors. The bulk of Jewish tradition regards her as a sexual predator. But Rashi's attribution of a more positive motive to her desires ought not be dismissed too quickly. This view connects Mrs. Potiphar back to Tamar and forward to Joseph's Egyptian wife, assumed by Rashi (though not by modern biblical scholars) to be Asenath:

> In order to relate the narrative of Potiphar's wife to the narrative of Tamar, also in order to indicate to you that just as this one [Tamar] acted with pure motives, so too, the other [Potiphar's wife] acted with pure motives. She had seen in her astrological signs that she was destined to have children from him [Joseph], but she did not know whether it would be from her or whether from her daughter.[17]

What became of Mrs. Potiphar? Was Potiphar in Genesis 39 the same Potiphera in Genesis 41, who gives his daughter Asenath to Joseph (or did Pharaoh command that)? Most modern Bible scholars have assumed that Potiphar, the *saris paro* (Pharaoh's courtier) in Genesis 39 and Potiphera, the *Kohen on* (Priest of On in Heliopolis) are two different people, but medieval scholars did not. Certainly the characterizations of Asenath in all postbiblical sources emphasize her chastity; there is no hint of any "like mother like daughter" thinking that occasionally captures rabbinic imagination at its most sexist.[18] Assuming that Potiphar and Potiphera are not the same and that Potiphar did not really believe his wife, we are left somewhat in the dark. As usually portrayed by artists, Mrs. Potiphar is a middle-aged grandam, but the situation is even more intriguing if she is a bored postadolescent, as Israeli painter Abel Pann imagined. This depiction makes the failed seduction a contrast not only to Judah and Tamar in Genesis 38, but an anticipation of Joseph's impending nuptials with Asenath.[19] Within the romance of *Asenath and Joseph*, who are the perfect power couple, lurks the idea that Joseph and Mrs. Potiphar were meant to be together. The fifteenth-century Persian poet Jami concludes his poem as follows:

> One night from Yusuf's hand in haste she fled;
> And limping to obtain release she sped.
> Behind he seized her garment as she flew,
> And by his hand her robe was rent in two.
> Sulaikha said to him: "In days of yore
> Thy robe from off thy body once I tore.
> Thou hast my garment now from off me torn,
> And I my crime's just punishment have borne.
> Of right and wrong I now no longer fear;
> In tearing robes we both stand equal here.[20]

Joseph's Actions: The Case for Probity

Until this point we have focused on Mrs. Potiphar. But an even more central concern of later commentators in Genesis 39 lies in the assessment of Joseph's motives, actions, and reactions to Mrs. Potiphar's seduction attempts. A variety of rabbinic texts marvel at Joseph's self-restraint, including one from the ongoing colloquy between Rabbi Yosi and a Roman aristocrat (Matrona) found in many talmudic and midrashic sources:

> A matron asked Rabbi Yosi: Is it possible that Joseph, at seventeen years of age, with all the hot blood of youth, could act thus?" Thereupon Rabbi Yosi produced the book of Genesis and read the stories of Reuven and Judah. If Scripture did not suppress aught in the case of these, who were older and in their father's house, how much the more in the case of Joseph, who was younger and his own master?[21]

How did Joseph resist Mrs. Potiphar's blandishments? In response to her first proposition, the text says flatly, "He refused" (Gen. 39:8). If Joseph had succumbed, said Rabbi Yosi, Torah would have said so. Yet Rabbi Johanon assumed that the two intended to consummate their relationship as did numerous other rabbinic sources. Why then did Joseph resist? Did images of his father appear over her bed stand; or was it images of Egyptian idols that repelled him? Was it filial piety or religious belief? Nehama Leibowitz adopts the position that Joseph's religious upbringing was decisive; for Leibowitz, the Joseph who rebuffs Mrs. Potiphar is consistent with the Joseph who teaches Pharaoh that wisdom and success follow those who believe in one God.[22] Joseph as a child might have been obnoxious toward his big brothers, but he was dutiful to his father, even obediently responding to his father's instruction to go find the brothers. Forwarding a similar argument, Nahum Sarna identifies three distinct components of Joseph's refusal: (1) the violation of his master's unbounded confidence, (2) the crime against his master's possession and dignity, (3) the sin against God that adultery constituted, widely recognized in the ancient Near East, and in rabbinic eyes, not only for Jews but also as one of the seven Noahide laws.

Adding to the desire to exonerate Joseph, ancient interpreters exaggerated the role of Joseph as a champion of sexual temperance. The unusual title they granted Joseph (*tzaddik*, a righteous man) can be interpreted as proof positive of his resistance to Mrs. Potiphar. Some flavor of that moralizing can be found in William Whiston's quaint translation of Josephus's *Antiquities*: "But this opposition of Joseph, when she did not expect it, made her still more violent in her love to him; and as she was sorely beset with this naughty passion, so she resolved to compass her design by a second attempt."[23]

In Josephus's reading Potiphar believes his wife's account, unambiguously considered her a woman of merit, and tossed Joseph in jail. Josephus presents Joseph's chivalry as extending to a conscious decision to refrain from defending himself, but trusting in God instead. Quite the opposite conclusion is reached in the Qur'anic version of this showdown. In the first place Joseph does defend himself verbally from the charge of attempted rape. In the Bible Joseph says nothing to Potiphar, but that does not suggest, as per Josephus, that he consciously decided not to present his case. Perhaps the matter was simply decided by Potiphar without any consultation—if the idea was to save face, this is entirely plausible. Faced with opposing accounts, one member of Potiphar's household suggests that the way to find the truth is to see whether the garment was torn from behind or in front. In the N. J. Dawood rendering of the Qur'an (devout Muslims are even more devoted to the Arabic original than are Jews to the Hebrew): "And when her husband saw Joseph's shirt rent from behind, he said to her: 'This is one of your tricks. Your cunning is great indeed! Joseph, say no more about this. Woman, ask pardon for your sin. You have done wrong.'"[24] Curiously this interchange precedes the banquet scene in which Mrs. Potiphar parades the glorious Joseph before the women of the city, a scene that gave rise to highly elaborate traditions. Only afterward does Joseph implore Allah (in some Muslim accounts Joseph tries hard to bring Potiphar over to Islam). Qur'an adopts a position only hinted at in the Bible: Joseph must be jailed to keep up appearances. "Yet despite the evidence they had seen, the Egyptians thought it right to jail him for a time."[25] Whatever the denouement to this scene, most readers would agree that it ends the drama of Joseph and Mrs. Potiphar. (But some readers pursued this scandal into prison where Mrs. Potiphar continued her fruitless quest.[26])

James Kugel's magnificent untangling of the postbiblical, cross-cultural traditions about Joseph's behavior in Potiphar's house renders the numerous exculpations and indictments of Joseph in much fuller detail than I can recount here.[27] A few examples will have to suffice to give the imaginative range of verdicts on Joseph's actions: In *Jubilees* Joseph breaks down the door to escape Mrs. Potiphar's clutches; the *Testament of Joseph* denies that Joseph even considered having sex with Mrs. Potiphar. *Targum Pseudo-Jonathan* concedes Joseph had impulses but insists he overcame them.[28] Josephus concurs; Joseph was a perfect gentleman. BT, Yoma 35b, imagines Joseph's reciting psalms to ward off each of Mrs. Potiphar's advances—many of the same psalms that make up a common morning prayer. It bears noting, then, that for several centuries after Genesis 39 was written, hardly anybody thought to read Joseph's refusal as anything other than what the biblical text plainly says: "he refused" (Gen. 39.8).

The Case for Joseph Courting Disaster

Other commentators thought that Joseph came perilously close to sinning. What prompted medieval and modern interpreters to view Joseph's actions more ambivalently? A careful look at the text enables us to see what critics of Joseph find fishy. Over "he refused" (*va'yima'ain*) Masoretic tradition places a *shalshelet*—a long, trilling note. To wit: he refused but thought about it. Joseph's speech then unfolds to proclaim his master's obliviousness to details of running the household, possibly hinting with the suggestive verb "to know" that Joseph could get away with sleeping with her. Joseph then proceeds to announce that he (Potiphar) has given everything into his charge (literally, "into his hand"); that there was no one greater in the household; and finally that "only you" he has withheld. Since Joseph has already noted their being married, is it not obvious that she cannot have him, nor he her, without committing adultery? As Mark Twain, one of the Bible's more cynical readers, commented, at least Mrs. Potiphar's version seemed plausible.[29] Joseph's demurral has the feel of "the young man doth protest too much." The reader skeptical of Joseph's virtue will find Gen. 39:11 equally troubling. Knowing full well that Mrs. Potiphar was not dissuaded by his initial rebuff (i.e., "she spoke to Joseph day after day") Joseph entered the house to do his work when none of the household was there. The use of the word *melachto* (creative work) raised doubt about exactly what Joseph intended to do, and the likelihood of someone so much in charge of affairs being unaware that he was alone with the mistress of the house seems implausible. Why did they have the day off? Were they at a pagan festival? And why did the text say "the people of the house," not just "the servants"? The text seems to emphasize that the place was cleared out. Even close-reading interpreters like Leibowitz and Sarna must acknowledge that Joseph was not terribly careful about distancing himself from sin.

But other interpreters are far less generous: they think Joseph courted this drama. These critics have read Joseph's self-aggrandizing speeches in Genesis 39 as preening incitement, though only Mark Twain, to my knowledge, goes so far as to imagine Joseph as having fulfilled Mrs. Potiphar's desires. "Joseph got into trouble with Potiphar's wife at last, and both gave in their versions of the affair, but the lady's was plausible and Joseph's most outrageously shaky." Leon Kass's analysis, as consistently hostile to Joseph as Nehama Leibowitz's is sympathetic, rests on the language Joseph used to turn her down: an excessive focus on his contributions to Potiphar's household and the trust that he enjoys.[30] But one must acknowledge that Joseph's self-aggrandizing self-description does not go much beyond the narrator who has previously told us of Potiphar that "he left all that he had in Joseph's hand."

Some Sages assume that Joseph intended to sin with Mrs. Potiphar, but overcame his desire to do so. The following text comes from a lengthy aggadic portion describing why the twelve tribes all deserved to have their names inscribed on Aaron's breastplate:

> R. Yohanan said: this verse teaches that the two of them had planned to sin together. "He entered the house to do his work." Rav and Samuel [disagreed]: one said it really means to do his work, the other said it means to satisfy his desires. He entered [and then it says] "And not one of the members of the household was present in the house." Is it really possible that no one else

was present in the large house of this wicked man [Potiphar?] It was taught in the school of R. Ishmael: that particular day was their festival, and they had all gone to their idolatrous rites, but she told them that she was sick. She had said that there was no day in which she might indulge herself with Joseph like this day! "And she seized him by his garment. . . ." At that moment the image of his father entered and appeared to him in the window. He said to him: Joseph your brothers are destined to have their names written on the priestly breastplate, and yours is among theirs. Do you want it to be erased and yourself to be called the shepherd of prostitutes? At once [he overcame his desires].[31]

The Credulous Mr. Potiphar?

We have examined only two of the three characters in this drama Who was Mr. Potiphar, and did he really believe his wife? We know very little about Potiphar, and most of that is packed into his threefold introduction. He is described here as "a certain Egyptian, Potiphar, a courtier of Pharaoh and his chief cupbearer." What exactly is a "courtier of Pharaoh"? Many sources identify that title (saris paro) as eunuch, which would add something to an understanding of Mrs. Potiphar's desire for Joseph.[32] Some midrashim, trying to connect Potiphar to Potiphera, imagine that Potiphar bought Joseph for sexual pleasure. If Potiphar was homosexual, that would also speak to Mrs. Potiphar's motives. In this far-fetched reading, God makes Potiphar castrated before he moves to Heliopolis and becomes Potiphera, Priest of On. Potiphar "chief steward" (sar ha-tabahim) appears to be related to food, and mitbah in modern Hebrew is kitchen; but the Potiphar household seems more like a self-standing economic unit than a catering office. Some midrashim render the title (sar ha-tabahim) as chief executioner rather than steward. Potiphar's titles are used only here—though eunuch and courtier, cupbearer and executioner, seem like very different jobs, we cannot be too sure what the text denotes.[33]

Why does Scripture introduce Potiphar as "an Egyptian man" (*ish mitzri*) three times (vv. 1, 2, and 5)?[34] Is this is a form of foreshadowing—the family of Israel will wind up in Egypt by the end of the book? Is it also a fulfillment of the prophecy to Abraham (Gen. 15:13)?[35] Or perhaps the emphasis on Egypt clarifies the fact that Joseph is no longer in the hands of Ishmaelites or Midianites (recall the confusing end of Genesis 37). Hirsch offers a more didactic explanation: namely, that the Bible refers to his being Egyptian repeatedly to highlight the contrast between Israelite and Egyptian mores.[36]

We have already seen that Potiphar takes a liking to Joseph, trusts him, and places his household's welfare in the latter's hands (all this, of course, will be preliminary to the far larger scope of control vested in Joseph by Pharaoh later). But Potiphar's next words express anger. "When his master heard the story that his wife told him," namely, "Thus and so your slave did to me," he was furious. Clearly Potiphar's anger resulted in Joseph's imprisonment. But reading between the lines, some rabbis believed they found evidence suggesting that Potiphar doubted Joseph's guilt. The first part of Gen. 39:19, "When his master heard the story *that his wife told him*," seems somewhat superfluous, since Potiphar and the reader already know that Mrs. Potiphar is doing the speaking. The end of Gen. 39:19 tells us that Potiphar was furious (literally, "his nose was burning"), but not at whom his wrath was directed. One can infer that Joseph is the object of Potiphar's anger, though no "at him" appears; but one can also conclude that Potiphar is angry at his wife, or simply at the awkward situation. Mrs. Potiphar, after all, was the speaker, and she had told her story quite differently to the servants, emphasizing Joseph's Hebrewness, and maybe laying a little blame on the master of the house, while with her husband she emphasizes Joseph's slave status and personal betrayal. Her words—crafted for two sets of listeners, reflects her intent to manipulate the situation and cast guilt on Joseph.

Can we believe that Joseph, that quintessential man of

words, kept silent when faced with the accusations? Joseph's response to the charge, although unrecorded in Scripture, would have been couched effectively. One can imagine something like Josephus's version of events. Recalling that no response from the household slaves is reported at all (which might have been something like "Let's tear that Hebrew son-of-a-bitch to pieces"), one suspects that Mrs. Potiphar's carefully chosen words to the household slaves failed to convince—especially if one posits some prehistory to her infatuation and sexual harassment. As we know, there is often a pattern to such behavior. Household servants, moreover, generally know the truth about their masters. One notes that Potiphar carefully "took" and "placed" Joseph in the prison specially designated for the king's prisoners. The doubling of the verbs and the repetition of this special term for royal prison emphasize Potiphar's continued tutelage of his favored servant. Modern commentators focus on the repetition of *beit ha-sohar* as a means of imparting Egyptian verisimilitude to the narrative, since imprisonment was a particularly Egyptian form of punishment. The narrative characterization of Potiphar's abiding interest in Joseph seems significant; Nahum Sarna cites one papyrus that refers to slaves committed to "the little prison of the Overseer of the Treasury." What an ideal place to have Joseph's abilities noticed![37] The continued use of the epithet "Joseph's master" supports the speculation that Potiphar believed Joseph and not his wife.[38] But the clincher is more obvious than grammar. Had Potiphar thought Joseph, a young Hebrew slave, to be his wife's rapist, would he not have had him summarily executed, just as Pharaoh did to the baker in the next chapter? The commentators are divided, but being thrown in the royal jail rather than being executed was certainly a fortunate turn for our hero. Joseph's three descents (the pit, Potiphar's house, the king's prison) have come to an end—and his ascent commences forthwith.

5

Joseph from Rags to Riches

Thrown into a pit by his brothers, and into a jail by Potiphar, Joseph makes his way from the bottom to the top. Once Joseph appears before Pharaoh in Genesis 41, he faces no more reversals of fortune—though his family relations, as we shall see, are far from smooth. Gen. 39:2 describes Joseph, while still a prisoner in a foreign land, as a "man of success," saying that "the Lord was with him" and "the Lord lent success to everything he undertook." Joseph displays prudence, innovation, problem solving, and dream interpretation.[1] Joseph's skill set prompted ancient authors to view him as a courtier and a role model, while some Bible scholars see Joseph as emblematic of the Bible's Wisdom tradition. With our protagonist situated in the diaspora, in a foreign court, and as an ethnic other, an audience before the Pharaoh seems like an improbable long shot. Joseph transforms this summons into history's most successful job interview. The extraordinary impression Joseph makes on Pharaoh and his counselors sets the stage for the former's remarkable ascent—the main theme in this chapter.

We have examined Joseph's skill as a dream interpreter: now we will see him turn this to best advantage. Remarkably Joseph proceeds to lay out a plan suited to the cycle of seven years of bounty and seven years of famine that the Pharaoh's dream portends. The plan wins immediate assent, and Pharaoh elevates Joseph to second in command over the land of

Egypt. Has the Pharaoh's gamble on this unknown Hebrew paid off? Yes! By the end of Genesis 41, Joseph's plan has succeeded wildly: "So Joseph collected produce in very large quantity, like the sands of the sea until he ceased to measure it, for it could not be measured" (Gen. 41:49). Midrash and medieval commentators were all impressed by Joseph's nerve (*chutzpah*) in articulating a carefully planned agrarian policy, for the most part differing only about the issue of whether this policy was implicit in the Pharaoh's dream, or whether Joseph saw an opportunity and seized it.

Since the reunion with his brothers and father qualifies as the climax of the Joseph story, the elaboration of Joseph's policies in Gen. 47:13–27 is easily overlooked—if any passage in the Joseph story, or in Genesis, can be called neglected, this one may qualify.[2] Narratively the passage from feast to famine provides the necessary background for explaining the descent of the family to Egypt, which afforded Joseph the opportunity to test his brothers' character. The fate of Israel's settlement in the area of Goshen further obscures the aftereffects of Joseph's polices, but they are striking. The reader sees that Joseph has done more than rescue Egypt from a onetime catastrophe; he institutes a new social system that avoids starvation but reduces the status of the Egyptian farmer relative to Pharaoh and the priests (Gen. 47:13–27).

Reading this passage in the light of Enlightenment ideas of governance, modern interpreters have been more critical of Joseph's initiatives than earlier commentators. Aaron Wildavsky, a political scientist, reads Joseph principally as a negative image of Moses, the nurturing father of a nation.[3] Wildavsky's indictment can be summarized simply. Joseph Egyptianizes fully, abandoning his Israelite identity in exchange for wealth and power. In so doing Joseph reduces the Egyptians to servitude, preparing the grounds for Israel's own enslavement.

This chapter also addresses the challenge of maintaining fidelity both to one's ancestral tradition and to one's adopted country—a perennial theme in Jewish history. Couched in the language of "dual loyalty," this challenge becomes a charge used by the enemies of Israel to allege bad faith. Casual readers may not appreciate that the Bible already addresses this theme in the later biblical books Esther and Daniel. And only scholarly readers are likely to appreciate that Esther and Daniel elaborate the turns of phrase, settings, and themes used in Genesis. How and why Esther and Daniel do this deserves some explanation; the borderline between revelation and interpretation turns out to be quite porous.[4] What these later books imply about Joseph's character may be debated: the portraits of balancing Jewish identity with devotion to foreign rulers found in Esther and Daniel seem to some like veiled criticisms of Joseph; to others they seem to be neutral or positive reflections.

At the end of this chapter we meet another woman briefly mentioned in the Bible who became an important figure in postbiblical literature: Joseph's wife, the mother of Manasseh and Ephraim, who appears in three verses in Genesis (47:42, 41:50, 46:20). As Joseph's companion and the mother of his two sons, Asenath naturally attracted attention. We know Joseph had challenging sibling relationships, but what was the vizier of Egypt like as a husband and as a father? How did his accommodations to Egypt translate into the private realm? What were later readers to make of this intermarriage, given that the Bible prohibits intermarriage in several texts (at Deut. 7:1–5, in Ezra, and in Nehemiah)? Egyptians, theoretically, may enter the community of Israel only in the third generation, yet Asenath's two children are adopted by Jacob (Genesis 48), effectively granting Joseph a firstborn's double portion. This seems like reward, not punishment. The various rabbinic sources dealing with the Joseph and Asenath handle this "intermarriage" in two principal ways: (1) Asenath was actually a convert to Judaism, or (2) Asenath was really Dinah's daughter and thus Jewish. Both suppositions require imagination. Their relationship inspired a novella that offers an intriguing view into romance and religiosity in the first centuries CE.[5]

Joseph's Path to Success

The Bible loves narratives in which characters rise and fall. Joseph starts as favored son, gets thrown into a pit by his brothers, and gets sold into slavery. "Brought down to Egypt," Joseph gains extraordinary favor in the eyes of Potiphar.[6] Mrs. Potiphar, unnamed in the Bible and the Qur'an, but known by later traditions as Zulaika, falsely accuses Joseph of attempted rape; Potiphar places Joseph in the royal jail.[7] Will Joseph pull himself up once again? Brought before Pharaoh by the steward, who conveniently remembers Joseph's skill as a dream interpreter, Joseph explains the dream that baffled Egypt's "magicians and wise men," then lays out a bold plan that will save the Egyptian nation from seven years of famine. Beginning in Gen. 41:33, Joseph skyrockets from unkempt prisoner to a decked-out vizier.

Joseph's elevation is sudden and to the Egyptian bystanders must have seemed extraordinary. The youthful Joseph of Genesis 37 displayed little diplomatic aptitude. The reader sees another side of Joseph's talents on display in Potiphar's house and in the royal prison, and in the latter Joseph's skillful negotiations between cupbearer and baker. Even if the cupbearer "did not think of Joseph; he forgot him" (Gen. 40:23), Joseph obviously made enough of an impression on this self-serving cupbearer that he conveniently remembered Joseph to Pharaoh, albeit as "a servant . . . a Hebrew . . . a youth" (Gen. 41:9–13). When he is brought before Pharaoh from prison, Joseph's "rags to riches" story accelerates.

The details of this elevation deserve our attention. Joseph recommends seeking a man of discernment and wisdom to oversee the land of Egypt. Joseph invokes the name of God five times in the speech preceding this policy prescription.

Pharaoh takes this seriously and concludes that the spirit of God animates Joseph's interpretation and policy. Many commentators have observed that Joseph and Pharaoh both realize that the dream was one dream, not two. Others note that the dream, obviously ominous, proceeding from good to bad both times—was interpretable, but the Egyptian advisors fear to tell Pharaoh the bad news or fail to imagine a solution to what they understood all too well. Carried away by his own high judgment of (or wishful thinking about) Joseph's link to divine guidance, Pharaoh repeats his approbation of Joseph's wisdom and discernment and hands him the reins of power. A series of verses (Gen. 41:41, 41:44, 41:45, 41:55) make explicit what the narrative suggests anyway: Joseph will run Egypt, and whether we call him viceroy or vizier or second in command pales in comparison to the obvious signs of favor Pharaoh bestows on him.

Again clothing plays a critical narrative role. Fleeing Mrs. Potiphar Joseph is stripped of his linens. Now Pharaoh garbs Joseph in fine linens and gives him a signet ring and a gold chain (possibly in contrast to Judah's turning over similar items of identity to Tamar). Nor does Pharaoh stop here: Joseph is installed as second in command and is given the royal chariot (*Air Force 2*), and the kingdom is ordered to salute him with the exclamation "*Abrek.*" The rabbis parse this otherwise unattested title as "father of the king" or "bend the knee." Pharaoh, who has shown himself willing to celebrate his own birthday by decapitating a baker and histrionically bemoaning the badness of cows in a dream (not everybody regards these details as parodic), extends his largesse to Joseph further by assigning him the name "Zaphenath-paneah"[8] and giving him Asenath, the daughter of Poti-phera priest of On, for a wife. In thirteen verses (Gen. 41:33–45), Joseph has been sprung from prison, given a bravura performance before the king of Egypt, received near-dictatorial powers, won lavish rewards, including a glamorous name change and a trophy wife.

Will Pharaoh change his mind as quickly as he made it up? Will Joseph retain his new, exalted status? Gen. 41:45–46 serves as a narrative breather, affirming that this is no dream: "Thus Joseph emerged as in charge of the land of Egypt—Joseph was thirty years old when he entered the service of Pharaoh the king of Egypt. Leaving Pharaoh's presence, Joseph travelled over all the land of Egypt."[9] As if to affirm this forward motion, we are immediately informed of the details of Joseph's successful land policy and the birth of his two children with Asenath, Manasseh and Ephraim (Gen. 41:37–46). By the end of the rich years, Joseph has put all preparations in place; made himself Egypt's indispensable man, just as Pharaoh had proclaimed; and become a well-contented husband and father.

Ancient Readers Appraise Joseph's Consolidation of Power

Joseph's skill set prompted admiration among ancient authors, who recognized that Egypt continued to serve as one of the great granaries of the ancient world well into Roman times. (In our day, by contrast, Egypt must import food to feed its population.) A long list of early interpreters known mainly to scholars praised Joseph and his reforms,[10] none more gushingly than the historian Artapanus: "And whereas the Egyptians previously occupied the land in an irregular way because the country was not divided, and the weaker were treated unjustly by the stronger, he [Joseph] was the first to divide the land and mark it out with boundaries and much that lay waste he rendered fit for tillage and allotted certain of the arable land to the priests. He was also the inventor of measures and for these things was greatly loved by the Egyptians."[11]

For Flavius Josephus, Joseph was nothing less than a role model.[12] Both were prodigies, both were proud of their high birth, and both succeeded in foreign lands, serving non-Jewish masters, Egypt and Rome, respectively. Josephus had ample reason to praise Joseph; his *Jewish Antiquities*, a Jewish history, largely retells the Bible in a way that would interest Josephus's Greco-Roman readers. Josephus does not write about every biblical character, but he does write about Joseph, on whom he bestows the stereotypical Roman virtues: wisdom, justice, prudence, courage, and piety:[13] "Joseph also died when he had lived 110 years; having been a man of admirable virtue, and conducting all his affairs by the rules of reason; and used his authority with moderation, which was the cause of his so great felicity among the Egyptians, even when he came from another country, and that in such ill circumstances also, as we have already described." At length his brethren died, after they had lived happily in Egypt.[14]

Separated from Josephus by eighteen centuries, many modern Bible scholars come to a similarly rosy judgment, albeit in different terms.[15] Gerhard von Rad, a giant of modern scholarship, saw Joseph as emblematic of the Bible's Wisdom tradition.[16] Some of the features of this tradition—reflected in biblical books as disparate as Proverbs, Ecclesiastes, and Job—as well as in ostensibly historical characters such as Solomon—share an admiration for prudence, moderation, persuasive speech, willingness to accept instruction, and sexual temperance. The absences in the Wisdom tradition might be equally striking: little talk of covenant, the promise of the land of Israel to the Patriarchs, or ritual and cultic matters—indeed many of the themes that seem to dominate the Pentateuch. So it is striking that we have in Joseph, at least according to von Rad, the most extended portrait of a biblical Wisdom figure. For von Rad this feature gives Joseph its universal appeal and surface secularity, despite Joseph's pious invocations of God: "[Wisdom texts] depict a man who by his upbringing, his modesty, his learning, his courtesy, and his self-discipline has acquired true nobility of character. He is, let us say it at once, the image of Joseph! Joseph, as the writer of the narrative draws him, is the very picture of such a young man at his best, well-bred and finely educated, steadfast in faith and well-versed in the world."[17]

Pregnant Pause: Joseph's Policies
Instituted and Intensified

As soon as Joseph interprets Pharaoh's dream, he proceeds to plan for the cycle of feast and famine (Gen 41:33–46). Pharaoh elevates Joseph immediately to second in command over the land of Egypt: he is the man for the job. After noting Joseph's age as thirty, the text tells us, twice, that he "went out" over the land of Egypt, implying, according to Nahum Sarna, that Joseph quickly familiarized himself with local circumstances and that his plan was immediately put into action. In *Understanding Genesis* Sarna treads a sensible line between assuming that Joseph had all the details planned from day one or that God's direction makes Joseph's efforts inconsequential. Gen. 41:53–57 stress the universal implications of this devastating famine. The word *aretz/aratzot* appears eight times, focusing readers' attentions on the inability to get sustenance from any other land, save Egypt, which this passage mentions seven times, but only in consequence of the prudence of Joseph, who is mentioned four times. The situation steadily worsens: "There was famine in all lands, but throughout the land of Egypt there was bread" (Gen. 41:54). And a mere three verses later: "So all the world came to Joseph in Egypt to procure rations, for the famine had become severe throughout the world" (Gen. 41:57). Literal-minded scholars have made the observation that agriculture in other lands has nothing to do with the Nile's annual flooding, the product of rainfall hundreds of miles to the south; the causes of this worldwide famine, if it indeed occurred, must have differed from place to place. But the hyperbolic language of the Bible points to the central role played by one man: "So all the world came to Joseph in Egypt to procure rations, for the famine had become severe throughout the world" (Gen. 41:57). Surely this passage serves in some measure to underscore Joseph's universal importance: the sun and moon and stars may not literally bow down to Joseph yet, but "all the

world" comes to him as a supplicant. One cannot help but suspect one last little wordplay on the part of the author between
"lishbor," often translated "to provision," and the *"bor"* (pit,
well, or dungeon) that Joseph had been thrown into in Genesis 37, was inhabiting at the beginning of Genesis 41, and has
subtly risen in his mind to the level of obsession, or at least a
humiliation to be exorcised.[18]

The personal dimensions of making his youthful dreams
come true, and removing the shame at being sold by his brothers, presumably lie behind Joseph's push for power; this assumption likely informed Josephus and some other ancient authors
who turn Joseph into a running narrative. But the stories of
family strife (Genesis 37) and rise to national dominance (Genesis 39–41) are formally separated, or better, juxtaposed, by
the biblical author. Treatments of this connection vary. In the
Testaments of the Twelve Patriarchs the brothers are consumed
with regret over their earlier treatment of Joseph. No hint of
Joseph's embarrassing backstory can be detected in the *Jubilees* version of his success:

> And Joseph ruled over all the land of Egypt and all the nota-
> bles of Pharaoh and all his attendants and all those who did the
> king's business esteemed him highly, for he walked in upright-
> ness, and he had no pride nor arrogance nor partiality and there
> was no bribery, for in uprightness did he judge all the people of
> the land. And the land of Egypt was at peace before Pharaoh
> thanks to Joseph, for the Lord was with him and gave him favor
> and mercy for all his family before those who knew him and
> those who heard about him, and the kingdom of Pharaoh was
> well ordered and there was no Satan and no evil.[19]

The Bible returns to elaborate Joseph's policies in Genesis 47. Narratively the passage from feast to famine provides
the necessary background explaining the descent of the family from Canaan to Egypt, affording Joseph the opportunity
to test his brothers' character. The attention paid to the fate

of the Israelite settlement in the area of Goshen (Gen. 47:1–12) has occasionally obscured the following passage that continues detailing the aftereffects of Joseph's policies, but they are fairly striking and deserve full citation.[20]

> Now there was no bread in all the world, for the famine was very severe; both the land of Egypt and the land of Canaan languished because of the famine. Joseph gathered in all the money that was to be found in the land of Egypt and in the land of Canaan, as payment for the rations that were being procured, and Joseph brought the money into Pharaoh's palace. And when the money gave out in the land of Egypt and in the land of Canaan, all the Egyptians came to Joseph and said, "Give us bread, lest we die before your very eyes; for the money is gone!" And Joseph said, "Bring your livestock, and I will sell to you against your livestock, if the money is gone." So they brought their livestock to Joseph, and Joseph gave them bread in exchange for the horses, for the stocks of sheep and cattle, and the asses; thus he provided them with bread that year in exchange for all their livestock. And when that year was ended, they came to him the next year and said to him, "We cannot hide from my lord that, with all the money and animal stocks consigned to my lord, nothing is left at my lord's disposal save our persons and our farmland. Let us not perish before your eyes, both we and our land. Take us and our land in exchange for bread, and we with our land will be serfs to Pharaoh; provide the seed, that we may live and not die, and that the land may not become a waste." So Joseph gained possession of all the farm land of Egypt for Pharaoh, every Egyptian having sold his field because the famine was too much for them; thus the land passed over to Pharaoh. And he removed the population town by town, from one end of Egypt's border to the other. Only the land of the priests he did not take over, for the priests had an allotment from Pharaoh, and they lived off the allotment which Pharaoh had made to them; therefore they did not sell their land. Then Joseph said to the people, "Whereas I have this day

acquired you and your land for Pharaoh, here is seed for you to sow the land. And when harvest comes, you shall give one-fifth to Pharaoh, and four-fifths shall be yours as seed for the fields and as food for you and those in your households, and as nourishment for your children." And they said, "You have saved our lives! We are grateful to my lord, and we shall be serfs to Pharaoh." And Joseph made it into a land law in Egypt, which is still valid, that a fifth should be Pharaoh's; only the land of the priests did not become Pharaoh's. (Gen. 47:13–27)

Why the Bible devotes fourteen verses to these policies has puzzled many commentators, but the reader sees that Joseph does more than rescue Egypt from a onetime catastrophe. He has instituted a new social system that avoids starvation, has instituted a 20 percent tax rate to provide for seed corn (the numbers three, five, and seven recur frequently in the Joseph narrative),[21] but reduces the status of the Egyptian farmer relative to Pharaoh and the priesthood. Joseph feeds the Egyptians, but he also concentrates power in the hands of Pharaoh.

Joseph's policies seemed providential to many medieval and modern commentators alike. Nachmanides comments that Joseph stored everything, grain and other foodstuffs, and doled it out so successfully that even nations that had not benefited from seven years of plenty came to Egypt to survive the seven years of deprivations. Samson Raphael Hirsch, often a follower of Nachmanides' expansive mode of commentary, finds the relocation of the Egyptian population a way of driving home the national crisis (and lessening the impact of possible resentment at the children of Israel—the true outsiders). Stressing that the population relocation was conducted "city by city," Naphtali Zvi Yehuda Berlin argued that Joseph wished to preserve the Egyptians' native social relations. In these readings, endorsed by Nehama Leibowitz, the Egyptians did not have their freedom taken by Joseph: they eagerly tried to barter it in exchange for food. In Gen. 47:19 the Egyptians plead, "Let us not perish before your eyes, both we and our land. Take us and our land in exchange for bread, and we with our land will be serfs to Pharaoh; provide the seed, that we may live and not die, and that the land may not become a waste." Gen. 47:20 announces the result: "So Joseph gained possession of all the farm land of Egypt for Pharaoh, every Egyptian having sold his field because the famine was too much for them; thus the land passed over to Pharaoh." Note that Joseph clearly rejects the offer of personal servitude and that the Bible highlights Joseph's role as servant of Pharaoh. Why does the Torah make a point of exempting the Egyptian priests from this land centralization policy? Leibowitz detects "the Torah's pillorying of the so-called justice and equality of Egyptian custom which left individuals sure of their livelihood, subsidized by Pharaoh with their land intact. Those who had were given more."[22]

Leibowitz juxtaposes Israelite social policy, noting not only the abhorrence of enslaving the fellow Hebrew and the reliance of the priestly tribe of Levites on the generosity of their fellow Israelites. Leibowitz seems uncomfortable with the details of Joseph's policies, but the biblical position is less clear. While the Bible lampoons Israelite ethnocentrism—"To me, O Israelites you are just like the Ethiopians" (Amos 7:7–8)—I think only a naive "presentism" would insist that the Bible invariably mandates equal treatment of the Israelite and the other. Joseph's preferential treatment toward his brothers is true nepotism—driven by kinship rather than affection. The colloquy between Joseph and his brothers in the preceding scene—touching on the topic of shepherds—indicates that Joseph's actions on his brothers' behalf are born of duty alone (Gen. 46:32–34). Although the ancient verdict on Joseph's role was usually positive, one midrash does not shrink from portraying Joseph as heartless. This midrash imagines a dialogue in between Joseph's command to the Egyptians to bring in their livestock (literally: their cattle; Gen. 47:16), and the continuation of the passage in Gen. 47:17 that specifies that Joseph gave them bread in exchange for their horses, sheep, asses, *and cattle*—everything save their land and their persons—which they offer Joseph in the next year of famine. This midrash imagines the Egyptians' desperation: "Some have died, some are sold, and we are left stripped of our wealth and treasures like a peeled onion."[23] This midrashic report on Joseph's flaws has been taken up with gusto by modern writers, as we shall see presently.

An Assimilationist? Modern Criticisms of Joseph's Character

Several modern interpreters have seen Joseph as a brilliant failure.[24] He Egyptianized fully, abandoning his Israelite identity in exchange for wealth and power; he reduced the Egyptian nation to servitude and in doing so prepared the grounds for Israel's servitude in Exodus; he fed Pharaoh's concentration of power at the expense of the populace, though not the Egyptian priests, and so on. Even the portraits of balancing Jewish identity and devotion to foreign rulers found in Esther and Daniel seem to Wildavsky more like veiled criticisms of Joseph than neutral or positive reflections.

Needless to say, biblical Hebrew has no word that directly corresponds to "assimilation," although modern Hebrew has several.[25] Nevertheless Genesis 41 blatantly raises Joseph's status as a Hebrew (Egyptian hybrid), and this will remain a theme for the rest of the Joseph cycle; we continue to be reminded of Joseph's outsider status and the theme of assimilation. Nevertheless the renaming, intermarriage, and visible Egyptianizing of Joseph in this chapter come as a bit of a shock. On the one hand this could all be taken as mainly external. After all if Joseph is to administer the nation he must be somewhat a part of it. On the other hand Joseph has spent thirteen years as a part of the Egyptian environment before coming before Pharaoh. His situation is very different from that of the Hebrew slaves in early Exodus, in which ethnic solidarity could be maintained and even cultivated—as many midrashim imagine. According to one tradition Israel kept its own names, language, and clothing.[26] Surely an intelligent lad such as Joseph had long since mastered Egyptian language and customs. Recalling that he showed up in Egypt in his skivvies (the "long-sleeved garment" having been torn from him), his dress, hairstyle, diet, and general appearance must have been considerably transformed. When the text reports in Gen. 42:7 that Joseph "estranged himself" from his brothers, there is no hint that Joseph needs to alter his physical appearance to be unknown to them. That his brothers do not recognize him gives evidence of his altered bearing, in part due to assimilation and in part due to his lofty status.[27] From what we know about immigration and assimilation in modern Jewish history, it is easy to believe that as Joseph reached the pinnacle of success his association with his new homeland strengthened.[28] Assimilation is more than a matter of intent and volition: it is also a matter of circumstances—how long one has been in residence, what job one has secured, how consistently the émigré must speak the language of his or her adopted country.[29]

We are given more than circumstantial evidence to cause us to suspect that Joseph's break with the past was profound; there is the naming of his two sons. Manasseh is named by Joseph as follows—"Menashe: For God has made me forget all my toil, and all my father's house." As Aviva Zornberg comments, the name contains a suggestion of contraction, shrinking. The past has been left—or so Joseph thinks—in the past. Ephraim is named—"Ephraim: For God has made me *fruitful* in the land of my *affliction*." The name of the second child is ambiguous, since fruitfulness and affliction certainly seem to point in opposite directions. But the tension between the two components seems to be resolved in favor of fruitfulness—an important theme in the Jacob's blessing of Joseph in Genesis 49. Zornberg links this tension of bounty and famine to Rashi's midrashic comment to 41:55, where the Egyptians cry out to Pharaoh for bread: "Because all the corn which they had stored, apart from that collected by Joseph, had rotted."[30] Rashi suggests that the mode of storage was as important as the plan itself. Joseph knew how to wrest a policy out of a dream; he knew how to preserve fruitfulness in the face of affliction. Joseph needed to assimilate, and the naming of his two sons points in the direction of making peace with his past and celebrating his new homeland. Joseph's piety, however, remains intact. Both these naming speeches invoke God.[31] And nobody calls him Zaphenath-paneah again.

The Road to Serfdom? Modern Criticisms of Joseph's Rule

Criticism lodged by Aaron Wildavsky and others stems not only from Joseph's personal accommodations to life in Egypt, but also his exercise of power in a foreign land.[32] Taking the two key passages regarding his rule together (Gen. 41:47–49 and 47:13–27), Wildavsky raises questions that should not be dismissed as mere narrative necessities. The availability of food in Egypt, but not Canaan, is necessary background to Jacob's pressuring his sons to go down and find provisions. The reader knows more than the characters on the critical point—it is none other than Joseph who holds the reins of power. Moreover the family focus in Genesis 42–45 diverts the readers' attention somewhat from Joseph's growing international importance. The narrative diverts the reader from contemplating that Joseph gained power at the beginning of the seven years of plenty; stated differently, Joseph has been ruling Egypt for a decade when Jacob's family relocates to Egypt.

Ten years is a long time to be in power, although Joseph will ultimately rule for a total of eighty years, from age 30 to age 110. (For those inclined to take biblical numbers as more symbolic than arithmetic, one could calculate this tenure as two whole generations, or more loosely, a very long time.) Joseph's critics focus on the passage that presents Joseph gathering the money, livestock, and land of the Egyptians. Only the priests were exempted from this centralization—they kept their lands and received tax support from Pharaoh (Gen. 47:22). Desperation forces the Egyptians to offer their personal freedom too (Gen. 47:19), and Joseph uses his power to relocate the population of Egypt from end to end. Wildavsky and others find these measures objectionable. In the words of Moses Pava, "We are arguing that there is a clear link between the Egyptian people's willingness to sell themselves into slavery in Genesis, and their acceptance of Pharaoh's plan to enslave Joseph's descendants in Exodus."[33] Pava, like Wildasvsky and Ivan Caine, view Joseph's consolidation of power in Pharaoh's hands, and consequent disenfranchisement of ordinary Egyptians, as contributing to Israel's plight as an enslaved population.

Perhaps the most damning judgment on Joseph's rule comes from Ivan Caine:

> This is a story in which the pagan potentate is depicted as benign, while the Hebrew hero, normally bearer of a high moral standard, is seen as behaving in a way that offends God. . . . The ethical judgment of Joseph is not affected by the assumption of many that the Bible speaks as though it reflects an actual state of affairs in Egypt, where Pharaoh owned all the land except the temple estates, and exacted a crop tax of twenty percent. We read from our own Scripture that our ancestor bore down on the Egyptians with a cruelty which is not ascribed to Pharaoh himself.[34]

Needless to say, these judgments contradict ancient appraisals and modern defenders of Joseph's policies as well. Unless one has enormous wealth and a good accountant, a 20 percent tax rate does not seem so bad. But a more learned case for Joseph can be made: "Indignation because of the people and the land of Egypt falling into dependency is misplaced. Joseph does not demand their subordination, but the Egyptians offer it. This is the true intention of the whole story. The book of Genesis is intended . . . as an introduction to Exodus."[35] There the main topic will be Israel leaving Egypt, "the house of bondage." *How* did this country become a house of bondage? For Benno Jacob, this is the reason for a detailed description of the "new" Egyptian economy; it serves as a transitional device.

Daniel and Esther and Joseph: Celebration or Censure?

Joseph appears many times in the Bible as the father of the tribes of Ephraim and Manasseh, with numerous references to the "House of Joseph" and the "Tribes of Joseph." Admittedly Joseph wanes in prominence as an individual, but claims about his erasure are overstated. To take a representative formulation, Ron Pirson asks, "Why is Joseph hardly mentioned outside Genesis? Why does Joseph not receive a portion of the land promised to his ancestors? And how did he come to lose his special position to Judah?"[36] But Joseph is referenced in Exod. 1:5, 1:6, 1:8, and Joshua 24. Moses' "Blessing" in Deut. 33:13–17 continues the praise of Joseph bestowed in Gen. 49:10. 1 Chron. 5:2 acknowledges Judah's political dominance but notes that the birthright has been given to Joseph. Psalm 105 celebrates Joseph's wisdom and rule. Some laws in Deuteronomy may well be written with Joseph's story in mind.[37] Above all Joseph's prominence in postbiblical literature suggests that he was never a forgotten character in ancient Israel—in fact allusions to Joseph in two late biblical books, Esther and Daniel, turn out to be fairly blatant.

Daniel and Esther are set in the diaspora, in the courts of foreign kings. Both books involve averting disaster; both contain considerable use of misdirection, which involves jailing and false accusations. The Jewish servant-savants Daniel and Joseph both interpret dreams that baffle the gentile dreamers; Daniel and Joseph both receive new names. Esther and Mordechai and Daniel make a didactic point out of preserving their Jewish loyalties, as did Joseph, albeit more subtly. For instance, whereas Joseph stresses God's role to Pharaoh, Mordechai refuses to bow down to Haman. Whereas Daniel stages a dramatic test to prove that he looks good on a kosher-vegetarian diet, we see Joseph eating separately from the Egyptians out of their abhorrence for him.

One can go beyond these general thematic similarities to indicate very precise verbal clues that Daniel and Esther are alluding to Joseph.[38] Both Gen. 40:20 and Esther 1:3 employ the unusual Hebrew word for drink-fest (*mishteh*) to picture the two heroes in the court of arrogant gentile kings. In Gen. 39:10 and Esther 3:4 we have the phrase "calling day by day" used to implore the heroes into sin: Joseph into adultery; Mordechai into apostasy. Judah in Gen. 44:34 and Esther in 8:6 use almost identical language to avert a disaster concerning the fate of Benjamin and the fate of the Jews, respectively. The description of Joseph as a "Hebrew" in Gen. 39:6 and Esther's dramatic revelation that she too is a "Hebrew" (Esther 2:7) employs the same loaded word—used mainly in the Bible to highlight an Israelite's ethnic-religious-geographic difference.[39] Likewise *saris* appears in Gen. 40:22 and Esther 1:3, where more a common word for servant would do. Joseph and Mordechai restrain themselves (*va'yitapek*; Gen. 43:31, Esther 5:10), but practically nobody else in Scripture does—and least not in that verbal construction. Both Joseph (Gen. 41:39–42) and Mordechai (Esther 6:1–12) are elevated from a dire situation. Esther 8:1–2 and Genesis 41:40–42 show the Jews are suddenly on top of the world, a comic likeness noticed by the rabbis. The opening scenes in Esther 1:1–2:4 seem patterned on the dramatic events of Joseph's rise to prominence. One could go on: the language, motives, and issues in the story of Joseph profoundly shape the books of Esther and Daniel.

Joseph, Daniel, and Esther may all be read as meditations on the difficulties of Jewish diaspora existence. This seems to be the consensus, but what should we make of it? Some have argued that Daniel is intended to satirize Joseph. Daniel remains a proud Jew whereas Joseph gives in and assimilates.[40] But Joseph calls the God of Israel to Pharaoh's attentions, gives his sons Hebrew names, eats alone, seeks his father's blessing, and asks to be buried in Canaan. Is it not just as likely that Daniel makes didactic the religious loyalty implied in Joseph? The argument for satire seems even more forced in the case of Esther, who, after all, changes her name, appearance, and eating habits, and, presumably sleeps with a gentile king. Nobody in the scroll of Esther mentions God, making Esther unique among the books of the Hebrew Bible. By contrast this makes the perpetually God-invoking Joseph a veritable model of piety.

The relationship of Esther and Daniel to Joseph remains debatable, but scholars agree that Jewish books from the Second Temple period often allude to and model themselves on the biblical texts that have become "canonical." To put this a little differently, the border between revelation and interpretation seems more porous than these terms suggest. Although later writers on the Bible did not consider Joseph as religiously central as the Patriarchs and Matriarchs, he became a prototype for more worldly circumstances. The ideal of the Jewish statesman, loyal to his birthplace and to his adopted country alike, has become a familiar one, from courtier Hasdai ibn Shaprut to diplomat Henry Kissinger. We all have our favorite—and least favorite—examples. Comparison is not equation, yet the British Jewish belletrist Maurice Samuel (1895–1972) likens Joseph to Benjamin Disraeli convincingly:

> He has been called the Disraeli of the ancient world. The comparison goes much further than is usually perceived and if it has not been done, someone should write two Plutarchian parallel lives of Victoria's Prime Minister and Pharaoh's Vizier. There are many differences between the two men, but the similarities are astonishing. Both were brilliant, and brilliant alike in their ability to irritate and to charm. Both were "foreigners," though Disraeli was second-generation English-born. Both were democratic conservatives concerned with the welfare of the masses as much as with the retention of traditional authority. The two

men even had, across the interval of more than three thousand years, a common bond in Egypt; Disraeli bought up the Khedive's shares in the Suez Canal, in a bold and irregular maneuver and thereby determined England's Egyptian policy forever after. The two men had a peripheral interest in the people of their origin, though in different degrees—and here again I touch on Joseph's deviation from his mission; again I point that though he was far more deeply involved than Disraeli in the fate of his people, Joseph gave his best to the country of his adoption.[41]

Joseph as Family Man: The Romance of Asenath

We know Joseph had challenging sibling relationships, but what was the vizier of Egypt like as a husband and as a father? How did his personal accommodations to Egypt translate into the private realm? Joseph's predecessors exercised their leadership within the family: he serves as a transitional figure to his successors, leaders of a nation. Joseph, Moses, and David may be compared as examples of the "shepherd-ruler" type, but the domestic downside of these three characters deserves notice.[42] The grumbling of Miriam and Aaron in Numbers 12, the need for Zipporah to circumcise their son Gershom, and her awkward reappearance from Midian at Mount Sinai give the impression of Moses as an overburdened leader who did not always attend to the home. David's political success came at a huge personal price, best seen in the unhappy fate of his children, not counting the fortunate Solomon.[43] Joseph ensured that his sons, Ephraim and Manasseh, were formally adopted in Genesis 48 (we will examine that later), but the details suggest that Jacob saw more clearly than Joseph the boys' respective qualities. Ephraim and Manasseh receive positive blessings from Jacob that do not drive a wedge between the brothers—quite a contrast with Jacob's father, Isaac, who struggles to find words to bless Esau. These biblical notices do not tell us a great deal about Joseph's private life, but for those willing to take later traditions seriously, an anonymous, undatable Greek novella provides a fully worked out and highly imaginative response.

"How the Egyptian Virgin Asenath Converts to Judaism and Marries Joseph" may be the most clunky title assigned this Greek-language romantic novella, which exists in whole or in part in no fewer than ninety-one manuscript versions.[44] In its third (or fourth) scholarly reconstruction, much of what earlier scholars thought they knew about this pseudepigraphic tale is questionable. Asenath, once attributed to between the first century BCE and the first century CE, was dated significantly later by Ross S. Kraemer, but the pendulum seems to be swinging back to the earlier date. Asenath's turn to Judaism seems less like a conversion and more like internal morale boosting for the Jewish community, possibly of Egypt, but possibly somewhere else. The many connections to the midrashic Asenath remain, but we know little about her. Nevertheless this biblical retelling, a surprisingly common genre in the first centuries BCE and CE, help us imagine a family side of Joseph about which Scripture is mainly silent.[45]

The anonymous author of *Asenath* takes a major liberty with the biblical text, which assigns Joseph a wife immediately, more or less a prerequisite and reward of rule. In the Bible Asenath is the daughter of Poti-phera, priest of On. In *Asenath*, as in Josephus and other Greek sources, Poti-phera is called Pentepheres and is assigned to the priesthood of Helioplis. Whether Poti-phera in Genesis 41 is the same person as Potiphar, Pharaoh's eunuch, in Genesis 39 has been debated. Modern scholars tend not to equate the two, in part because of the unlikely event that a eunuch would have a daughter. Asenath herself is introduced in this tale as follows: "And the daughter of Pentepheres was a virgin about eighteen years old, tall, in the bloom of youth, and beautiful, surpassing any virgin in the land. And she was in no way like the daughters of the Egyptians but was in all ways like the daughters of the Hebrews. For she was tall like Sarah, and in the bloom of youth like Rebecca, and beautiful like Rachel; and the name of the virgin was Asenath."[46]

Needless to say, this piece of exegesis varies in its fidelity to scripture. While Rachel is declared beautiful, and while Rebecca must have been in great shape to water all those camels in Genesis 24, Sarah's height goes unremarked. Recalling our discussion of the Canaanite Tamar, it seems pretty clear that Asenath is being positively characterized in the same fashion as Tamar and Ruth—non-Israelite women likened to the Matriarchs. What are we to make of the line "And she was in no way like the daughters of the Egyptians but was in all ways like the daughters of the Hebrews"? Not much—it is a setup. Overcome, like other women, by Joseph's beauty, Asenath is rebuffed by the chaste Joseph on the grounds that she is an idolater, and an ethnic other.[47]

Joseph's resolve to resist this latest advance is overcome when Asenath, turned iconoclast, smashes her household gods of gold and silver.[48] (Recalling Rachel's theft of Laban's household gods? Abraham's smashing of his father idols?) Asenath destroys and distributes the idols as charity. Like Esther and Daniel, Asenath fasts, dons sackcloth and ashes, and does something that the biblical Joseph never does—for all his invocations to the Lord—she prays to God. A heavenly messenger feeds her a magical honeycomb, and she is cleansed of idolatry. This impediment removed, the two pure virgins marry in a splendid wedding, and she immediately conceives Manasseh and Ephraim. Asenath becomes a model convert, invoking God later in the tale to foil an abduction scheme by Pharaoh's son. Kraemer comments, "Presumably Joseph and Asenath live happily ever after, more or less."[49] This romantic tale, however bathetic, supports the rabbinic reading of a still Hebraic Joseph, as does Rembrandt's magnificent *Jacob Blessing the Children of Joseph*, which imagines Asenath serenely standing by as her sons are blessed by Jacob.[50]

A more Oedipal account of Asenath's origins may be found

in rabbinic midrash, handily woven together in Louis Ginzberg's *The Legends of the Jews*. Ginzberg, with the translational and editorial assistance of Henrietta Szold, Zionist hero and founder of Hadassah, took midrashic traditions from many centuries and wove them into a running "rabbinic Bible." Having explained the cryptic name Zaphenath-paneah as an acrostic, midrash does the same for Asenath. Here is the version according to Ginzberg and Szold:

> The name of Joseph's wife pointed to her history in the same way. Asenath was the daughter of Dinah and Hamor, but she was abandoned at the borders of Egypt, only that people might know who she was, Jacob engraved the story of her parentage and her birth upon a golden plate fastened around her neck. The day on which Asenath was exposed, Potiphar went walking with his servants near the city wall, and they heard the voice of a child. At the captain's bidding, they brought the baby to him, and when he read her history from the golden plate, he determined to adopt her. He took her home with him, and raised her as his daughter. The Alef in Asenath stands for On, where Potiphar was priest, the Samek for Setirah, Hidden, for she was kept hidden on account of her extraordinary beauty; the Nun for Nohemet, for she wept and entreated that she might be delivered from the house of the heathen Potipher; and the Taw for Tammah, the perfect one, on account of her pious, perfect deeds.[51]

Although the story is not from Scripture, one could imagine the tale of Asenath, in either its pseudepigraphic or midrashic versions, as providing a deft transition from the end of Genesis 41 to the beginning of Genesis 42. Joseph names his two boys in celebration of his newfound status. Joseph thinks he has put the past behind him; he is dead wrong. Joseph entered Egypt as an enslaved teenager, proved his mettle to Potiphar, to the chief jailor, and to Pharaoh. He negotiated setbacks, including two instances of physical assault—one of them sexual assault, yet composed himself, stood before Pharaoh, uttered some inconvenient truths, and directed an agrarian policy to address a worldwide famine. (We have included Gen. 47:11–27 to give the full picture of Joseph's governance.) Joseph's rule won near-universal approval among most ancient commentators. Modern critics of Joseph as a Jew and as an administrator have been much harsher but have not made their case beyond a reasonable doubt, nor have all been persuaded that earlier centuries had him wrong. The Bible sees Egypt as a land of servitude, but one could as easily interpret Joseph as mitigating rather than exacerbating that quality. At the end of Genesis 41 Joseph stands at the acme of accomplishment but is only midway through life. At the height of his powers, he now confronts his brothers in their hour of need.

6

Testing, Dreaming, Punishing

In the end the brothers pass the fraternity test with flying colors. But Genesis 42–44 relates a drawn-out back and forth between Canaan and Egypt, between Jacob and the brothers, between the brothers and Joseph. The brothers bring Simeon down to Egypt and see him imprisoned. Then, after considerable resistance on Jacob's part, they must bring the favored child, Benjamin, down to Egypt too. Judah delivers an effective speech to Jacob (Gen. 43:8–10), a stark contrast with Reuben's pledge that if Jacob gives them Benjamin and they fail, Jacob may kill Reuben's own two sons, Jacob's grandchildren, in retribution.[1] The plot twists in these chapters cannot be easily summarized: the journeys, the colloquies with Jacob, the inconsistent behavior of Joseph, bordering on the bizarre, and the brothers' increasingly obvious repentance all demand scrutiny.

A lengthy banquet scene follows immediately after Joseph lays his eyes on Benjamin. Joseph leaves the room to cry; he will cry again in Gen. 45:2a and Gen. 50:17b under different circumstances. The Egyptians eat separately, the brothers eat separately, and Joseph eats separately. When combined with the uncanny seating according to age, and the double portion served Benjamin, readers ancient and modern alike wondered if the brothers suspect Joseph's real identity. Another deft characterization is offered here: for all his power and status,

Joseph remains a foreigner in Egypt, a perception highlighted by the term "Hebrews" in this passage, a usage for Israelites indicating ethnic otherness.

Above all, commentators differ over Joseph's motives. Does he seek punishment (Adar)? Does he test the brothers' repentance (Maimonides)? Does he attempt education by a strict application of measure-by-measure choreography with Benjamin in his stead (Abravanel, Adar)? Or does Joseph perceive that he may now fulfill the dreams of his youth (Nachmanides, though he also affirms the educational intent of Joseph's tests)? Maurice Samuel, among other modern authors, considered Joseph's behavior in these chapters downright sadistic—a charge not lightly levied or dismissed. When faced with such a profusion of opinion from such talented readers, must we choose?[2] I do not think so. Meir Sternberg offers a different perspective: "Why does Joseph torment his brothers? Since this gap forces a choice between inference and incoherence, no reader can afford to ignore it; and many have left their closures on record. Their motivations of Joseph's conduct have always proceeded along four main lines: punishing, testing, teaching and dream fulfillment. Predictably enough, however, each line is wrong because all are right. In characteristic biblical fashion, no hypothesis can bridge the discontinuities and resolve the ambiguities by itself."[3] Putting Sternberg more simply, the texts and gaps invite readers to abstract multiple teachings. Since more than one conclusion can be reasonably drawn, a full accounting of a biblical story ought to take all legitimate readings into consideration.

Biblical style remains doggedly open ended. The commentator determined to find the only solution possible errs when he or she imagines that uncertainty is a flaw to be rectified. Following Sternberg's caveat not to reduce Joseph's motivations to a single psychological cause, we will closely follow the intricate action of Genesis 42–45.[4]

Canaan, Meet Egypt

While things are going splendidly for Joseph in Egypt, they are not going well for his birth family in Canaan:

> When Jacob saw that there were food rations to be had in Egypt, he said to his sons, "Why do you keep looking at one another? Now I hear," he went on, "that there are rations to be had in Egypt. Go down and procure rations for us there, that we may live and not die." So ten of Joseph's brothers went down to get grain rations in Egypt; for Jacob did not send Joseph's brother Benjamin with his brothers, since he feared that he might meet with disaster. Thus the sons of Israel were among those who came to procure rations, for the famine extended to the land of Canaan. (Gen. 42:5)

The lengthy encounter of the brothers, culminating in Joseph's revealing his identity, occupies three chapters (Genesis 42–45) and constitutes the dramatic highpoint of the Joseph cycle. Naturally we have not heard from Jacob in the preceding chapters since the action is focused on Judah (Genesis 38), and at greater length Joseph (Genesis 39–41). But Jacob has been ineffective up to this point. Despite his disapproval of the slaughter of the Shechemites, he stood dumb in the face of Simeon and Levi's final question, "Should we let our sister [Dinah] be treated like a whore?"[5] Jacob in Genesis 37 seemed blind to the poisonous relationships in his own family. We have seen the astonishment of many commentators that Jacob would send Joseph to seek his brothers, but now he is determined not to repeat this mistake with Benjamin. These silences cast into high relief the reality that Jacob continues as Patriarch. The action begins back in Canaan with Jacob literally coming back to his senses after the trauma of Joseph's loss: "When Jacob *saw* that there were food rations to be had in Egypt" (Gen. 42:1)"; "'Now I hear,' he went on, 'that there are rations to be had in Egypt.'" Sight, sound, and hunger (taste) engage him. Jacob's renewed assertiveness offers hope for remedying the severity of the family's situation, which we had been prepared for by the twofold mention of a worldwide famine in Gen. 41:56–57, reiterated in Gen. 42:5, "Thus the sons of Israel were among those who came to procure rations, for the famine extended to the land of Canaan."[6]

Gen. 42:3 begins, "So ten of Joseph's brothers went down to get grain rations," wording that subtly anticipates the fact that the brothers have repented of their former lack of fraternity, an especially pointed reference, since they are described as the "sons of Jacob" in verse 1. The seeming redundancy of the word "ten" allows the reader a moment to "do the math" and set the ten apart from Joseph, and from Benjamin, described here as "Joseph's brother" (achi Yosef). As Joseph's full brother through Rachel and as a child at the time of Joseph's disappearance, Benjamin's fraternity to Joseph is unimpeachable. Jacob's rationale for keeping Benjamin back is stated—Benjamin may come to some disaster (ason), but Jacob's introductory phrase, "For he said/thought" (ki amar), leaves open the question of whether Jacob actually stated this out loud or merely thought about the fate of his youngest son.[7] The brothers do not challenge Jacob's decision. They accept Jacob's suspicion as justified, even though it displays the same favoritism toward this son of Rachel that Jacob felt for her other son, Joseph. The brothers' acknowledgment of their earlier sin finds increasingly pronounced expression and their acceptance of Jacob's favoritism becomes explicit—in Genesis 44, this favoritism becomes an arrow in Judah's rhetorical quiver—which finds its target in Joseph's powerful attachment to this father and his full brother, Benjamin.

Joseph's Self-Alienation

In Gen. 42:6 Joseph's power over Egypt occupies less attention as the action returns to the familial domain, but we are told that Joseph now governs the land. The terms describing Joseph (*hu ha-shalit* [vizier] and *hu ha-mashbir* [dispenser of rations]; "Now Joseph was the vizier of the land; it was he who dispensed rations to all the people of the land [Gen. 42:6]) may suggest now realized functions, for these are *not* the official titles Pharaoh bestowed on Joseph in Genesis 41.[8] Seven years of plenty and two years of famine have transpired since the Hebrew youth was summoned from prison, and the reader gets the impression that Joseph has been exercising his power freely. In Genesis 42–45 Joseph never consults Pharaoh or any officers of the Egyptian court. In the climactic scene Joseph commands the Egyptians to leave him with his brothers, and in his first reassurance speech to them he emphasizes that he is "father to Pharaoh," "lord of his house," and "ruler of over Egypt." If one includes his instructions to his brothers what to tell Jacob, in Gen. 45:9, "Now, hurry back to my father and say to him: Thus says your son Joseph, 'God has made me lord of all Egypt,'" then we have *four* expressions in this telling speech that testify to Joseph's seemingly unlimited power.[9]

With few preliminaries the brothers are magically transported into Joseph's presence, where they "bowed low to him, with their faces to the ground" (Gen. 42:6). As with the crystallization of Joseph's rule, the Bible passes on the opportunity to explain how these ragged Hebrews managed to secure an audience with the viceroy, who is providing the whole world with sustenance. The narrative compresses this potentially dramatic action in favor of highlighting the fraternal encounter. This sparseness presents a telling contrast with the brothers' return trip to Canaan, which offers the narrator an extended opportunity to plumb the brothers' soul-searching and confessional mood. Midrashic scholar Louis Ginzberg indicates how a more discursive literature might set the scene:

> At the gates of the city of Egypt, the brethren of Joseph were asked what their names were, and the names of their father and grandfather. The guard on duty happened to be Manasseh the

son of Joseph. The brethren submitted to being questioned. . . . On the evening of the day they entered Egypt, Joseph discovered their names in the list, which he was in the habit of examining daily, and he commanded that all stations for the sale of corn be closed, except only one. Furthermore, even at this station no sales were to be negotiated unless the name of the would-be purchaser was first obtained. His brethren, with whose names Joseph furnished the overseer of the place, were to be seized and brought to him as soon as they put in appearance.[10]

Joseph saw his brothers and declines to reveal himself. Two Hebrew words highlight his decision: "and he recognized them but he acted like a stranger to them" (va'yikarem va'yitnaker).

The first verb in this phrase (va'yikarem) has been a key one throughout the Joseph story; the second verb (va'yitnaker) has the same root (nun-khaf-resh) but is conjugated in the rarely used reflexive form—Joseph has made himself unrecognizable—or as NJPS puts it quite rightly, "he acted like a stranger to them." That is, he keeps his distance.[11] But there seems to be no physical effort at concealment here—no makeup or costume or the like. Rather, in his regal bearing, in his Egyptian apparel, in his use of an interpreter (Gen. 42:23), and in his mature manhood he simply failed to make himself known. The midrashic speculation that Joseph now wore a beard, a typical instance of "judaizing" biblical characters, runs counter to the text at Gen. 41:14. Joseph knew enough to appear before the king of Egypt clean shaven.[12] The word "to make himself strange" also carries the modern Hebrew connotation of "estrangement" or "alienation." In other words Joseph was not yet prepared to reconcile. This condition is reiterated in the next verse with yet another doubling of the verb "to recognize" (l'hakir). Recognition and knowledge, two themes that have been with us since Genesis 37, come together here explosively.[13]

At this juncture Joseph recalls "the dreams he had dreamed about them" (Gen. 42:9).[14] Robert Alter notes that we are given a look into the head of a character, a rarity. This exception is appropriate to the uncanny nature of this occurrence. The brothers now "bowed low to him, with their faces to the ground," which satisfies the first dream of the bound sheaves in Gen. 37:7.[15] The fulfillment of the second dream, involving all eleven brothers, and the sun (Jacob), and the moon (Bilhah, or alternatively, the entire household), requires a more aggressive posture on Joseph's part.[16] He provides it. Joseph's pent-up frustration and resentment comes tumbling out of him: "you are spies; you have come to see the land in its nakedness" (Gen 42:9b). The accusation is psychologically acute: Joseph was stripped, if not naked then close to it, by the brothers before they threw him into the pit, and Potiphar's wife stripped him in anticipation of sexual relations. The brothers do not know about this second incident and never relate to the first in terms of nakedness. The brothers' conception of their crime does not encompass the shame it caused it Joseph, but the latter's various and inconsistent retellings of that incident point to that feature. Additionally, as Sternberg comments on Joseph's accusations of his brothers' spying, they correspond to Joseph's tattletales early on and the likely fraternal reprisals.[17]

This cycle of accusation and denial prompted the rabbis to invent a lengthy colloquy in which the brothers explain that they have searched all houses of prostitution in Egypt for their lost brother. When challenged by Joseph to explain why a child of Abraham, Isaac, and Jacob would be in a house of ill repute, the brothers respond that he was sold as a sex slave to Potiphar. When he challenges them further, the brothers reply they would use violence to rescue him. Joseph now plays his trump card. As Ginzberg has it: "Now see how true my words were, that ye are spies. By your own admission ye have come to slay the inhabitants of the land. Report hath told us that two of you did massacre the people of Shechem on account of the wrong done to your sister, and now ye have come down to Egypt to kill the Egyptians for the sake of your brother.[18]

Note that the narrator skillfully keeps in the background the supposed purpose of their visit: to get provisions for starving family. The focus is instead on the brothers' relationship; their physical survival is a given. Faced with Joseph's hard words, the brothers reply with unwitting accuracy, "We are all one man's sons" (Gen. 42:11). Joseph, apparently unimpressed with their response, repeats his accusation of spying for a third time, only to be told this time, "We thy servants are twelve brethren, the sons of one man in the land of Canaan; and behold, the youngest is this day with our father, and one is not" (Gen. 42:13). The irony could hardly be greater: They are still, despite everything, twelve brethren. Benjamin is with his father, although it is not clear that Joseph believes them. Even more paradoxically Joseph is not nonexistent—he is standing right there in front of them.[19]

Spying and Crying

Joseph insists they are spies. His almost Abbott and Costello–like non sequitur in Gen. 42:14—"It is just as I have told you: You are spies!"—indicates that their words are not good enough. Joseph will put them to the test, and inflict a little punishment in doing so. He places them all in custody for three days. Perhaps the three is arbitrary; Joseph simply wants the brothers to experience that specific aspect of his own suffering—incarceration. But that seems unlikely given the symbolic significance attributed to numbers in the Joseph story. Maybe the duration is nothing more than Joseph's mental calculus: three denials, three days. One does not get the sense Joseph languished in the pit for three days, though it would make for a neat "measure for measure" equation. Christian expositors drew exactly that conclusion, reading backward from Jesus's three days in the tomb.[20] Robert Sacks documents the instances of "three days" in the Bible, which, he contends, "always mark a period of doubt and wonder."[21] Even more threatening, Joseph tells them, in harsh terms, "you must bring me your youngest brother, that your words may be verified and that you may not die" (Gen. 42:15–16, 20). The wordplay between *"asaf"* (gathered, an allusion to the name Joseph) and *"asar"* (imprisoned) is likely intentional. Verse 18, in which Joseph settles for the imprisonment of only one brother (Simeon) and the promise of Benjamin, marks, in the view of biblical scholar James Ackerman, a turn from punishing to testing. Will they simply abandon Simeon to his fate and flee back to Canaan? Or will they act as a family and settle for nothing less than all or none? We will turn our attention to the brothers' attitude momentarily, but a final, visible marker of Joseph's emotional distance from the brothers manifests here, his hidden tears. "He turned away from them and wept" (Gen. 42:22).

Joseph will weep again, three times before the climactic Genesis 45, once more, presumably, when he falls on Jacob's neck at the father-son reunion, and once more near the end of Genesis, when his brothers beg for his forgiveness. (No doubt Joseph wept many more times in his life, but these are instances Scripture narrates.) Weeping comes easily to Joseph, as it did to his parents. Robert Sacks writes, "With the exception of David, Joseph weeps more than any other Biblical character. Up to this point his tears have been shed alone. They were the tears of a man who knows more than other men, and it is hard to say whether they were tears of joy or sadness. [At this point the god, Joseph, master magician, reveals himself as a human being and vainly tries to reestablish contact with his brothers.]"[22]

This first time, "He turned away from them and wept," I would attribute the tears not only to "deep natural sympathy for his brothers," as Elie Wiesel did in *Sages and Dreamers*, but also to the release of pent-up emotions, however mixed, that naturally attend the conclusion of their first encounter. Joseph cried, but was still far from calling an end to the test: the continuation of the verse has Simeon bound "before their eyes," hardly the act of someone overcome by sympathy. Fair enough: even Joseph cannot know for sure what will happen next as they head back to Canaan at this juncture—perhaps they will leave Simeon in chains.

The second time Joseph cries, it is the sight of Benjamin specifically that prompts his tears. Many commentators link Joseph's second weeping with compassion: "Joseph made haste because his compassion for his brother overwhelmed him and he felt a need to weep, and he entered the room and wept there" (Gen. 43:30). In this instance Joseph must struggle to keep himself in check as conveyed by the double use of the verb to weep, and the use of the verb "va-yevakkesh" rendered here by NJPS as "on the verge of," though this verb ordinarily conveys desire, something like, "and he sought."[23] This occasion conveys Joseph's compassion for Benjamin, not necessarily all the brothers.

In the third instance, when revealing himself to them all, Joseph weeps loudly enough to be heard by the Egyptians sequestered in another room. It is a nice touch, narratively, that Pharaoh's house hears about it; this does not seem like ordinary behavior for their controlled and controlling vizier. Finally Joseph cries again in Genesis 50, when the brothers display a staggering lack of trust in his intentions following Jacob's death. These tears are bitter ones, unexpected and unplanned. In short Joseph's encounters with his brothers seem significantly punctuated by weeping, and like the various weeping of his parents, encompass compassion, relief, and self-pity. Weeping in the Hebrew Bible signifies strong emotion rather than any particular emotion: sadness, joy, relief, and more.

Pangs of Conscience

Even before heading back home, the brothers begin their repentance:

> They said to one another, "Alas, we are being punished on account of our brother, because we looked on at his anguish, yet paid no heed as he pleaded with us. That is why this distress has come

upon us." Then Reuben spoke up and said to them, "Did I not tell you, 'Do no wrong to the boy'? But you paid no heed. Now comes the reckoning for his blood." They did not know that Joseph understood, for there was an interpreter between him and them. He turned away from them and wept. (Gen. 42:21–24)

This collective admission is a deft way of conveying a collective act of repentance and also gives us a critical piece of information: until now we assumed that Joseph had lain silent in the pit, unconscious or traumatized. Now we learn—assuming that the brothers have not elaborated on the crime—that Joseph entreated them and they did not hear. Without anyone mentioning Joseph by name, again, a delightfully apt way of characterizing their bad consciences, Reuben declaims his anger at their refusal to hear his entreaties so many years ago on Joseph's behalf. With the phrase "and also behold his blood is required" (v'gam damo hinay nidrosh) we are reminded of the bloody imagery of the primeval (fraternal) murder of Abel and the divine dictum in Gen. 9:5–6 that whoever spills the blood "dam" of a man his blood will be required (yidrosh). Fortunately Reuben has overstated the actual crime. Joseph is right there, along with his interpreter, and moved to tears by their words. But we have one dream still to fulfill and a test with Benjamin as the subject to be conducted. Joseph hardens his heart and binds Simeon before their eyes and keeps him as a hostage.

Nachmanides' comment to 42:21 explores their guilty consciences with typical nuance:

It is obvious that the brothers now considered their display of cruelty toward Joseph as deserving of a greater punishment than the sale itself since it was their blood-brother who was imploring and prostrating himself before them and they remained unmoved. Scripture, however, did not relate [that imploring] there, either because it is naturally understood that a person would implore his brothers when falling into their grip when their intention is to harm him. . . . It may be the desire of Scripture to speak only

121

briefly of their sin . . . or it is possible that it is characteristic of Scripture to speak briefly about a matter in one place and elaborate on it in another place.[24]

But Scripture may be offering a confused narrative deliberately, much like the end of Genesis 37. It is not that Joseph's pleas are briefly recorded in Genesis 37 and then elaborated here; we are simply not told that Joseph said anything in Genesis 37. Hence we do not know if Joseph indeed spoke or was traumatized into silence. We do not know if the brothers truly ignored his pleas, or if they imagined those pleas years later.

Joseph dispatches the nine brothers back toward Canaan and Jacob with provisions. Along the way, however, they discover that their payment for the corn is still in their sacks. The phrase ("they trembled one to another/a brother"; *harad ish el achiv*) is used again, this time to convey fear at what the mad Egyptian might do to Simeon when he finds out he has been ripped off in this grain deal gone bad. Verse 28b—"What is this that God has done to us?"—quite naturally troubled traditional commentators, implying in a simple reading a distinct lack of faith in God's justice. Rashi, indeed, accepts this as the simple sense: "To cause us to be falsely accused." Does the narrator intend a veiled rebuke to their religious faith by this verse (42:28b)? Does it look bad in comparison with Joseph's repeated insistence that God is responsible and beneficent? Is the brother's refrain, "we are upright men" (*kaynim anachnu*), addressed to Joseph, repeated in different forms three times in the preceding verses, self-directed as well? Are they upright?

The following passages of Genesis yield an affirmative response, giving truth to their assertion, "we are upright men."[25] But other commentators, considering that the brothers' repentance commenced only a few verses earlier, disagreed with these pejorative undertones, reading it as an exclamation of dismay. Rabbi Jacob Zvi Mecklenburg, taking advantage of the traditional chanting of the verse, which pauses at "this" (*zot*), argues that the sentence should be divided at this point to make it into a second, freely offered admission of guilt. In other words Mecklenburg rereads the text as "What is this? God has done [it] to us!" Far-fetched though this reading may be, traditional commentators were acute in their observation that only when returning home to Jacob minus Simeon does the connection between their prior actions and current situation really hit home. Bible scholar Meir Weiss writes: "The recalling of this long buried episode here, at this juncture, represents the awakening of the brothers' conscience. Joseph's heartrending pleas for mercy more than they emanate from the pit now well up from the depths of their own hearts. This constitutes the underlying intention of the narrative in citing this detail here. It is meant to reveal what was going on in the consciousness of the brothers at the moment indicating their remorse."[26]

Telling Jacob the Patriarch

After casting Joseph in the pit, the brothers had evasively allowed Jacob to assume the worst. Now the brothers take a more direct, though not fully direct, approach:

> When they came to their father Jacob in the land of Canaan, they told him all that had befallen them, saying, "The man who is lord of the land spoke harshly to us and accused us of spying on the land. We said to him, 'We are honest men; we have never been spies! There were twelve of us brothers, sons by the same father; but one is no more, and the youngest is now with our father in the land of Canaan.' But the man who is lord of the land said to us, 'By this I shall know that you are honest men: leave one of your brothers with me, and take something for your starving households and be off. And bring your youngest brother to me, that I may know that you are not spies but honest men. I will then restore your brother to you, and you shall be free to move about in the land.'" (Gen. 42:29–34)

The brothers' retelling of these events to Jacob merits scrutiny. What seems to be simple repetition reveals much about their mindset. They neglect to mention that they were imprisoned for three days; they play down the seriousness of Simeon's incarceration; they do not say that Joseph thrice accused them of spying, refusing to accept their denials; they underreport the ominous tone in Joseph's threats; they fail to report the details about finding money in their sacks. The brothers' consideration for their aging father's feelings presumably plays a role in their edited account.

As Nachmanides observed, the glossing of their encounter with the mad vizier also struck them as a necessary tack to convince Jacob to let them have Benjamin, a necessity if they were to survive the famine. This plan, however, proves to be a tough sell to Jacob. Reuben's offer of his two sons as a bail bond for Benjamin draws no response at all from Jacob—as if killing his own grandchildren could compensate for losing his youngest son! Since Reuben is the oldest and Benjamin is the youngest, Reuben's children and Benjamin were probably about the same age. This may also be yet another way of letting us know that Reuben really is not the man to lead the family.[27]

The speech of Jacob that concludes this chapter could hardly be more provocative, or insulting. He begins by saying, "My son will not go down with you." Note the emphasis on the singular "my son" and the absence of the identifier "your brother." Jacob continues, "his brother is dead," which may refer only to the fact that Joseph and Benjamin are full brothers, but may insinuate far more. Jacob's comment, "He [Benjamin] only remains," must rankle. What, then, the brothers may reasonably ask Jacob, are we and all our children, your grandchildren? Jacob's speculation, "If some harm should befall him on the way that *you* are going," can be read as more insinuation. "Then you will bring down my gray hairs with sorrow to the grave [Sheol]," a virtual repetition of Genesis 37, in which

Jacob refused to be comforted for the loss of Joseph, and proclaimed that he would go down to Sheol in mourning. Thus Genesis 42 ends with Jacob ratcheting up the difficulty level of the "test" that Joseph has prepared for the brothers. The brothers return to Egypt knowing that Jacob's life also turns on their performance. That test begins to unfold in the next chapter. Judah's speech to Jacob suggests that severe famine is a necessary but not sufficient condition for Jacob to part with his beloved Benjamin.

Sheol, that dark and gloomy place, may also point to the national component in this invocation of mourning. So Nachmanides concluded his reading of Gen. 43:14: "The intent of this text is to suggest that Jacob's going down to Egypt alludes to the present exile at the hand of Edom, and the prophet Jacob saw this matter at its very inception and so he prayed about it in a general way, which was applicable to the moment as well as to the future. This verse according to their interpretation contains a great mystic thought. Jacob was saying, 'And G-d Almighty,' by the Divine attribute of justice, *give you compassion* that is before him,' meaning, 'He should direct you upward from the divine attribute of justice to that of compassion.' The student versed in the mystic teachings of the Torah will understand."[28]

The Brothers' Luncheon

Judah's speech to Jacob and Jacob's reluctant permission to the brothers to take Benjamin with them will be dealt with in the next chapter. The brothers' preparations, under Jacob's watchful eyes, and with some explicit instructions from the Patriarch, take several verses. But the description of the brothers' second descent into Egypt, which would have taken chapters in Greek legend, occupies only one verse in the text: "They made their way down to Egypt, where they presented themselves to Joseph" (Gen. 43:16). We have been granted considerable insight into their thought processes on the trip up to

Canaan, and the narrator allows us to imagine further rumi-
nations on their part. Joseph sees Benjamin and orders his
servant to prepare lunch. This unnamed character, who does
whatever Joseph tells him to, shows compassion to the brothers
on his own initiative. Not only does he reassure them, "Your
God and the God of your father must have treasure in your
bags for you. I got your payment"; but he gives them water to
bathe their feet and food for their animals (Gen. 43:23–24).
That this servant "is privy to Joseph's scheme" does not dimin-
ish his words or deeds.[29] He is his master's servant but seems
intent on making these starving Hebrews comfortable. Here
is another sympathetically drawn Egyptian.

Encountering Joseph in his home, the brothers make their
obeisance. We are told a second time that they bow down "to
the ground" (Gen. 43:26). James Ackerman notes that since
Benjamin is with them this time, Joseph's youthful dreams are
one step closer to fulfillment. Initially Joseph is all smiles, making inquiries about "your father" and "your youngest brother."
Joseph invites (commands?) them to dine with him at lunch,
but the brothers are frightened—perhaps because they have
been singled out among all prospective grain shoppers and perhaps because they know that Egyptian lords kept dungeons
in their homes.[30] Possibly, however, they have come to the
reasonable conclusion that Joseph is rather unpredictable. In
Gen. 43:20–24 the text has the brothers explain the presence
of their money to Joseph's unnamed servant, who reassures
them. Yet these verses also stretch out the dramatic tension—
even with Simeon returned it must have been a long morning
waiting for Joseph's return. The text doubles back on itself at
this point to focus on Joseph's reaction to his youngest sibling.
Seeing Benjamin again, Joseph once more is brought to tears
and leaves the room (Gen. 42:24 and 43:29).[31]

Although only three verses, the luncheon offers an unusual
affair to visualize—well worth reproducing:

They served him by himself, and them by themselves, and the Egyptians who ate with him by themselves; for the Egyptians could not dine with the Hebrews, since that would be abhorrent to the Egyptians. As they were seated by his direction, from the oldest in the order of his seniority to the youngest in the order of his youth, the men looked at one another in astonishment. Portions were served them from his table; but Benjamin's portion was several times that of anyone else. And they drank their fill with him. (Gen. 43:32–34)

We have three parties (Joseph, the brothers, and the Egyptians) all eating separately. The text informs us at this juncture (Gen. 43:32) that Egyptians will not eat with Hebrews. This is an interesting piece of social history, which also serves as a corrective to any assumption that Joseph has been fully integrated into Egyptian society. He may be very powerful, but he is still an outsider, regarded by natives as inferior. As Herodotus reports, Egyptians would not eat with Greeks because they ate cows, forbidden food to Egyptians. Being shepherds who ate sheep, the same taboo would presumably apply (Herodotus, *Persian Wars* 137). Visualizing this scene is a way of stressing Joseph's alienation: "They served him by himself" (Gen. 42:7). Joseph is not an Egyptian, but neither is he part of the family circle—and in many ways, he never will be.

Joseph may be parading his status over his brothers, but mainly he uses the meal to test the brothers' acceptance of his preferential treatment of Benjamin. The theme of favoritism, ubiquitous in the Joseph cycle, far from being rejected here, is carried through to the very end of Genesis. Seating them in order of age, to their astonishment, Joseph gives Benjamin a portion five times the size of the others. Earlier we asked why Joseph imprisons the brothers for three days; we should now ask: why does Benjamin receive five portions? Perhaps to correspond to the fifth part of grain that Joseph gathered from the Egyptians?

It is Louis Ginzberg's *Legends of the Jews* that reports that Joseph, Asenath, Ephraim, and Manasseh each gave their portions to Benjamin so he had five. This tradition obviously builds on the elevation of Ephraim, Manasseh, and Asenath into major characters—a reasonable development as they are Joseph's wife and children. While some commentators suggest that the brothers naturally took seats in age order and their astonishment was occasioned only by their preferential treatment vis-à-vis the other starving supplicants, Rashbam's explanation that their wonder also centered around Joseph's knowledge of their age seems more plausible. Please note the use of two different verbs conveying "to drink" (*va'yishtu*) and "to get drunk" (*va'yishkaru*). NJPS renders this half of the verse, "And they drank their fill with him." The second half of this verse prompted the further speculation that Joseph and the brothers foreswore wine in the years in between their early crime and this meal; Joseph on the basis of his separation, the brothers on account of their regret.[32] But this verse, especially in this NJPS translation, understates the anxiety level: the brothers thought they would need a stiff drink to get them through the ordeal—and they were right.

Following Rashbam's reading that the brothers were surprised that Joseph knew their birth order, an obvious question emerges: did the brothers begin to suspect Joseph's identity? Demonstrably they have long since tied the unfolding events to their prior treatment of Joseph. And, curiously, although we are told they all ate separately, we are also told in Gen. 43:34 that they drank their fill *with him*. These are small hints. In any event the luncheon is certainly an appropriate setting for Joseph's penultimate test and for Judah's impassioned advocacy, which is the subject of Genesis 44.

The "Benjamin Conundrum"

Benjamin, from different perspectives, serves as the emotional focal point of Joseph, Judah, and Jacob. Yet Benjamin seems deliberately uncharacterized, as if to emphasize his role as a blank screen for other characters' projections. The biblical technique of leaving a character unnamed or in the background is a common one.[33] In Genesis 24, for instance, the servant assigned to find a bride for Isaac is not named, though we assume him to be Eliezer, Abraham's faithful servant, mentioned earlier in Gen. 15:2. Benjamin, unlike the loquacious servant, gets no line of dialogue in this entire narrative. Surely there is no hint of the wolf-life character portrayed in Jacob's blessing of Benjamin in Genesis 49. Nor do we sense the future of Benjamin's tribe in Genesis 42–45, which will be full of violence and heroism. That Benjamin is a "Rachel" tribe that aligns with Judah politically later on has been long observed. Yigal Levin, who calls this the "Benjamin Conundrum," explains the narration here as a way of displaying Judah's great concern for Benjamin following the breakup of the United Monarchy—and justifying Judah's subsequent suzerainty over Benjamin's descendants.[34] As attractive as this proposal may be, an exclusively political reading clashes with Joseph's sincere affection for Benjamin before and after the former's self-revelation.

Throughout the ages commentators and artists have been dissatisfied with the biblical portrait of Benjamin—with some justification. While Benjamin is the youngest son, he cannot be a child. Benjamin is born in Genesis 35—before the beginning of the Joseph cycle. He must be a young man at least. The text in Gen. 46:21, which names Benjamin's children, suggests he is older than a twenty-something. We ought not to be too literal about genealogies, yet this seems amiss. (A distinguished artistic tradition acknowledges Benjamin's key role: in Lorenzo Ghiberti's *Gates of Paradise* Benjamin sits on Joseph's lap; for Girodet de Roucy-Trioson, *Joseph Recognized by His Brothers*, Benjamin is the brother who recognizes Joseph—his arm points toward Joseph, in clear contradiction of the biblical text that makes Joseph the one who reveals his identity.[35])

Another interpretation of Benjamin comes from Ambrose,

Bishop of Milan, who composed a *Life of Joseph* (*De Josepho*), likely originating as a sermon sometime in the late 380s. For Ambrose, as for many of the Church Fathers, Joseph is a prefiguration of Jesus; this maneuver is expected and not particularly novel.[36] More interesting, Ambrose envisions Benjamin as prefiguration of Paul. Ambrose was a champion of the allegorical method, akin to "*remez*" in the fourfold rabbinic sense of a scriptural verse.[37] While Benjamin remains Benjamin in the literal sense, in the allegorical sense Benjamin prefigures Paul, a member of the tribe (Rom. 11:1), and a latecomer to the Jesus movement. Likewise Benjamin was held back, a late arriver on the scene, coming down to Egypt only on their second journey. Joseph speaks to the brothers harshly when Benjamin is absent; with Benjamin on hand he speaks to them kindly. Allegorically Paul's arrival and message to the gentiles softens Jesus's attitude toward the Hebrews (Ambrose is engaging in allegory, not history.) Benjamin was unaware that the silver goblet had been stashed in his sack; Paul had been initially unaware of Jesus's true status. Ambrose adds many "moral" and "mystical" interpretations to the allegorical equation of Benjamin and Paul. "Thus our sight is directed by the guidance of our mind. And so, holy Joseph, saw Benjamin his brother; he remembered him, he looked for him, he almost had seen his brothers in Benjamin's absence because the sight of them was of no help whatsoever. Neither was he satisfied only to have seen him; as if not known him, Joseph asked 'Is this your youngest brother?'"[38]

Ambrose continues, "Joseph saw them and Benjamin his brother by the same mother. The Hebrews are seen now and they are seen by Christ, who is the true Joseph, when they come with the figure who symbolizes Paul. And Joseph speaks to them gently and mildly, inviting them to take food together. Earlier, however, when they came without Benjamin he did not even recognize them but turned away from them, as it is written, and he spoke harshly to them. For they did not recognize him by whom they were recognized."[39] Ambrose continues to unfold Benjamin's story allegorically. While his Christological tones will not resonate with Jewish readers, Ambrose, like many other readers, finds something missing in the biblical Benjamin.

Whatever Joseph's motives, which have been variously assessed, he employs one last test, planting his silver (*kesef*) divining cup in Benjamin's sack of food. Divining cups, in which oil (or some similar liquid) was dropped in water and then interpreted, were common in the ancient Near East. The irony of that particular item has long been observed. After all it was for twenty pieces of silver (*kesef*) that Joseph was sold in Genesis 37. So in the rabbis' moral economy of "measure for measure" (*midah k'neged midah*) it only makes sense that as Joseph was tormented for silver, the brothers should be too. But there is another irony here. The Hebrew Bible generally inveighs against all nonkosher (*treyf*) forms of trying to determine or influence God's intentions, most famously in Deut. 18:9–14. Here in Gen. 44:5 and 44:15 one of the words used in Deuteronomy for forbidden divination (*nahash*) is employed, first by Joseph's servant, and then by Joseph himself. In effect Joseph is telling the brothers: "How did you think you'd get away with fooling me?" Of course Joseph does not need to practice divination to determine the identity of the brothers: We have been told since the start of the reunion that he knows exactly who they are. Moreover Joseph did not need to use divination even in interpreting dreams—that's what made him stand out from the Egyptians. This parallel links the connection between divination versus revelation, monotheism versus idolatry, Israel and Egypt. This confrontation recalls the interaction of Laban and Rachel, who disrespects her father's idols. Do the brothers doubt Benjamin's innocence just a bit, as some midrashim suggest? If so that only makes their unwillingness to abandon Benjamin more striking.

Having completed this set-up, by placing the divining cup

in Benjamin's sack, Joseph sends out his servant to confront them.[40] The brothers, anonymously, collectively, and foolishly, repeat Jacob's ill-considered statement to Laban regarding the household idols that had been stolen by Rachel: "But anyone with whom you find your gods shall not remain alive! In the presence of our kinsmen, point out what I have of yours and take it" (Gen. 31:32). Jacob of course did not know that Rachel had stolen them. While the narrator does not directly connect Jacob's words to the death of Rachel, later interpreters certainly did make that connection. Here the narrator uses similar language, albeit, happily, with a very different outcome:

> He [Joseph's cupbearer] overtook them and spoke those words to them. And they said to him, "Why does my lord say such things? Far be it from your servants to do anything of the kind! Here we brought back to you from the land of Canaan the money that we found in the mouths of our bags. How then could we have stolen any silver or gold from your master's house! Whichever of your servants it is found with shall die; the rest of us, moreover, shall become slaves to my lord." He replied, "Although what you are proposing is right, only the one with whom it is found shall be my slave; but the rest of you shall go free." (Gen. 44:6–10)

Some commentators have considered Joseph rather cruel to drag out the testing so far. After all, by the end of Genesis 43 we know that Jacob is alive, that Benjamin is alive, and that the brothers are not willing to leave any of their family (even the violent Simeon) dangling. Why, then, does not Joseph reveal himself at the luncheon described above? As usual no direct answer is forthcoming. Perhaps we can note that Jacob still has not bowed down to Joseph, and hence the dreams are only incompletely fulfilled. Perhaps again Joseph is not entirely convinced of his brothers' attitude toward Benjamin. Naturally they presented a united front when confronted with the vizier of Egypt, but what happens behind the scenes? Presumably, young Joseph was not mistreated by his brothers in their father's presence—only when he was alone did they display their full animosity. Don Isaac Abravanel writes, "Why did Joseph denounce his brothers? Surely it was criminal of him to take vengeance and bear a grudge like a viper. Though they had meant evil God turned it to good. What justification then had he for taking vengeance after twenty years?"[41]

Joseph: Sadist or Tzadik?

Abravanel's censure notwithstanding, a significant tonal difference exists between medieval and modern critics regarding Joseph's treatment of his brothers in these chapters. Maurice Samuel indicts Joseph for cruelty toward his aged father and his clueless brothers. Joseph indulges the urge to make himself the center of a theatrical drama. He does this at the brothers' expense, and Samuel utterly rejects Thomas Mann's portrayal of these tense scenes as innocent fun. Samuel writes:

> We leap over for a while to the closing acts of the Joseph drama. Many years have gone by. Joseph has become governor of Egypt, and his brothers come before him out of famine-stricken Canaan to by corn. . . . And how does Joseph behave toward his brothers? He responds at once to the obvious, irresistible dramatic suggestiveness of the situation. You can almost hear him say to himself: "This is too good to pass up!"[42]

Coming to the test of the brother's fidelity to Benjamin, Samuel drives home his indictment:

> If you have forgotten the details of the story, if you think that Joseph is now satisfied, that having had his innocent little revenge, he calls the shocking comedy off, then you do not know your man. The actor has an insatiable appetite for encores, especially if he is acting out himself. Joseph practically repeats the first act, with Benjamin now in the cast. The details vary a little, the spirit and technique are now the same; and Joseph weeps again, and again enjoys his tears.[43]

Poet Alicia Ostriker reimagines the feel of these chapters:

Finally the day arrives for which we have all been waiting. Joseph's brothers come down to Egypt during the famine. They are here to buy grain. Everyone at home is on the verge of starvation. The officials send them with all the other petitioners to make their request of the prime minister, sitting draped in his magisterial robes. Do they recognize this prime minister? No. Does he recognize them? What do you think. Does he tease them? What do you think. Torment them? What do you think. Heap grain on them, feast them, refuse to take their money, accuse them of theft, refuse to release them unless they bring their youngest brother Benjamin to court while—the old father at home laments that if he loses Benjamin, Rachel's only other son it will bring down his gray hairs with sorrow to the grave—and when Joseph sees the boy Benjamin does he hide himself in an antechamber to weep? What do you think.[44]

In Genesis 41 Joseph has made peace with his past, or at any rate, moved beyond it, and his reactions to his brothers, to the unfolding events, sometimes drawn as a simple cat-and-mouse game, arguably show Joseph wrestling with his own past, not only that of his brothers. Was this final test really necessary? For Samuel and Ostriker the answer is obvious: no. By this point the testing only serves a psychological need on Joseph's part, and not an admirable one. But this is not obvious. Isaac Arama, author of *Akedat Yitzhak*, maintains: "Evidently, Joseph's intention had from the outset been to test them to see whether they still hated him or regretted their deed. He saw no other way of doing it except through his brother Benjamin, to observe how they would react when they saw him in distress and danger. To that end he thought up on the spur of the moment, the stratagem of the cup. But since Benjamin was not with them he had to abuse them and trick them into bringing him."[45]

Even Abravanel, who was quite critical of Joseph's cruelty, accepts the necessity of verifying the brother's true feelings: "In spite of the feelers that Joseph had put out through accusing his brothers of being spies he still could not be sure whether they loved Benjamin or still nursed hatred for the children of Rachel his mother. He particularly wanted to put Benjamin to the test by the cup to see if they would try to save him. At the same time, he was concerned that perhaps his brothers might imagine that Benjamin had indeed stolen the cup just as Rachel stole the idols from her father. Perhaps on account of this they would say: 'The soul that sins shall die,' and not make every effort to plead for his life, not because they hated him but because of their shame for what he had done. Joseph with this in mind ordered their grain and their money to be placed together with the silver cup."[46] For Samson Raphael Hirsch, another defender of Joseph, his teaching of the brothers served to bring about a fair appraisal of *both* the brothers and of Joseph as sons of Israel.[47]

Elie Wiesel endorses this positive view of the biblical Joseph.[48] For Wiesel, Joseph the tzadik achieved his status despite his upbringing.

> He wasn't born a tzadik or raised as one. Jacob was inattentive; his brothers lacked fraternal feelings; even Judah did his mitz-vahs in a mealy-mouthed half-hearted way. Joseph persevered and became special nonetheless. And in the face of knowing that ultimately, politically, he would fail: Joseph knew—and who was in a better position to know—that to be the first Jewish prince, to be the first to liberate Jews outside their homeland, would be difficult and unrewarding. A descendant of Judah's was to wear the crown of Jewish sovereignty, symbolizing eternal promise and eternal dawn.[49]

Was the biblical Joseph as aware of either Judah's eventual role as family leader or the challenges of diaspora Jewish existence as Wiesel suggests? This may be questioned; Joseph was a dreamer, maybe even a tzadik, but no source I know calls him a prophet. Joseph was certainly surprised by his brothers' reappearance and took advantage of the chance to see his dreams through to fulfillment. His testing seems at times designed simply to punish, at times designed to test whether the brothers will treat Benjamin better than they treated him. Joseph's full brother, Benjamin, plays a prominent role. But he is not a fully drawn character—the focus remains on Joseph and the brothers. But what happens next is clear. The narrator turns to Judah to present the final argument on the brothers' behalf. Judah's rhetorical triumph prompts Joseph's self-revelation.[50]

7

Judah in Joseph

When the mysterious wrestler and God renamed Jacob "Israel" in Gen. 32:29 and 35:10, respectively, he becomes the eponymous father of the nation, and so the sibling competition seems to be resolved. In theory all will share in the paternal blessing. As Devora Steinmetz writes, "Jacob then, is more than a father; he is the patriarch, Israel. As a patriarch, he is able to talk not only of the present but of the future. . . . Jacob, as the patriarch Israel, accomplishes what no father in Genesis has been able to do."[1] By the end of Genesis this is true, but the conflict does not feel resolved—sibling tensions continue, and many readers have the sense that Joseph (oldest son of the beloved, younger wife) is battling for preeminence with Judah (fourth son of the less loved, older wife).

Joseph's authority over Egypt becomes the vehicle for Israel's national salvation, and Joseph, not Judah, is alluded to in the beginning of Exodus. Joseph remains the protagonist. Yet many readers agree that Judah also emerges as a leader in these chapters. Like Joseph, Judah is a man of words, one of the most effective speakers in Genesis. Judah convinces both Jacob and Joseph, neither of them pushovers, to do something they are disinclined to do, just as he got his brethren to abandon homicide for a cash sale, back in Genesis 37. Judah gets the longest, climactic speech in Genesis—the one that finally prompts Joseph's emotional self-disclosure. The story of Judah and Tamar, the longest Judah narrative in the Bible, casts him in a pretty poor light, but readers have found a distinct moral turning point in Judah's admission, "She is more in the right than I" (Gen. 38:26).[2] We will focus on Judah in this chapter, seeing what light he casts on his younger brother.

Leah's Fourth Son

When the Bible provides a naming speech, a good reader will pay attention to it. Leah names her children; this maternal naming is common despite the patriarchal bias of the text as a whole. (As we have seen, Rachel names Joseph and tries to name Ben-oni, who is renamed Benjamin in Gen. 35:18.) Biblical scholar Ilana Pardes notes that each of Leah's first three sons bears a name that reflects her marital frustrations with Jacob. Although the naming formula is the same for Yehudah (Judah), and although Leah once again invokes the Lord, Judah's name contains the four consonants of the Tetragrammaton and so suggests a change of heart.[3] Leah's "praising the Lord," the meaning of Judah, shows a shift away from Leah's resentment at failing to win her husband's affections. Judah, in other words, is born under a lucky star relative to his older full brothers. Leah has not given up on Jacob entirely. She trades some mandrakes found by Reuben with Rachel for Jacob's sexual favors (Gen. 30:16), but she has broadened her agenda. We readers are told that Leah stops bearing at Gen. 29:35; when she too becomes aware of this at Gen. 30:9, she appoints her handmaid Zilpah to be her surrogate. Leah's naming of Gad (lucky) and Asher (happy), offspring of Zilpah, bears no hint of the resentment she expressed with the birth of her first three biological sons. But they are children of handmaids and younger. Judah does not need to displace Gad and Asher the way he does his own full brothers.

Judah's leading role in at the end of Genesis 37, when Joseph is in the pit, deserves a second mention. As will become paradigmatic, the brothers prefer his solution to that of the eldest brother, Reuben (37:27b), and as usual Reuben falls short at the fateful moment. Did he leave the brothers in pique after they accepted Judah's suggestion? His resentful statement a few verses later invites speculation: "When Reuben returned to the pit and saw that Joseph was not in the pit, he rent his clothes. Returning to his brothers, he said, 'The boy is gone! Now, what am I to do?'" Did Reuben fail to grasp that there were too many variables to simply leave Joseph in the pit and come back to fetch him later? Reuben is a man of action—but often unreflective action. By contrast Judah effectively heightens the enormity of the crime and proposes an alternative. The last word of Gen. 37:25, *mitzraymah*, indicates that the (famously anachronistic) camel caravans are already heading toward Egypt.[4] Thus Judah makes a plan based on a piece of information that all his brothers knew about equally. Using the epithetic language "our brother" to describe Joseph, Judah changes the verb from the original "conspired to kill him" (*va'yitnaklu oto la'hamito*; root: *mem-vav-tav*) to "murder him" (*naharag*; root: *heh-resh-gimmel*), highlighting the enormity of the intended crime. Then, having drawn a grim visual picture of "covering up his blood" (Gen. 37:26b), Judah proposes an alternative: a sale that will bring tangible benefit. Whatever the exact amount paid by the Ishmaelites, twenty pieces of silver according to the Masoretic text, Judah's sordid solution offers an effective alternative to murder and rids the brothers of the obnoxious Joseph.

Judah's "solution" has immediate and long-term implications for the family. The continuation of the story has Judah's "going down," and those readers who consider Genesis 38 integral to the overall narrative have seen Judah's departure as reflecting alienation from his brothers. (Benjamin is the only brother born in Canaan; Judah and Joseph are the only brothers who marry outside the clan of Abraham.) In the long run, however, Judah has much to gain from the sale and enslavement of Joseph, just as Reuben had much to gain from being personally responsible for returning Joseph to Jacob's care.[5] The pioneering midrash scholar Judah Goldin explains that with Reuben and Simeon/Levi already in disfavor, Judah has displaced sons number one through three. Only Jacob's personal favorite, Joseph, presents a threat. That Judah's plan wins out in Genesis 37 will foreshadow later events—he repeatedly has his way.

Jacob remains the Patriarch, but it is Judah who convinces Jacob to take action. It bears repeating that the initial, collective attempts to relieve their dire situation failed. Simeon has been held captive; the unpredictable Egyptian vizier demands Benjamin too; they are still facing starvation. It seems that individual effort is needed now that collective effort has failed. Reuben, the firstborn, steps forward first and breaks the chorus line. Still in Egypt, Reuben bitterly reproaches his brothers: "Then Reuben spoke up and said to them, "Did I not tell you, 'Do no wrong to the boy'? But you paid no heed. Now comes the reckoning for his blood" (Gen. 42:22–23). Reuben's exact words in Gen. 37:21–22 were a little different, and one may read his sincere but somewhat abstract "let us not take life" and "shed no blood" as being more concerned with general principles and his sense of responsibility to his father than empathy with Joseph, who is neither mentioned by name nor by the epithet "our brother."

If this seems like overreading, it is supported by Reuben's speech to Jacob. Now, back in Canaan, Reuben attempts to persuade Jacob to entrust him with Benjamin as follows: "You may kill my two sons if I do not bring him back to you. Put him in my care, and I will return him to you" (Gen. 42:37). Reuben's offer of his two sons as a bail bond for Benjamin, once again, draws no response at all from Jacob—as if killing his own grandchildren could compensate Jacob for losing his youngest son! (Since Reuben is the oldest and Benjamin is the youngest, Reuben's children and Benjamin were presumably about the same age. This may be yet another way of letting us know that Reuben really is not the man to lead the family.)

The speech of Patriarch Jacob that concludes this chapter could hardly be more provocative, or insulting. Jacob begins by saying, "My son [Benjamin] will not go down with you." Note the emphasis on the singular "my son" and the absence of the identifier "your brother." Jacob continues, "for his brother is dead," which may refer only to the fact that Joseph and Benjamin are full brothers, but may insinuate far more. Jacob's comment, "He [Benjamin] only remains," must rankle them. Now the brothers may reasonably wonder about Jacob's attitude toward the rest of them. Jacob's speculation, "If some harm should befall him on the way that you are going," can easily be read as more insinuation. "Then you will bring down my gray hairs with sorrow to the grave [Sheol]," a virtual repetition of Genesis 37, in which Jacob refused to be comforted for the loss of Joseph, and proclaimed that he would go down to Sheol in mourning.

Genesis 42 ends with Jacob ratcheting up the difficulty level of the "test" that Joseph has prepared for the brothers. Two lives are at stake, Benjamin's and his own. That test begins to unfold in the next chapter. In a nice use of indirection, both Reuben (42:37) and Judah (43:4–13) refer to Benjamin only indirectly, while Jacob breaks through the euphemistic "brother" and "boy" to call Benjamin by name (Gen. 43:14).[6]

Judah Emerges as Leader

In Genesis 43 Judah emerges as the most effective brother. By the end of Judah's first speech (43:4–5), Jacob has been given an ultimatum: only with Benjamin in hand will they descend again to Egypt to meet the mad vizier. What changes Jacob's refusal in Gen. 42:36–38 to his acceptance in Gen. 43:14? Nehama Leibowitz, echoing earlier traditions of Jewish exegesis, writes, "Simeon's plight, imprisoned in foreign parts, awaiting release, did not move him, neither did his son's entreaties nor Reuben's appeal. The hunger of the little ones finally broke his resistance."[7] Bible scholar James Ackerman focuses on the content of Judah's rhetoric as holding the key. He notes that Judah emphasized generational continuity. Judah here (43:8) quotes Jacob's own earlier statement in 42:2, "So that we will live and not die," which focuses on the whole family, then Jacob, then the children. Judah culminates his opening statement with the words, "also our little ones" (*gam-tapeynu*). Judah presents Jacob's favoritism as the stumbling block to their collective survival, even as he recognizes his father's authority. But Judah does not leave it at that. He evokes legal rhetoric to "pledge" himself for Benjamin's safe return, using the same wording that he used when he left his cord, signet ring, and staff with Tamar.

Jacob, called Israel here, finally relents. He tells the brothers to prepare the choicest products of the land as a gift of submission and a double share of money. What else can Jacob do? He invokes *El Shaddai*, the archaic name of God used mainly by the Patriarchs, and makes peace with the uncertain outcome.[8] With a doubling of the verb, Jacob declares, "If I am bereaved, I am bereaved" (Gen. 43:14). In the course of these final words, a peculiarity in the text appears. Instead of reading, "that he may release to you your other brother," which would be an appropriate reference to Simeon, the text lacks a letter. The simple referent in the verse is to Simeon, but the hint in the verse is to another brother: Joseph. In Hebrew the letter *heh* serves as the definite article marker. The text at Gen. 42:14 should read: *"achichem ha-acher."* Instead the text reads simply *"achichem acher,"* which could be rendered something like "that he may release to you—an other brother." Perhaps this can be read as an act of unwitting prophecy on Jacob's part, which is reminiscent of the brothers' statement that they were all "sons of one father" (Gen. 42:13)—thereby including Joseph in their words, even as they assumed him to be "merely" the vizier of Egypt.

Judah's Rhetorical Masterpiece

Descending to Egypt a second time, Judah has a difficult task. He will need to convince Joseph to release Simeon, satisfy his ominous curiosity about Benjamin, and secure the food they still need. The mission does not start well. Benjamin is framed in the matter of the silver divining cup, and Judah must respond. He does. In a dramatic threefold declamation he asks, "What can we say to my Lord? How can we plead, how can we prove our innocence?" Please note that the brothers are innocent of the crime of which they have been accused. Judah refuses to throw Benjamin to the wolves but immediately and decisively makes them all "servant(s) or "slave(s)" (*eved/avadim*)—picking up on a thematic word that has been used since the beginning of their reunion. "Slave" is an appropriate theme word given the subsequent fate of Israel in Egypt. Judah's admission, "God has uncovered the crime of your servants," acknowledges, in the presence of the original victim, and with Benjamin ostensibly the character at risk, their prior sin regarding Joseph. Pointedly ignoring Joseph's reference to the role of divination here, Judah affirms that the Lord of the Universe has revealed their crime—not a silver goblet and a trained diviner. No wonder the rabbis applauded Judah's perception of the accusation—unjust in the particular, but a call to repentance generally.[9] Rejecting Joseph's suggestion to imprison only Benjamin, the putative goblet thief, Judah, launches into the single longest speech in Genesis:

> Then Judah went up to him and said, "Please, my lord, let your servant appeal to my lord, and do not be impatient with your servant, you who are the equal of Pharaoh. My lord asked his servants, 'Have you a father or another brother?' We told my lord, 'We have an old father, and there is a child of his old age, the youngest; his full brother is dead, so that he alone is left of his mother, and his father dotes on him.' Then you said to your servants, 'Bring him down to me, that I may set eyes on him.'

We said to my lord, 'The boy cannot leave his father; if he were to leave him, his father would die.' But you said to your servants, 'Unless your youngest brother comes down with you, do not let me see your faces.' When we came back to your servant my father, we reported my lord's words to him. Later our father said, 'Go back and procure some food for us.' We answered, 'We cannot go down; only if our youngest brother is with us can we go down, for we may not-show our faces to the man unless our youngest brother is with us.' Your servant my father said to us, 'As you know, my wife bore me two sons. But one is gone from me, and I said: Alas, he was torn by a beast! And I have not seen him since. If you take this one from me, too, and he meets with disaster, you will send my white head down to Sheol in sorrow.' Now, if I come to your servant my father and the boy is not with us—since his own life is so bound up with his—when he sees that the boy is not with us, he will die, and your servants will send the white head of your servant our father down to Sheol in grief. Now your servant has pledged himself for the boy to my father, saying, 'If I do not bring him back to you, I shall stand guilty before my father forever.' Therefore, please let your servant remain as a slave to my lord instead of the boy, and let the boy go back with his brothers. For how can I go back to my father unless the boy is with me? Let me not be witness to the woe that would overtake my father!" (Gen. 44:18–34)

Judah comes to terms with the issues that have divided the family since their youth, deals with their current situation, and points a way toward resolving them. Thirteen times the word *eved* (slave or servant) appears, six times the word *adon* (master), and fourteen times the word *abba* (father), including the last word of the speech. A quick read of this speech implies Judah's subservience—not a surprising stance for a hungry, threatened, Hebrew petitioner to the vizier of Egypt. A closer reading, however, reveals an undercurrent of resentment and resistance, not at all surprising considering the treatment that they have received from the vizier. After his opening words Judah's account is focused on the family of Jacob, not on the greatness of Joseph; that he does not even deign to repeat the charge that they were spies and the half verse "you who are the equal of Pharaoh" (Gen. 44:18),[10] ostensibly the highest praise, could easily contain a barbed reproach. In a variety of retellings, the rabbis imagine Judah's plea rather as a verbal combat between the two brothers, whose stories contend for domination in this narrative and in the subsequent history of the nation.

Judah's speech, a model of ethos, pathos, and logos, merits close attention. Judah's description of Benjamin as the beloved son of Jacob's old age is exactly the language used by the text to describe Jacob's feelings for the young Joseph and takes us back close to the origins of the family tragedy. Judah's comment that the boy cannot leave his father lest he die concedes the critical link between the father and son and plays on another pair of key thematic words in chapters 44–45: life and death. This is reinforced later in the speech in the moving phrase *"v'nafsho keshurah v'nafsho,"* which NJPS renders, "Since his own life is so bound up with his" (44:30b).[11] Judah also quotes Jacob's speech in Canaan, "You know that my wife bore me two sons," acknowledging before a presumed stranger (Joseph) that their father counted the two sons from his favorite wife (not their mother!) of greater importance than the ten men standing in the vizier's presence. He quotes, using the same onomatopoetic words as in 37:33, Jacob's verdict on Joseph's fate, as if Jacob's words on that terrible occasion, "Joseph is torn, torn-to-pieces," had stuck in Judah's head all these years. "And his brother is dead" constitutes the first time any of the brothers have voiced this without euphemism.

Several phrases from Genesis 37 reappear here in different guises, as if to alert the reader that we are indeed approaching the climax of the story begun so many years ago. Judah makes a final gambit. Citing his legal obligation, a nice touch considering that Joseph insisted only the guilty party should be punished and that Judah had pledged himself to Jacob for Benjamin's safety, Judah offers himself in Benjamin's place. The brother responsible for Joseph's sale into slavery volunteers to become a slave himself. As young men the brothers came before Jacob reporting the loss of a favorite son. As a mature man and as a father who has himself lost two sons, as he did in Genesis 38, Judah cannot bear the terrible prospect of facing Jacob without Benjamin, his father's now favorite son.

Philosopher-rabbi Roger Klein contends that the Joseph cycle has four levels: individual, familial, national, and theological. This particular speech can certainly be interpreted on all four levels. Individually Benjamin and Jacob are so close that the fate of one is inseparable from the fate of the other. The family, which will not survive as a family if the meaning of this verse is not acted on, is framed by linkage of the aged Patriarch and the youngest son, whose very presence is a constant reminder of the fate of the son whom the brothers did away with so long ago. Nationally their continuation depends on Joseph's help; hence his evaluation of the brothers' relationship between Benjamin and Jacob. Theologically the test that the brothers passed with flying colors turned on their acceptance of this special, spiritual relationship between the Jacob and Benjamin.

Judah as *Ba'al Teshuva*: A Rabbinic Perspective

Traditional Judaism has found in Judah's speech, beyond superlative rhetoric, a profound meditation on transgression and repentance. Judah's utterance to Joseph in Gen. 44:32, "I shall stand guilty before you forever," is nearly a citation of his comments to Jacob in Gen. 43:9, when he convinces Jacob to send Benjamin with him. In the words of Eliezer Benmozegh: "This figure of speech contains a valuable lesson, teaching us something not otherwise explicitly alluded to in the Torah: that there is no punishment outside of the sin. Sin itself is its own punishment in the Divine scheme of judgment and serves the purpose of reward and punishment. This is the meaning of 'then shall I bear the blame to my father forever (44:32).'"[12] Maimonides, following the midrashic tradition, focuses on the moral symmetry of Judah's *teshuva* with his past transgression, highlighting its sincerity and its completeness. Maimonides' well-known definition of the penitent (*ba'al teshuva*) as one who, when faced with the same temptation, resists, seems to be exemplified by this situation.[13] Judah and brothers could have betrayed Benjamin as they did Joseph but refrain from doing so at all costs. To the obvious objection that the brothers are now grown men with children of their own (and therefore not really in the same situation as Maimonides imagines), Rav Joseph Soloveitchik avers: "There can be a certain sequence of events that starts out with sin and iniquity but ends up with mitzvot and good deeds. The future transforms the thrust of the past. This is the nature of that causality operating in the realm of the spirit."[14]

Modern commentary emphasizes the literary effectiveness and propriety of Judah's remarks, no one better than Meir Sternberg:

To Joseph, of course, the speech reveals even more than the speaker intended: the official version of his own death, the reason for the delay in the brothers' return, the pain his testing as well as his fate must have given. More important, if to a listener ignorant of the family situation and record, the brothers' attitude as expressed by their leader would appear admirable. Then to one in the know it surely manifests nothing short of a transformation, from subnormal to abnormal solidarity. That the sons of the hated wife should have come to terms with the father's attachment to Rachel ("my wife") and her children is enough to promise an end to hostilities and a fresh start. That the second of these children should enjoy his brothers' affection is amazing. But that Judah should adduce the father's favoritism as the

147

ground for self-sacrifice is such an irresistible proof of filial devotion that it breaks down Joseph's last defenses. . . . Nor is this a one-sided but rather a double and causally motivated enlightenment: having discovered their character, Joseph discloses his identity. One anguished cry about the patriarch draws out another, "I am Joseph. Is my father still alive?"[15]

Did Judah Know It Was Joseph?

Let us raise one last question about this speech: did Judah know to whom he was talking? According to the simple sense, no. What drama remains should Judah have already intuited speaker's true identity?[16] Benno Jacob acknowledged that Judah suspected that something was off, but not what.[17] Leon Kass goes farther, "Even more to be wondered at, although Judah probably does not know (as far as we can tell) before whom he stands and to whom he speaks, he makes a speech perfectly suited to move and instruct his brother Joseph."[18] But the text hints at some level of awareness. The use of epithets "father," "brother," and "servant" sound like personal appeals rather than abstract justice. Why would an Egyptian vizier care if Jacob's soul were bound with Benjamin's? Why would the pointed reference to Benjamin and Rachel as being Jacob's favorites, an extraordinary acknowledgement that love is irrational and does play favorites, be expected to move Pharaoh's lieutenant?

Judah and the brothers surely realize that they are missing some critical piece of information: just as Judah pleads guilty generally, but not to the charge of stealing the divining cup, it seems unlikely that the brothers think Benjamin did so, and implausible that Joseph is acting fairly. The fact that Joseph sat alone at the banquet must have caused reflection, as did the double portion given Benjamin at the banquet and the order of seating by age, which "astonished the brothers" (Gen. 43:33). Perhaps Judah subconsciously recognized Joseph; the narrator was surely capable of such subtlety. If Judah knew he faced his long-lost brother, would that have made his speech less impressive? What seems beyond doubt is that Judah's stepping forward here not only provokes Joseph's third set of tears and his self-revelation, but it also signals their reconciliation and its cosmic importance: "It is the privilege of the righteous that when they come together, peace descends upon the world. . . . Joseph and Judah provide an example."[19]

Judah's Speech in Tradition

Many midrashim detect Judah's rhetorical genius in the lengthy speech Judah delivers in Genesis 44:18–34 but tend to expand it in a way that takes the confrontational undertone and makes it a direct challenge, audible for "four hundred parasangs."[20] Or, as another midrash comments, "Just as Pharaoh decrees and does not fulfill his decree, so dost thou decree and not fulfill. As Pharaoh lusts for males, so dost thou for Benjamin. As Pharaoh is a king . . . so is my father a king in the land of Canaan."[21] Yet another midrash goes even further:

> My lord has asked his servants—from the beginning didst thou come down upon us with a pretext. From many countries did they come down to Egypt to buy corn, and thou didst not question anyone of them. Peradventure we came to take the hand of thy daughter? Or thou are of a mind to wed our sister? Even so we hid nothing from thee. Joseph replied to him: Judah! Wherefore art thou the spokesman of your brethren, whereas I see in my divining goblet that thou hast brothers older than thyself? Answered Judah: All that thou seest is due to the bond that I stood for him.[22]

Nehama Leibowitz draws an apt distinction between the scriptural and the postscriptural: "Judah, in the original biblical petition only hints at injustice, indirectly. In the Midrash, he beseeches, threatens and denounces whilst Joseph aggressively answers him back in mocking and ironic tone."[23]

149

Joseph—Finally—Reveals His Identity

The climax of the Joseph story begins with Joseph's stage management of his self-revelation: "Have everyone withdraw from me!" (Gen. 45:1). It is entirely appropriate that Joseph should be alone with his brothers given the intensity and intimacy of what he has to say. Once again Joseph is reduced to tears, and we must wonder at the contrast between the self-contained young man who rose to the pinnacle of Egyptian society and the mature ruler who now feels free vent to his pent-up emotions.[24]

Joseph's long-delayed self-revelation, "I am Joseph" (Gen. 45:3b), is followed by a second utterance, "I am your brother Joseph" (45:4b). I second Robert Alter's verdict that source critics who attribute this double exclamation to two different sources (E and J) suffer from literary tone deafness. The text explicitly tells us that the brothers were dumbfounded, and given all that has transpired, who could doubt that Joseph would feel impelled to repeat himself—adding that telltale epithet, "I am *your brother* Joseph"? Alter comments that the drama of this situation virtually necessitates Joseph's repetition to the incredulous men. The first self-revelation, to begin with, gives us the narrator's account, which uses the reflexive form of the verb "to know," in this case *b'hitvadah*, (to make himself known). This verb form reverses the use of the reflexive form of the verb *va'yitnaker* (to make himself a stranger, or to make himself unknown) in Gen. 42:7. In contrast to the narrator's report, verse 3 gives us Joseph's actual words. Direct speech is simply more dramatic than omniscient narration, and drama is what the situation demands.

Joseph's expostulation in Gen. 45:3—"Does my father yet live?"—need not be explained by one source being unaware that another source has just described Jacob as being alive—if not quite well—in Canaan, as Judah's speech suggests. As a more plausible choice, in this context, one should read Joseph's remarks to his brothers as anticipating the now assured reunion with his father and his incredulous joy at the prospect. Not surprisingly the brothers are initially speechless, and Joseph tells them to approach and repeats his comment. The contrast between the verbally adept Judah and their collective stunned silence now is most effective. Only when Joseph commits himself to the physical gesture of crying and hugging Benjamin and then all of them are we told by the text, "With that he embraced [fell on] his brother Benjamin around the neck and wept, and Benjamin wept on his neck. He kissed all his brothers and wept upon them; only then were his brothers able to talk to him"(Gen. 45:14–15).[25] What Joseph says to the brothers next, a reassurance speech, bears comparison with a second reassurance speech delivered in Genesis 50; we will examine the speeches together later on.

Awkward Reunions

After the dramatic self-revelation of Joseph the biblical text naturally returns to reunions and reconciliations of Genesis's first family. As if to remind the reader of Judah's established role among the brothers, the text records, "He [Jacob] had sent Judah ahead of him to Joseph, to point the way before him to Goshen" (Gen. 46:28). The long-awaited reunion of Joseph and Jacob that follows is shockingly brief: "So when they came to the region of Goshen, Joseph ordered his chariot and went to Goshen to meet his father Israel; he presented himself to him and, embracing him around the neck, he wept on his neck a good while. Then Israel said to Joseph, "Now I can die, having seen for myself that you are still alive" (Gen 46:28–30).

Nowhere does Goethe's reproach that the Joseph narrative is too short seem to me more warranted than in these scant three verses, although commentators seem more focused on the grammatical difficulty about who cried on whom than on its surprising brevity. The grammar is indecisive: looking at the verbs and pronouns, annoyingly singular, one cannot tell subject from object. Rashi (and Robert Alter) hold that the copious tears were shed by Joseph, expressing years of pent-up emotion, while Jacob was busy reciting the Shma (Rashi, not Alter). Overlooking the grammatical difficulties with the alternative, and suggesting that Jacob's eyes had already dimmed, Nachmanides finds it more likely on psychological grounds that the father would be more overcome with emotion than the son.[26] But psychology is an inexact science. Taking their lives into account, Samson Raphael Hirsch overturns Nachmanides' verdict in favor of Rashi's:

> Joseph not Jacob wept. Joseph wept liberally, but Jacob's tears had long since dried up. Joseph continued to weep even after Jacob had already begun conversing with him. These little touches mirror the true situation. Jacob had lived lonely and isolated and his whole life had been centered on mourning for Joseph. Joseph had experienced many changes of fortune. These had not let him dwell on his homesickness. But the encounter with his father as he fell on his neck aroused in him nostalgic memories of him twenty years earlier and all these feelings surged out in tears.[27]

The place name Goshen appears twelve times in Genesis 46–47 as the region in which Joseph settles the brothers. The rationale for this has also elicited comment, but we will focus on Joseph's warning that the brothers should describe themselves as keepers of cattle (*anshe mikneh*; Gen. 46:32, 34) rather than sheep herders (*roeh tsoan*), because the Egyptians consider shepherds abhorrent (Gen. 46:34). We have no other Torah verses shedding light on cattle breeders, and no evidence that Egyptians despised shepherds. Is there some memory in Gen. 46:31–34 of shepherd versus cattlemen hostility, akin to the farmer versus rancher strife of the American West? Is there an entire "shepherd ethics" incompatible with the ethics of a settled agriculturalist? Whatever the roots of these self-descriptions it cannot be accidental that Joseph stresses to his brothers that they should say "both we and also our fathers" are keepers of cattle (Gen. 46:34), and that his brothers retort "both we and also our fathers" have been shepherds (Gen. 47:3)! Are the brothers being ornery, forgetful, or subconsciously resistant to Joseph's overwhelming dominance? To dismiss all this as accidental, or as an unintended consequence of poor editing, strikes me as unlikely, especially when we recall the introductory verse Gen. 47:2, "And from the pick of his brothers." As Robert Alter comments, "The Hebrew prepositional phrase *miqtseh ehaw*, has elicited puzzlement, or evasion, from most translators."[28] As midrash realizes, Joseph is stage managing the scene—with mixed results.[29]

The same awkwardness seems apparent in the passage in which Joseph introduces Jacob to Pharaoh, that is, his father to his boss. Considering the emphatic way Joseph inquires after Jacob's well-being with his brothers, it seems curious he introduces five of his brothers before Jacob. But Jacob has always been a difficult character, and his answer to Pharaoh's polite greeting is vintage Jacob: "Joseph then brought his father Jacob and presented him to Pharaoh; and Jacob greeted Pharaoh. Pharaoh asked Jacob, 'How many are the years of your life?' And Jacob answered Pharaoh, 'The years of my sojourn [on earth] are one hundred and thirty. Few and hard have been the years of my life, nor do they come up to the life spans of my fathers during their sojourns.' Then Jacob bade Pharaoh farewell, and left Pharaoh's presence" (Gen. 47:7–10).

Jacob's Blessing of Judah in Genesis 49

The biblical text returns to Judah once more in Genesis, in the deathbed valedictory address bestowed by Jacob on all twelve sons. These valedictions (benediction and malediction alike) abound in cryptic elements, mix past and future, and blend individual incidents in Jacob's son's lives with much later dispositions of Israel's tribes. We will take a second look at Genesis 49 as a portrait of Joseph later in this book, but let us look briefly at its implied characterization of Judah. Since scholars agree this oracle follows poetic form, we reproduce it accordingly:

> You, O Judah, your brothers shall praise;
> Your hand shall be on the nape of your foes;
> Your father's sons shall bow low to you.
> Judah is a lion's whelp;
> On prey, my son, have you grown.
> He crouches, lies down like a lion,
> Like—the king of beasts—who dare rouse him?
> The scepter shall not depart from Judah,
> Nor the ruler's staff from between his feet;
> So that tribute shall come to him
> And the homage of peoples be his.
> He tethers his ass to a vine,
> His ass's foal to a choice vine;
> He washes his garment in wine,
> His robe in blood of grapes.
> His eyes are darker than wine;
> His teeth are whiter than milk. (Gen. 49:8–12)

Judah will possess lion-like strength, his territory will be fertile, and his brothers will praise him, a play on his name. More remarkably, from the point of view of the preceding narrative, Jacob states, "your father's sons shall bow low to you" (Gen. 49:7b), effectively reversing the obeisance done to Joseph, first in the latter's youthful dreams, and then in actuality. Jacob's utterance, "On prey, my son, you have grown," may remind readers of the doubling of that verb (*tet-resh-peh*) when Jacob pronounces Joseph's supposed fate. Likewise the dipping or dying of a garment in wine may refer to the use of the bloodied garment to deceive Jacob back in Genesis 37.

We are next confronted by a flood of vivid images—milk, blood, and wine, which call to mind the vitalism of Judah that can cross the border morally—and which some commentators think implicit in the idea of tethered ass, ordinarily destructive, but helpless against the productivity of Judah's vine. That vine (*sorek*) also reminds the reader of a detail in the narrative, for Wadi Sorek is in Timnah region, the site of Genesis 38, Judah's longest Bible scene. Judah's competition with Joseph, whose blessing in Genesis 49 also occupies five verses, seems implicit in these lines. Jack Miles's provocative *God: A Biography* finds this comparison blatant. To Miles, Judah's political power will be through violence, but Joseph's personality remains far more attractive.[30]

Judah and Joseph beyond Genesis

Joseph and Judah die in Genesis, and later references to them in the Bible mainly refer to their roles as the respective, eponymous founders of their tribes.[31] Two passages stand as exceptions to this purely "tribal" treatment of the two brothers; both examples point to the ironic outcome of the contending brothers. While Ephraim, Joseph's son promoted by Jacob in Genesis 48, will be very important to the Northern Kingdom Israel, these tribes will be scattered by the Assyrians. The descendants of Judah will ultimately stand at the head of the nation. Literary scholar Gabriel Josipovici compares Joseph's words in Genesis 50:19–21, that it all worked out according to God's plan, with the concession speech delivered by Shimei to King David, "I am come the first this day of all the house of Joseph to go down to meet my lord the king" (2 Sam. 19:20). Josipovici notes, "Nevertheless, it turns out that David belongs to the house of Judah; and we have seen how Shimei, one of Saul's followers, will come to David as he returns in triumph to Jerusalem and say: And we have seen how David dealt with Shimei." The end of Genesis does not anticipate the eventual emergence of Judah as the triumphant tribe, and Josipovici concludes that biblical irony is broader than usually conceived. The patterns are never wholly available to the biblical characters, but that does not invite contempt on our part, for we are not omniscient either. Josipovici concludes, "In light of all this even Genesis 50 has to be thought about again. God did mean it for the good, but even Joseph could not see what it was that God meant."[32]

The second passage that seems more than just tribal is the prophet Ezekiel's images of the conjoining of the two branches of the nation represented by Judah and Joseph. Once again rule will pass to Judah, but only after both brothers have contributed to the effort.[33] The passage comes in Ezekiel directly after the famous image of the valley of the dry bones. The images are related: they represent, respectively, the revival and unification of the nation. The two sticks represent all the tribes, though here only two matter: Joseph and Judah.[34] Unlike Genesis 49, which reflects sibling competition still at work, in Ezekiel's day the dominant partner is no longer in doubt. David, Judah's descendant, described as the "Lord's servant" in this passage, will rule as shepherd over one nation. The reiteration of oneness or unity, repeated often in this passage, seems the perfect complement to the reconciliation of the brothers, the climax of the Torah portion Va-yiggash, and here, in the accompanying haftarah (Ezekiel 37:15–28):

> The word of the Lord came to me: "Son of man, take a stick of wood and write on it, 'Belonging to Judah and the Israelites associated with him.' Then take another stick of wood, and write on it, 'Belonging to Joseph (that is, to Ephraim) and all the Israelites associated with him.' Join them together into one stick so that they will become one in your hand. When your people ask you, 'Won't you tell us what you mean by this?' say to them, 'This is what the Sovereign Lord says: I am going to take the stick of Joseph—which is in Ephraim's hand—and of the Israelite tribes associated with him, and join it to Judah's stick. I will make them into a single stick of wood, and they will become one in my hand.' Hold before their eyes the sticks you have written on and say to them, 'This is what the Sovereign Lord says: I will take the Israelites out of the nations where they have gone. I will

gather them from all around and bring them back into their own land. I will make them one nation in the land, on the mountains of Israel. There will be one king over all of them and they will never again be two nations or be divided into two kingdoms. They will no longer defile themselves with their idols and vile images or with any of their offenses, for I will save them from all their sinful backsliding, and I will cleanse them. They will be my people, and I will be their God. My servant David will be king over them, and they will all have one shepherd. They will follow my laws and be careful to keep my decrees. They will live in the land I gave to my servant Jacob, the land where your ancestors lived. They and their children and their children's children will live there forever, and David my servant will be their prince forever. I will make a covenant of peace with them; it will be an everlasting covenant. I will establish them and increase their numbers, and I will put my sanctuary among them forever. My dwelling place will be with them; I will be their God, and they will be my people. Then the nations will know that I the Lord make Israel holy, when my sanctuary is among them forever."

With Judah's emergence as a leader, hardly predictable from his status as Leah's fourth son or from his earlier encounter with Tamar, the brothers manage to pass their fraternity test with Benjamin.[35] Judah's speeches to Jacob and Joseph address injured parties. In the case of Joseph, Judah's long speech contains lots of supplication and some reproach, although rabbinic sources exaggerate these notes of reproach well beyond the simple sense. As often, from a rabbinic point of view, the issue is religious as well as literary. Judah's penitence, his status as a *ba'al teshuva*, (a penitent) constitutes a moral requirement for reconciliation with Joseph. Did Judah or the other brothers understand the nature of this drama staged by Joseph? Not entirely, but Josipovici seems correct in concluding that the Bible keeps even Joseph, the great stage manager of these scenes, somewhat in the dark. I find no verse that hints at

Joseph's awareness that Judah will one day lead the nation, as suggested by Genesis 49 and by Ezekiel 37. With Joseph's identity and status now revealed, the tension between the brothers might seem resolved. But rifts over past failures remain. One of these reemerges presently between Jacob and his favored son.

8

The Return of Rachel

If forced to choose the most intriguing verse in the entire Joseph narrative, I would opt for Gen. 48:7—transliterated and translated below—in a noble attempt to convey the fraught tone of an obvious interjection: "the reference to Rachel's death has no recognizable relation to what follows or precedes."[1] Source critics argue that this passage belongs with the original notice of Rachel's death in Genesis 35, or, with some additional integrating verses (which are now assumed to have been lost), into the adoption scene of Ephraim and Manasseh, which this verse clearly interrupts. But arriving at the simple sense of this verse is difficult. One might begin by noting the ironic context. Jacob, settled in Goshen, requests burial in remote Canaan in the family tomb purchased by Abraham, knowing full well that he buried Joseph's own mother, Rachel, in a kind of no man's land. The pillar Jacob sets up to mark Rachel's tomb reflects his enduring affection but also has the practical purpose of marking a previously undistinguished spot.[2] Since Jacob was headed east to west, why did he fail to bury Rachel in the family crypt at Mahpelah in Hebron? Some commentators stress the practical difficulties of transporting Rachel to the cave of Mahpelah: he oversaw a large household and many animals; the road was in disrepair; honor requires immediate burial; there were no embalmers, and the weather was hot; and so on. But one could retort that Jacob surely could have *reburied* Rachel in Hebron. Here is the sole verse we will examine in this chapter:

Va'ani b'voi mi-padan, meyta alai rahel b'eretz k'na'an ba'derekh b'od kivrat-eretz lavoh efratah va'ekbi'reha sham b'derekh efrat—hi beit lechem.

I [do this because], when I was returning from Paddan, Rachel died, to my sorrow, while I was journeying in the land of Canaan, when still some distance short of Ephrat; and I buried her there on the road to Ephrat—now Bethlehem. (Gen. 48:7)[3]

Adding to the difficulty of discerning the simple sense of the verse, we have Jacob's inscrutable tone, introduced by the halting *"va'ani b'voi m'padan."*[4] This tone suggests pain, guilt, and resentment.[5] The pain, emphasized by Samuel Dresner, stems from Jacob's sadness at losing his beautiful wife too soon. The guilt feelings may emerge from Jacob's failure to bury Rachel in the "right" place, but possibly for the role he had played in her demise, both as the father of Benjamin (she died in childbirth) and, as more frequently noted, for condemning the thief of Laban's household idols to death in Gen. 31:31–32 (the thief was Rachel). In this reading Jacob makes amends for Rachel's early demise by the adoption of Ephraim (sounds like Ephrat?) and Manasseh.[6] But just as much as guilt, the tone expresses Jacob's resentment at the untimely death of the love of his life. A more literal translation of the text than NJPS's would be Rachel died "on me" or "unto me." This preposition, *alai* (also used in Gen. 11:28), may reflect defensiveness, or perhaps something worse. Jacob's solipsism at this moment may strike some readers: he has lived to good old age (not old enough in his eyes), seen children and grandchildren, and received preferential treatment from both "my son the vizier," as it were, and even Pharaoh. Perhaps "Rachel your mother" would have been a more sensitive way to refer to her when talking to Joseph on this occasion.

Other peculiarities in this verse may be observed. The narrator's identification of Ephrat with present-day Bethlehem constitutes one of those etiological notices that scholars relish as evidence of historical development within the Bible. The double mention of Ephrat, along with the doubling of the phrase "on the way" (ba'derekh/b'derekh) in Genesis 48 invited midrashic explanation, especially as this word was absent from the earlier account of Rachel's death.[7] Two additional features heighten the mystery of this verse. First, Jacob's utterance blatantly interrupts the adoption narrative of Joseph's sons—but why here exactly? Second, in a narrative sense this verse does not tell us anything new, since Rachel's death has already been narrated at greater length in Genesis 35:[8]

> They set out from Bethel; but when they were still some distance short of Ephrath, Rachel was in childbirth, and she had hard labor. When her labor was at its hardest, the midwife said to her, "Have no fear, for it is another boy for you." But as she breathed her last—for she was dying—she named him Ben-oni; but his father called him Benjamin. Thus Rachel died. She was buried on the road to Ephrath—now Bethlehem. Over her grave Jacob set up a pillar; it is the pillar at Rachel's grave to this day.

Rachel's role in Joseph's story differs from the other women in the Joseph cycle (e.g., Tamar, Potiphar's wife, Asenath, Serah bat Asher). She is one of the Matriarchs and an important character in her own right. Readers see Rachel as a daughter, mother, sister, and wife. In all these roles she reveals strong character. Contrary to the stereotype of the hovering, helicopter Jewish mother of Philip Roth's novels, Rachel is outstanding in Genesis 37–50 by her absence; our verse intrudes, perhaps, to convey Rachel's presence as felt by the characters in the story—or at least Jacob and Joseph, husband and son.

Joseph's Missing Childhood

Scripture focuses on certain events, leaving other developments to the imagination of the reader. Rachel gave birth to Joseph in Genesis 30 and died giving birth to Benjamin in Genesis 35. What happened in the time that passed from Genesis 30–35 is vividly narrated: the incident of the spotted and speckled sheep, the decision to leave Laban and return to Canaan, the wrestling match that leads to Jacob's renaming as Israel, and the reunion of Jacob and Esau rank as highpoints of narrative style. But of Rachel's relationship with Joseph, the son she sought so badly, nothing remains. Her rise to preeminence within Jacob's household must be teased out from the narrative in which she is mentioned before Leah (Gen. 31:4, 31:14), from the safety spot in which Jacob placed Rachel and Joseph (Gen. 33:2, 33:7), from the disappearance of Leah from the narrative until her death notice, and that too is ambiguous.[9] Later sources reflect Leah's secondary status vis-à-vis Rachel—in the climactic passage of the book of Ruth, 4:11–13, Rachel is mentioned first,[10] and many midrashim that relate Rachel's barrenness (*akarah*) to her being the principal (*ikkarah*) of the family.[11] Childhood in the Hebrew Bible is a complicated status to nail down precisely. Birth and weaning narratives abound, as do tales of infancy. Youth is often noted as a preliminary to some great acts—think of David, or Joseph, for that matter. But childhood does not get much textual play in the Hebrew Bible—Hannah brings little Samuel a new cloak every year while he attends Eli in Shilo; Ishmael is banished with Hagar to the wilderness; the boys who mock the prophet Elisha are mauled by bears.[12]

There is every reason to think that the seventeen-year-old Joseph remembered his mother vividly; certainly his older brothers would have. Jacob, we may assume, mentioned Rachel often (the novelist Thomas Mann assumes this too). While the relations between handmaids and wives were not easy, as the example of Sarah and Hagar demonstrates, it seems likely that Bilhah would have spoken of Rachel her mistress, and Joseph probably got wind of Reuben's attempt to take Bilhah as his wife, an attempt on Reuben's part to enhance his status as the firstborn of Jacob (*bekhor*) by taking the deceased

Rachel's handmaid.[13] While the sororal competition between Leah and Rachel was fierce, the sisters began their voyage back to Canaan willingly. Leah may have wanted more affection from Jacob than he was willing to deliver, but her naming speeches for Judah, Gad, and Asher shows her coping successfully with that lack. Leah suffered the rape of her daughter in Genesis 34 and the premature death of her sister in Genesis 35.[14] Not too many characters would be unaffected by those kinds of trauma, and there is no reason to think tender-eyed Leah falls into that hard-hearted category.[15] To summarize, while we must turn mainly to postbiblical readers for Rachel's role after her demise, it does not seem like much of a stretch to presume some legacy for such a powerful woman.[16]

The verse at the heart of this chapter (Gen. 48:7) indicates that Jacob certainly remembers Rachel many years after her death (which we might have expected given their passionate relationship), and the similar physical appearance of Joseph and Rachel. That the Bible uses the same language invites several further inferences, including the most obvious: when Jacob sees Joseph he may be reminded of his beloved, deceased wife. This is not given as a further cause of either Jacob's favoritism, or as evidence of some darker emotion,[17] but it is hard to ignore the possibility.

Revelation and Interpretation: Jeremiah's Great Midrash

Rachel's ascendancy may be traced in Genesis, in Ruth, and of course in postbiblical literature. But the critical moment in Rachel's afterlife took place in the early sixth century BCE, benefit of the prophet Jeremiah.[18] Jeremiah's midrash on Rachel's fate was no doubt inspired by the loss of the Kingdom of the North in 722/721 BCE, led by the tribe of Ephraim, Rachel's distant descendant. Jeremiah 30–31, usually dated to the immediate post–587/586 BCE destruction, sounds a more hopeful note than the remainder of Jeremiah, and is often termed the "scroll of consolation" by modern scholars.[19] The prophecy here is dominated by the elevation of Rachel and the restoration of Ephraim, the sorry history of these two characters notwithstanding.[20]

> Thus said the Lord: A cry is heard in Ramah—Wailing, bitter weeping—Rachel weeping for her children. She refuses to be comforted for her children, who are gone. Thus said the Lord: Restrain your voice from weeping, Your eyes from shedding tears; For there is reward for your labor—declares the Lord: They shall return from the enemy's land. And there is hope for your future—declares the Lord: Your children shall return to their country. I can hear Ephraim lamenting: You have chastised me, and I am chastised. Like a calf that has not been broken. Receive me back, let me return, For You, O Lord are my God. (Jer. 15:18)

Poignantly Jeremiah's utterance picks up on Rachel's struggle to give birth (Gen. 30:1) and on her travails giving birth to Benjamin (Gen. 35:16–18). Disaster has befallen Ephraim, here, as often, symbolic of the northern tribes at large, but God's love and compassion led to severe punishment, not abandonment. Ephraim will be turned back to God and restored. Jeremiah's imaginative leap has had an enduring impact. God's comforting Rachel lies behind many midrashim devoted to Rachel's intercessory tears, behind Matthew's account of the slaughter of the innocents in Matt. 2:18, and behind the kabbalistic practice of Tikkun Hazzot—an all-night vigil in which the sisters and co-wives Rachel and Leah are invoked as symbols of exile and redemption.[21] Fans of Herman Melville will remember Ahab's cruel refusal to aid the *Rachel's* lost sailors and the closing lines of *Moby Dick*: "Buoyed up by that coffin, for almost one whole day and night, I floated on a soft and dirge-like main. The unharming sharks, they glided by as if with padlocks on their mouths: the savage sea-hawks sailed with sheathed beaks. On the second day, a sail drew near, nearer, and picked me up at last. It was the devious-cruising Rachel that in her retracing search after her missing children, only found another orphan."

164

Rashi: Jacob's Prophetic Burial, Before and After?

In between Jeremiah and Rashi lie some midrashim we will turn to at the end of this chapter. Anthologically no one can compare with Rashi, who preserved earlier midrashim and pressed them into service of explaining the verse. In this case Rashi's choice of traditions is revealing:

> Rashi: [va'ekbireha sham] And I buried her there and I did not carry her even to Bethlehem to bring her into the land of Israel. And I know that you have a complaint in your heart against me [alai]. However, know that by the word of God did I bury her there, that she might be of aid to her children when Nebuzaradan exiled them and they passed by there; there would Rachel come out of her grave, crying and beseeching for them mercy, as it is stated, "A voice is heard in Ramah," and the Holy One Blessed Be He answers her, "There is a reward for they work," sayeth the Lord, "And they children shall return to their own border." (Jer. 31:15–16)[22]

Rashi presents Gen. 48:7 as if God gave Jacob a direct, divine command in order to validate the prophecy uttered by the prophet Jeremiah, hundreds of years after Jacob, Rachel, and Joseph are all long gone. Rashi's egregious anachronism offers an example of the rabbinic principle, "There is no before or after in Torah." In other words, since God gave the entire Torah, one can, when occasion demands, disregard chronology in the course of exegesis. Not all rabbis approved of the principle's overuse, Nachmanides included. After all, if one begins to move sequence in a narrative, where does one stop? What serves as the control mechanism on rearranging biblical stories? For Nachmanides there *is* a before and an after in Torah; he proposes a different reading this passage.

Nachmanides' Dissent: A Hint Is Not a Prophecy

Nachmanides connects the proposition "on me" or "to me" (*alai*) to Jacob's large holding of livestock, children, and

165

grandchildren—Jacob had to press on to reach the city of Eph-
rat/Bethlehem in haste. But an obvious question may be posed:
why did not Jacob return and rebury Rachel, exactly what Joseph
will request of his brothers at the end of Genesis 50? Nachmanides responds to Rashi's reading:

> Now I do not know the meaning thereof. Was Rachel buried out-
> side of the land? Forbid it! She died within the land, and she was
> buried there, just as it says here in the parashah: Rachel died by
> me in the land of Canaan. And there in the narrative of her death
> it is still more clearly written, And Jacob came to Luz, which is
> in the land of Canaan—the same as Beth-el and there was still
> some way to come to Ephrat, and Rachel died there on the way
> between Beth-el and there was still some way to come to Eph-
> rath, and Rachel died on the way between Beth-el and Bethle-
> hem Ephrata in the Land of Israel.[23]

For Nachmanides Rachel's burial in the land of Israel is critical for another reason: it addresses the thorny issue of whether
the Patriarchs observed the laws of the Torah, even though
these had not been given until Sinai, and how they knew these
laws in the first place (Gen. 26:5). In this case the clear prohibition against marrying two sisters (Lev. 18:18) would seem
to cast Jacob in the light of a transgressor. But Nachmanides
justifies Jacob's behavior on the basis of these commandments
being applicable in the land of Israel only. Since Jacob married
Rachel and Leah outside the land of Israel, he did not violate
this "don't do" commandment. Law, not affection, explains this
choice. But this comment implies a secondary connection to
Rachel's tragic death and her reentering the land. Nachmanides concludes his dissent from Rashi:

> Now it is my opinion that these words are but words of apol-
> ogy as Joseph already knew that Rachel died on the road and
> was buried in the land, and that honor was paid to her when she
> died. But the reason Jacob did not transport Rachel to the cave

of Machpelah was so that he should not bury two sisters there, for he would be embarrassed before his ancestors. Now Leah was the one he married first, and thus her marriage was permissible, while he married Rachel out of his love for her and because of the vow he made to her.[24]

Why Was Rachel Such a Potent Intercessor?

Why did Jacob fail to return and rebury Rachel? Joseph requests this of his brothers at the end of Genesis 50, and it transpires. Rabbinic authors assume the reader's familiarity with Jeremiah, who first elevated Rachel to the role of mother of the nation, and cast her in the role of sympathetic intercessor.[25] The biblical Rachel lobbies on her own behalf (see Gen. 30:1, 30:14, 31:35) but also on behalf of her children as the collaboration with Leah demonstrates. "Then Rachel and Leah answered him, saying "Have we still a share in the inheritance of our father's house? Surely, he regards us as outsiders, now that he has sold us and used up our purchase price. Truly, all the wealth that God has taken away from our father belongs to us and to our children" (Gen. 31:14–16). That Jacob makes his decision to leave Laban's house directly after Joseph's birth, asks Rachel and Leah, not Leah and Rachel, for their consent, that Rachel and Leah, not Leah and Rachel answer, suggests that the younger sister has already gained preeminence over the older sister, as in so many fraternal Genesis narratives.

An extreme reconciling of Rachel and Leah comes from one of the openings of *Lamentations Rabbah*—it has been ably discussed by many scholars. Nevertheless no discussion of their sororal competition and their ultimate reconciliation as mothers of the nation, whether in Jeremiah's eyes, the author of Ruth, or those of the rabbis, should ignore this remarkable midrash set against the backdrop of looming exile in Jeremiah's case, exile long protracted in the case of *Lamentations Rabbah*:

The matriarch Rachel broke forth into speech before the Holy One, blessed be He, and said, Sovereign of the Universe, it is revealed before Thee that thy servant Jacob loved me exceedingly and toiled for my father on my behalf seven years. When those seven years were completed and the time arrived for my marriage with my husband my father planned to substitute another for me and wed my husband for the sake of my sister. It was very hard for me, because the plot was known to me and I disclosed it to my husband; and I gave him a sign whereby he could distinguish between me and my sister, so that my father should not be able to make the substitution. After that I relented, suppressed my desire, and had pity upon my sister, that she might not be exposed to shame. In the evening they substituted my sister for me with my husband, and I delivered over to my sister all the signs which I had arranged with my husband. . . . More than this, I went beneath the bed upon which he lay with my sister; and when he spoke to her she remained silent and I made all the replies in order that he should not recognize my sister's voice. I did her a kindness was not jealous of her, and did not expose her to ahem. And if I, a creature of flesh and blood, formed of dust and ashes, was not envious of my rival . . . why should thou, A King who lives eternally and are merciful, be jealous of idolatry in which there is no reality, and exile my children and let them by slain by the sword and their enemies have done with them as they wished! Forthwith the mercy of the Holy One, blessed be He, was stirred, and He said, "For thy sake Rachel, I will restore Israel to their place." And so it is written, "A voice is heard in Ramah."[26]

In Ilana Pardes's reading this midrash reconciles the sisters, a message she finds in the book of Ruth as well, with Naomi and Ruth reversing the expectations of tensions between mother-in-law and daughter-in-law. Both Pardes and Dvora Weisberg elaborate the gender dimension in this midrash, which includes failed attempts to bring about the end of the exile on the part of the Patriarchs and Moses. Rachel's personal example of compassion (*hesed*) toward her sister Leah succeeds where the various male-voiced appeals to strict justice (*din*) fail to move God to action. This midrash is, without doubt, a very moving one; how far from the character of the biblical Rachel, I will leave to the reader's judgment.

Joseph's devotion to his mother is nowhere stated in explicitly in Scripture, though this verse may imply it. But midrash captures Joseph's likely sentiments and casts Joseph in his mother's role as lamenter for the nation:

> O mother, mother who bore me, arise and behold how your son has been sold into slavery with none to take pity upon him. Arise from your sleep, O Mother, and behold the cruelty of my brothers who tore me from my father and sold me into slavery. . . . "Arise O mother, awaken from your sleep and comfort my father whose spirit ever broods over me." So Joseph lamented at the grave of his mother, until, spent, he lay there sobbing, immovable. Suddenly, from deep within the earth was heard a tearful voice: "Joseph my son, my son Joseph. I heard your cry; I saw your tears; I felt your grief. My son, trust in the Lord and wait upon him. Do not fear, for the Lord is with you, and he will deliver you from all evil. Go down to Egypt my son. Fear not, for the Lord is with you, my son."[27]

This midrash imagines Joseph passing by Rachel's grave on the way down to enslavement in Egypt. (It serves as a bookend for another midrash that imagines Joseph, returning from the burial of Jacob in Canaan, passing by the very pit into which he was thrown by the brothers.) In this first midrash above Joseph implores Rachel to behold the brothers' cruelty. In a famous midrash, *Lamentations Rabbah,* Rachel implores God to witness the cruelty of the nations in contrast to her loving-kindness to her sister. This midrash also echoes God's necessary reassurance to Jacob that the latter may indeed descend to Egypt, despite God's contradictory warning to Isaac on this very subject.[28] Rachel knew there is a rightness in Jacob's marrying two wives, for this world, which is a world of division and separation, does not lend itself to total unity. If Jacob had only the one wife of his desire, the family and the nation would have been unified; the basic split of the people into two kingdoms (Judah from Leah, and Ephraim from Rachel), a split that will endure till messianic times, would have been avoided. But because Rachel saw that such a split is congruous with the nature of this world, she suppressed her love and jealousy. She, therefore, is uniquely qualified to plead that God similarly forgive Israel for a sin—idolatry, the "rival wife"—that is the direct outcome of the fragmented reality of this world. She is most personally tutored in the pain of incompleteness; God listens to the weeping that teaches Him about the world He has created.[29]

Aviva Gottlieb Zornberg considers this mysterious reference to Rachel's death, in the process of adopting Ephraim and Manasseh, a critical psychic crisis, from which Jacob recovers and launches into his famous valedictory address in Genesis 49. He is blocked by anxiety over the future, by his assembled progeny, and by remembrance of the past, embodied in the fate of his deceased wife. Is this the simple sense, the *peshat*, of Genesis 48:7? Surely not, but maybe it is something close to what the Catholic medieval tradition called the *sensus plenior*, the full sense. Gen. 48:7 may be read as a biblical glitch. It may also be read as a glimpse into the ability of biblical characters and even individual verses to inspire subsequent readers.[30]

9

Adopting Ephraim and Manasseh

The last parashah in Genesis is called "And he lived" (Va-yehi).[1] Intentionally or not this title is ironic since the portion focuses on the deaths of Jacob and Joseph. The traditional Jewish division into weekly portions may be preferred here to the familiar arrangement into chapter and verses.[2] As convenient as the latter may be for rapid location, Gen. 47:28 begins a new train of thought, carried through until the end of the book of Genesis. Centuries of readers have noted the dramatic contrast between the brief death reports of Abraham (Gen. 25:7–10) and Isaac (Gen. 35:27–29) and the expansiveness of the text here. Nahum Sarna explains this difference by the special circumstances of Jacob's demise. He is in Egypt, not Canaan; he is far from the Cave of Mahpelah, not nearby. Jacob's blessing is transferred to the entire family, not just to one son. His passing marks the end of the family saga—from here on the Torah will be principally about the nation Israel. Thus Jacob's dispositions demand more focus. All this is true. Yet one feels that the character of Jacob—difficult, resilient, agonistic, and histrionic—provides an ideal personality for this drawn-out presentation of illness, old age, and death.[3]

Meir Sternberg notes that for all the Methusalahs in early Genesis, descriptions and discussions of old age appear only with the patriarchal narrative. Sternberg believes that Jacob's old-age narrative presents a variation on a biblical type scene.

We see Abraham in full possession of his faculties, dispensing appropriate blessings, settling his estate, and being buried with his principal wife. In what erroneously appears to be Isaac's death-bed scene, we have blindness, confusion, a purloined blessing, and a wife's intervention. But Isaac does not die. He lives on for another twenty-two years, makes it to 180 years old, and is "buried by his sons Esau and Jacob," a notice that reflects birth order and preference.

Jacob, in a highly choreographed scene (Gen. 48:13–15), blesses Ephraim (the younger brother) before Manasseh (the older brother). Jacob thus runs the risk of Joseph's anger and violates ancient custom.[4] But here Jacob's decision to violate norms, unlike his earlier dealings with Esau, or even his intent to marry a younger sister, brings him no personal advantage. Jacob, though blind, sees that Ephraim will be the greater tribe. In Sternberg's words, "Jacob, then, does the right thing for the right reason."[5] He dies a better man than he lived, continues Sternberg, and in so doing transforms not only the family and the nation, but also our expectation of the death-bed scene. Jacob's fading vision is not connected to his insight on this occasion (versus Tieresias of Greek legend), but neither is it a metaphor for a failure of vision overall as in Isaac's favoritism of Esau.

After arriving in Egypt Jacob lives another seventeen years, but the biblical text is remarkably silent about those years (Gen. 47:28). Given the formality of the relationship between Jacob and Joseph evidenced in this Torah portion, the need to make official the Israelite status of Joseph's sons (Jacob's grandsons), and the fears of the brothers after Jacob's death, one does not get the feeling that the family got together regularly for Shabbat dinner, though many midrashim argue against that impression. The acknowledgement of the brothers' earlier crime against Joseph, of course, never gets reported by the text. One midrash even suggests that Joseph kept his distance from Jacob simply to avoid the possibility of the awkward subject of how he wound up in Egypt in the first place.[6]

This tradition seems plausible: the first details of the reunion focus on Joseph's status, Jacob's health, the fate of lost ones, and the rising offspring. Joseph remains the dreamer, the charmed youth, the operator who can get results, the man with a successful plan, but one who remains one step removed. Joseph collaborates with the brothers (e.g., they bury Jacob together, Joseph supports them, and he asks for their help in reinterring his bones in Canaan), but he is not one of them—how could he be, given his remarkable life? Joseph's relationship with his father, as we observed last chapter, remains complicated. We can sense the tension:

> And when the time approached for Israel to die, he summoned his son Joseph and said to him, "Do me this favor, place your hand under my thigh as a pledge of your steadfast loyalty: please do not bury me in Egypt. When I lie down with my fathers, take me up from Egypt and bury me in their burial-place." He replied, "I will do as you have spoken." And he said, "Swear to me." And he swore to him. Then Israel bowed at the head of the bed. (Gen. 47:29–31)

Please Don't Bury Me in Egypt

Jacob asks Joseph to swear that he will not bury him in Egypt. Remarkably Joseph's first answer, already one of compliance, "I will do as you have spoken" (Gen. 47:30b), does not quite reassure Jacob. He insists that Joseph swear it, and Joseph does so (Gen. 47:31). The mode of swearing involves Joseph's placing a hand "under the thigh," presumably a euphemism for the penis. (Abraham swears his servant to find a wife for Isaac in the same way [Gen. 24:1–14], although the servant must swear to God, whereas Jacob does not ask this of Joseph.) One may speculate in two directions. Either Jacob fully confided in Joseph, understanding that any oath involved God, implicitly or explicitly. Or one may speculate that after so many years in Egypt, Jacob was not entirely sure what would come out of Joseph's mouth. Would his favorite son have gotten accustomed to swearing in the name of the gods of Egypt?[7]

Jacob's formal bowing at the head of the bed, like the formal initiation, "If I have found favor in your eyes" (Gen. 47:29), reminds us of the way the chariot-enthroned Joseph approaches Jacob (Gen. 46:29) and implies a power relationship at odds with our expectations of this patriarchal text—certainly at odds with Jacob's authority in Genesis 42–44. Some have suggested that Joseph cannot do obeisance to his father because there are Egyptians all around and he is vizier of Egypt—in other words cannot blow his cover. In this reading Joseph would be an obedient son if he could. In this scene we confront Joseph, a powerful man in his prime, and Jacob an aging father, but still head of his clan.

A puzzling declaration begins Genesis 48:1: "Sometime afterward, Joseph was told 'Your father is ill.'" Several facets of this declaration troubled the rabbis. Why does Joseph not know about his own father's condition given the preceding scene in which Jacob prepares Joseph for his death? The question of who is looking after Jacob's well-being may be directed toward all his sons: Joseph comes to visit, but where are the other brothers, who are not running a country? The picture drawn here does not convey intimate familial relationships. What significance do we attach to the intervening time between Jacob's insistence on Joseph's swearing to bury him back in Canaan and this revelation of Jacob's illness?

"Sometime afterward" (Gen. 48:1a) obviously introduces a passage of time—but of what duration? Rashi makes a distinction between v'achar and v'acharei in Gen. 15:1, where he states that v'acharei signifies a long time afterward. Sarna reads this notice differently, insisting that this comes right after the beginning of the oath commenced in the previous chapter. Sarna finds support in other rabbinic traditions; he suggests that this chapter comes right after the swearing ceremony chronologically as well as canonically. The anonymously delivered report says only that Jacob is ill. Instead of buying a bunch of flowers, Joseph assembles his sons and heads out to receive the death-bed blessing. How did Joseph know that the end was approaching? Visiting the ill (*bikur holim*) is a major obligation in Judaism—but every reader senses from the onset that this scene is the final meeting of father and son.

Adopting Joseph's Egyptian Sons

Joseph arrives with his sons, and Jacob summons his strength, a continuation of the theme of life warding off death. If news that your son is still alive brings you renewed life, as the narrator tells us regarding Jacob and Joseph ("the spirit of their father Joseph revived" [Gen. 45:27]), then your grandsons' dutiful attendance should bring strength as well. Perhaps Jacob, who sits up in bed in deference to Joseph's status, will need his strength to contradict the wishes of his puissant favorite—for Joseph comes with Manasseh and Ephraim, in order of age, expecting the eldest to be blessed (Gen. 48:1). Of course, even in his first naming of his grandchildren, Jacob makes it clear that his preference will contradict that of birth order: "Ephraim and Manasseh shall be mine no less than Reuben and Simeon" (Gen. 48:5).[8]

By this point in Genesis, even the first-time reader would not place a bet on the firstborn actually getting his due. Genesis is full of firstborn sons being passed over for more deserving siblings, the legal rights of the firstborn son to a double inheritance in Deut. 21:15–17 notwithstanding.[9] Why does this theme play so prominent a role? Certainly it points to God's ability to foresee the future and guide the fortunes of the nation, contrary to the usual expectations. But why should this particular exception get so much play? (I admit that I am partial to the explanation that, being latecomers to the ancient Near East compared to the Mesopotamians or Egyptians, the Israelites found the reversal of primogeniture theme irresistible.)

Jacob begins his blessing of Joseph's sons by invoking a special name of God (El *Shaddai*) and reporting the latter's promise of fertility and possession of the land of Canaan. The Canaanite background stress of this passage has been duly noted: perhaps this is a subtle way of not explicitly mentioning the awkwardness of Egyptian-born and Egyptian-bred sons of Joseph being elevated to the status of boys born from the clan of Abraham and in the land of Paddan-Aram. Jacob formally adopts the two children of Joseph into the family of Israel, granting them equal status to his own children— Reuben and Simeon, the two oldest. As Sarna notes, the formalities of adoption include Jacob being called exclusively by his family-national name (Israel), a formalized interrogation of the father (Joseph), a formal embrace, and of course explicit language letting all know that this adoption has been formalized. Verse 6, "But progeny born to you after them shall be yours; they shall be recorded instead of their brothers in their inheritance," seemingly referring to subsequent children born to Joseph in Egypt, has rightly puzzled commentators ever since.

Commentators can only guess, however, because we have no reference to these children in the Bible, if Asenath bore them at all. Generally Jewish commentators regarded this blessing as a part for the whole. Since Jacob blesses Joseph, it is as if the sons of Joseph are included as well. Some commentators understand this blessing to refer to other members of the "House of Joseph," that is, clans calling Joseph their father, but not included in the nation Israel.[10] Other commentators think this verse refers to a future eventuality;[11] still others believe that it literally refers to Joseph's grandchildren.[12]

Interpreting this scene as an ancient Near Eastern adoption ceremony clarifies another utterance that Jewish tradition finds problematic, "Noticing Joseph's sons, Israel asked, 'Who are these?'" (Gen. 48:8). The Bible scholar Aviva Zornberg describes this as "one of the most startling moments in the entire Torah."[13] But the moment is startling only if one does not see that Jacob's question is part of a formal, legal procedure. One does not simply skip parts of a sacred ritual. For medieval scholars, who did not have numerous ancient Near Eastern analogues at their disposal, one can understand the confusion. Thus the striking supposition found in one midrash: "Did he really not recognize them?" Concluding that he did recognize his grandsons, the midrash continues and finds a reason for Jacob to have had a sudden blockage, a loss of memory. This midrash offers a radical answer: "He [Jacob] saw Jeroboam ben Nevat and Ahab ben Omri—idolators, who would descend from Ephraim; and the holy spirit departed from him."[14] In other words, responding to both Genesis 48 and Genesis 49, in which Jacob is presumed to be acting with divine inspiration, a prophetic glance at the idolatrous history of the Northern tribes Ephraim and Manasseh makes Jacob blank out. (We will return to the rabbinic traditions surrounding Jacob's utterances in Genesis 49 shortly.)

Sarna finds the acknowledgement of the legal adoption process an answer to rabbinic perplexities, and a riposte to those source critics who consider Jacob's failure to recognize his grandsons seventeen years after entering Egypt explicable only by positing multiple traditions. One might add that Sarna's line of thought militates against the notion that Jacob is appropriating Ephraim and Manasseh away from Joseph and away from Egypt—that the elevation of Joseph's two sons is tantamount to his demotion in Joseph's own status.[15] One biblical genealogy implies that Manasseh and Ephraim were born, respectively, in Transjordan and in Israel—clearly contradicting the Genesis narrative that has them born in Egypt. This segment ends, "In these dwelt the sons of Joseph the son of Israel" (1 Chron. 7:14–29). While this text may be a gloss to emphasize "the eternal bond between Israel and its land," as David Rothstein writes, the text offers no support the notion that Joseph somehow "lost his sons" in the process of their acquiring a double portion.[16]

Jacob's Cross Handed Blessing

Jacob's poignant recollection of Rachel in Gen. 48:7 and his question "Who are these?" (Gen. 48:8) create a pause in the action. The conclusion of the adoption ceremony gives prominence to Jacob's blessing:

> And Joseph said to his father, "They are my sons, whom God has given me here." "Bring them up to me," he said, "that I may bless them." Now Israel's eyes were dim with age; he could not see. So [Joseph] brought them close to him, and he kissed them and embraced them. And Israel said to Joseph, "I never expected to see you again, and here God has let me see your children as well."
>
> Joseph then removed them from his knees, and bowed low with his face to the ground. Joseph took the two of them, Ephraim with his right hand—to Israel's left—and Manasseh with his left hand—to Israel's right—and brought them close to him. But Israel stretched out his right hand and laid it on Ephraim's head, though he was the younger, and his left hand on Manasseh's head—thus crossing his hands—although Manasseh was the first-born. (Gen. 48:9–14)

The second half of the adoption ceremony, interrupted briefly by Jacob's blessing of Joseph in Gen. 48:15–16, reminds us of other blessings, most especially Isaac's, whose eyes were also failing (in Isaac's case "dim with age," in Jacob's case "heavy with age"). In both cases the "hand" plays an important part physically: it is Jacob's disguised hand that receives the blessing Isaac intended for Esau, it is Jacob's crossed hands that bestow the preferred blessing on Ephraim. Right and left are used seven times in this passage—Joseph knows that in his family the rights of the firstborn can be compromised. More striking than the absence of obvious favoritism on Jacob's part is that both boys receive a meaningful blessing. Symbolically Jacob includes the words "Bless the lads" (et ha-na'arim; Gen. 48:16). Although Joseph initially protests, "Not

so, Father," he accepts Jacob's disposition; neither boy protests. How different from Esau's anguished cry in the earlier
narrative! One can see in the lack of hostile reaction to this
disinterested parental preference a resolution of sorts of the
fraternal strife theme that has been with us since Cain and
Abel (Genesis 4). A more ironic reading is that the paternal
blessing simply did not matter to two boys raised as Egyptian
princes. But Thomas Mann certainly understands the politics
of Jacob and Joseph's past:

> "I know, my son, I know it well," he said. "And you are to let it be.
> You rule in the land of Egypt and take your fifth in taxes, but in
> these things I rule and know what I am doing. Do not fret. This
> one and he raised his hand a bit will also increase and become
> a great people; but his little brother will be greater than he and
> his seed will be a multitude of nations. What I have done, I have
> done, and indeed it is my will that it become a proverb and say-
> ing in Israel, so that whenever someone wishes to bless, and he
> shall say, 'God make you as Ephraim and Manasseh. Let Israel
> take note.' As you have commanded," Joseph said.[17]

Fathers and Sons . . . and Grandsons

As the adoption ceremony draws to a conclusion, it is Joseph's
turn to bow down to the ground (*artzah*). The words Jacob
uses to reassure Joseph (Gen. 48:19), "I know my son, I know"
(*yadati b'ni yadati*), possess an undeniably magnificent finality.
Jacob's lucid vision as to the true preservers of his family and
nation, at the end, ennoble a life that has been somewhat less
than exemplary. Jacob's double "I know, I know" recalls the
scene at the Jabbok River when Jacob awakens and exclaims,
"God was in the place, and I, I did not know" (Gen. 28:16).
Gen. 48:13–14 and 17–20 give a very explicit choreography, turning on the right-left repetition, of Joseph's placing the boys in
such a way that the elder (Manasseh) would get the blessing
for the firstborn. But Jacob, having another outcome in mind,

crosses his hands, and over Joseph's objections (Gen. 48:18) blesses Ephraim with the promise that "his offspring will be plentiful enough for nations" (Gen. 48:19, 48:20b). The great blessing of being remembered belongs to both of Joseph's sons: "By you shall Israel invoke blessings, saying: God make you like Ephraim and Manasseh" (Gen. 48:20). With these very words, generations of Jewish fathers have blessed their sons before sitting down for the Friday night meal.

We have focused on the resolution of fraternal conflict over blessings within the house of Israel. James Kugel alerts us to a different problem: the apportionment of the firstborn's double portion to Joseph's sons. The early interpreters responded to this challenge of Jacob not obeying Torah, Kugel tells us, by reading Jacob's reward against the punishment he levied against Reuben for his indiscretion with Bilhah.[18] Joseph can receive a double portion via sons only when Reuben forfeits his rightful place: "The sons of Reuben the firstborn of Israel for he was the firstborn; but because he polluted his father's couch, his birthright was given to the sons of Joseph the son of Israel, so that he is not enrolled in the genealogy according to his birthright; though Judah became strong among his brothers and a prince was due from him yet the birthright belonged to Joseph" (1 Chron. 5:1). The Chronicler displays fine footwork, explaining why Reuben lost his firstborn status yet still appears as first in many genealogies, why Judah enjoys dominant political status, and why Joseph, notwithstanding his descendants' exile long before the Chronicler wrote, received the birthright.[19]

Genesis 48:15–16, "And he [Jacob] blessed *Joseph*," intrudes rather roughly into this scene, which focuses, after all, on the status of Joseph's sons, not Joseph himself. The translators of the Bible into Greek (the Septuagint) and Latin (the Vulgate) changed the text to read, "He blessed *them*" and "*the sons of* Joseph," respectively. Robert Alter considers the Masoretic text illogical to refer to Jacob's blessing of Joseph, but the Hebrew text really does not offer any invitation to this sort of emendation, and thus the rabbis were stuck with the dilemma. Sarna writes, "Traditional commentators explain that a father is the vicarious recipient of blessings bestowed on his children."[20] Considering that the tribes Ephraim and Manasseh, collectively referred to as the House of Joseph, will eventually be destroyed by the Assyrians in the eighth century BCE, this seems like a consolation prize. Jacob invokes Abraham and Isaac, recalls the angel that has redeemed him, and asks that the youths be called in his name.[21]

Going Back to Shechem: The Mysterious "Portion"

The end of chapter 48 has Jacob announcing his imminent demise and reassuring Joseph, paralleling God's reassurance to Jacob as he prepared to go down to Egypt (46:2–4), "Then Israel said to Joseph, 'I am about to die; but God will be with you and bring you back to the land of your fathers. And now, I assign to you one portion more than to your brothers, which I wrested from the Amorites with my sword and bow. God will be with you and bring you back to the land of your fathers.'" (Gen. 48:21–22). The second person plural form of "you" in Genesis 48:21–22 (imachem, etchem, avoteichem) is doubly appropriate here, first, because we readers know that the period of Egyptian servitude is only beginning; it will be another four hundred years for the Exodus to take place. The plural here pointedly refers to distant descendants; Jacob's own sons will die and be buried in Egypt. Second, it is doubtful that a promise to Joseph himself to return to Canaan, if couched in the singular, would be comforting. Joseph has had far better luck in his adopted country.

The difficult phrase "one portion more than to your brothers" has perplexed Bible scholars ancient and modern. On first glance this cryptic verse seems to signify that Ephraim and Manasseh will each receive a full portion, making a double portion for the whole House of Joseph. One may also hear a hint of reproach directed toward the other brothers in Jacob's assertion, "I assign to you one more portion (*shechem*) than your brothers" (Gen. 48:22a). Might the Hebrew word *shechem* recall a deed that Jacob has never quite forgiven—the rape of Dinah in Shechem and his sons' violent reactions? Only Jacob's young son Joseph, presumably similar in age to Dinah, played no part in the massacre of the Shechemites in Genesis 34.[22] The portion granted to Ephraim and Manasseh would thus be poetic compensation for Joseph's earlier innocence. One tradition, which regards Asenath as the daughter of Dinah, considers the gift of the town of Shechem, modern day Nablus, literal compensation for the dowry promised Dinah long ago, "Ask of me a bride price ever so high" (Gen. 34:12).[23]

The narrator might be thinking of Joseph's ultimate resting place—the issue of Joseph's bones is a major one for text and tradition.[24] Alter reads *shechem apayim* as an expression of Jacob's determination to include Ephraim and Manasseh in Israel: "I have given you with single intent."[25] Alter finds the most usual renderings, "portion" and "shoulder," without textual warrant. Alter prefers to render this phrase as an idiom, an adverbial clause supporting Jacob's intent.[26]

If one considers Genesis 48 an adoption ceremony, we have an act of radical inclusion. Despite an Egyptian mother, birth, and upbringing, Ephraim and Manasseh are, and will always be, part of Israel, even after their conquest by Assyria. That dictum is the beating heart in the Jeremian passage on Rachel's weeping that we examined in the last chapter in reference to Jacob and Joseph.[27] The switching of birth order, no longer surprising by this point in Genesis, pales in importance to the bestowal of Jacob's blessing on both sons of Joseph. Having settled the fate of his grandsons Ephraim and Manasseh, Jacob turns to all twelve of his sons in one of the most enigmatic and ancient texts in the Bible.

10

Jacob's Valedictory

Genesis 49 consists of addresses delivered by Jacob, upbraiding his sons for their shortcomings, praising them for their virtues, and offering a preview of the fate of their descendants. A sustained piece of ancient poetry, Genesis 49 is paralleled by Moses' Blessing (Deut. 33:1–29), which comprises most of the last weekly portion of the Torah. Modern Bible scholars are nearly unanimous in treating this poem as distinct from the rest of the Joseph cycle. Traditional commentators, who assumed the unity of the Torah, did not have that liberty, but they were no less aware of the peculiarities of this text, beginning with Jacob's unequal treatment of his sons, quantitatively and qualitatively. Highlighting how often different biblical readers through the ages have responded to the same textual quirks has been a main purpose of this book, but my goal is hardly novel. Regarding "The Testament of Jacob," as he judiciously calls this passage, Nahum Sarna comments:

> In origin the collection of aphorisms about the tribes [Genesis 49] is not a unity, and no inner thread of logic binds the diverse elements together. The individual tribal traditions embedded in the poetry are undoubtedly independent of each other and relate to widely separate and discrete situations. This was fully recognized by the medieval Jewish exegetes, who were quite aware of the fact that some aphorisms appear to refer to past

individual acts of the eponymous ancestor, the remote hero from whom the tribe derived its name, while others allude to tribal history hundreds of years later. *Modern scholarship has added almost nothing to the great variety of medieval exegesis in its attempt to unravel the historic background of the sayings, except that the medievals treated these as prophetic, whereas the modern would be generally inclined to view them as retrojections from later historical reality.* [my emphasis][1]

Sarna acknowledges the origins of Genesis 49 as independent of the Joseph cycle and views it as another instance of Genesis preserving ancient materials at odds with later historical developments.[2] Modern Jewish Bibles have at least avoided misnaming the entire section "The Blessing of Jacob," as found in some translations, including the New English Bible. Some of Jacob's pronouncements surely sound more like reproach than praise. Midrash and the medieval commentators treat Genesis 49 as prophecy; modern scholars regard it as retrojection, but commentators of all eras have struggled to make sense out of Jacob's words.

Messianic Muddles

The chapter begins, "And Jacob called his sons and said, 'Come together that I may tell you what is to befall you in days to come'" (*acharit ha-yamim*; Gen. 49:1). The phrase *acharit ha-yamim* probably meant little more than "in the future" or "sometime in the future," in the days of the writing of Genesis. This is crucial because commentators as early as the Dead Sea sectarians assumed Genesis 49 should be read in a messianic vein.[3] Taking this phrase, along with the even more enigmatic *ad ki-yavo shilo*, to refer to the messianic end of days, commentators inevitably searched for the messianic implications of these verses. For the rabbis the messianic messages in Jacob's utterances were this-worldly and political. Gen. 49:10 reads:

The scepter shall not depart from Judah,
Nor the ruler's staff from beneath his feet;
So that tribute shall come to him
And the homage of peoples be his.

Christian interpreters understood Shiloh as a proper name and a title, clearly referring to Jesus.[4] Jewish exegetes understood this verse, with Shiloh often rendered as "tribute will come to him" (*shai-lo*), as a phrase rather than a cryptic name, and as more generally referring to the hegemony the tribe of Judah will someday enjoy, rather than the Messiah. Alternately some Jewish exegetes assumed this referred to another biblical character, occasionally identified as Machir, Manasseh's son (Joseph's grandson!) and ancestor of Gideon the judge.[5] Despite rejecting the Christian understanding of this verse, the rabbis had a problem with Genesis 49 generally—how to square a distinctly messianic opening with distinctly nonmessianic judgments of his sons' characters and actions, which form the body of Genesis 49.[6]

One rabbinic response, which cleaves closely to the original meaning of "in days to come," imagines Jacob reflecting on the fidelity of Abraham and Isaac, and wondering if his descendants would show the same loyalty to the One God in the future. These rabbis reread "Assemble and Hearken" (Gen. 49:2) as "Hear," the opening word of the central affirmation in Judaism (the *Shma*). Jacob's children reassure him by reciting the first line of the *Shma*, and Jacob quietly responds, as we do in synagogue, "Blessed be the Name of his Glory for ever and ever." This solution created its own problems: do we recite this verse in honor of Jacob, or do we not recite it since it is not part of the *Shma* itself, given by God to Moses? The solution is to recite the phrase, but sotto voce.[7] Using the obscure opening of Gen. 49:1–2 as a textual basis to explain the choreography of the recitation of the *Shma* might seem exegesis enough—but, of course, more remained to be said.[8]

Orthographic Hints of Jacob's Prophetic Crisis

Rashi attempted to explain the seeming contradiction between Jacob's desire to disclose what will come and failure to do so by reference to the graphic layout of this last Torah portion of Genesis, which shows only a one-letter gap separating the beginning of the Torah portion, "And he approached," from "And he lived."[9] Aviva Zornberg notes: "Rashi asks, 'Why is this *parashah* closed?'" By this Rashi means that there is no space at all marking the parashah break. This is in fact the only instance where not even a minimum nine spaces separate the new parashah from the previous one."[10]

Zornberg explains Rashi's two answers to this problem: "For when Jacob our father died, the eyes and the hearts of Israel were *closed* because of the affliction of the bondage with which the Egyptians began to afflict them. Another explanation: Jacob desired to reveal the end to his sons but it was *closed* from him."[11]

We do not need to presuppose Jacob's prophetic failure. After all the Pharaoh had just finished settling Jacob's family in Goshen on very generous terms—no beginning of bondage here, even if dark clouds start to gather in the final chapter of Genesis. Rashi may be reading the parashah too strongly in the context of Exod. 1:8–12, where a different Pharaoh institutes the Israelites' national enslavement. Even if Jacob was bestowed with prophetic insight at this moment, nothing in the text suggests that his offspring shared this epiphany.

Rashi's second answer—that Jacob intended to convey the messianic end time—is both mystical and tantalizing. Zornberg cites a midrashic parable likening Jacob's desire to tell his sons about the end of days to a king's servants who wished to impart secrets of the monarchy on his death bed. In both cases a vision of the ruler "blocked" or "closed" the impulse.[12] Jacob contents himself with confirming the need to hold God in awe. Zornberg quotes *Sefat Emet,* which held that exile could have its purifying effect only were the end *not* known in detail. The Jew must believe in the coming of the Messiah, though he may tarry.[13]

When we enter into the specifics of the blessing, some characters seem better described by the valediction than others. Reuben, the firstborn, is downgraded, "you shall excel no longer" (Gen. 49:4), for his sexual indiscretion with Jacob's handmaid Bilhah, just as he is in Gen. 35:22. (Indeed some observers have noted that Jacob seems even angrier on his death bed than he seemed to be at the time of the transgression.) Benjamin, on the other hand, is described as a "ravenous wolf" (Gen. 49:27), which makes sense in light of that tribe's ferocity in Judg. 18–21 and in some of its more famous figures, such as the bellicose King Saul and pugnacious Mordecai—but has nothing to do with the Benjamin figure in the Joseph story. Zebulon, Issachar, Dan, Gad, and Asher occupy the middle section, receiving a few verses each. The blessing on Judah, as noted earlier, probably alludes to certain unsavory incidents in his life, but the overall coloration is certainly positive, is very political, and seems more connected to Judah's eventual role as progenitor of the tribe of King David. While Judah's name includes the word "praise" and his brothers' descendants will bow down to King David in time, these are not actions narrated anywhere in Genesis.[14]

Judah and Joseph, the two key brothers, naturally receive the lion's share of Jacob's attention. But let us take a brief look at the malediction that Jacob latter delivers to Simeon and Levi. Imagine an old Jewish man exclaiming in disgust, "Simeon and Levi are a pair" (Gen. 49:5), and you have got the mood of the opening. In fact the word used for pair, *achim*, literally means "brothers." One midrash spins this in a positive way, noting that they were truly brothers to Dinah, having avenged her rape by Shechem (Genesis 34), but not brothers to Joseph, as they instigated his sale to the Midianites. The next line, "Their weapons are tools of lawlessness," precludes a definite conclusion, but Sarna's view, that it alludes to the pseudoselling of Dinah and the use of that sale as a pretext for manslaughter, makes sense.[15] Certainly the entire focus of Jacob's malediction is their role in the slaughter at Shechem—presented here as the reason for these tribes to be scattered in Israel and deprived of a specific tribal allotment. Since God sometimes rewards zealotry (see the case of Phineas in Numbers 25), the rabbis were intrigued that these two merited condemnation.

Rabbi Naphtali Berlin maintained that the circumstances of Phineas's act and the actions of Simeon and Levi explain the different responses. Berlin's principle is a good one, but it is hard to see how it applies here. After all in Genesis 34 Simeon and Levi are given the last word, "Should one deal with our sister [Dinah] as with a harlot?" Two other modern commentators regard the pragmatic distribution of zealotry as the key. Citing Aristotle's view that anger and temper may be necessary for bravery and courage, one medieval exegete contended that all the tribes needed a little of the zealotry found in dangerous quantities in Simeon and Levi. Samson Raphael Hirsch, who lived in Bismarck's Germany, considered zealotry dangerous in a strong nation, but critical for a politically powerless people. Hirsch thought zeal essential for Jewish survival in exile.[16] These interpretations seem to underrate the real anger in Jacob's malediction as well as his intent to punish. One may distinguish between a human being's intent and a divinely directed outcome. Nachmanides saw Jacob's moral outrage as real:

> Jacob implied that Simeon and Levi were brothers in deed and counsel. Jacob disapproved of their massacres of the Shechemites because, in so doing, they had committed violence against people who had done them no wrong but had, on the contrary, entered into a covenant with them and circumcised themselves. Perhaps they would sincerely acknowledge the true God and become part

of the House of Abraham and of the souls they had gotten. The Patriarch was also disturbed at the defamation of the Name of God that might ensue, that it might be thought that the deed had been committed at His prompting, that a prophet of the Lord should be suspected of lending his hand to violence and pillage.[17]

Both Jacob and Moses Bless Joseph

Modern scholarly isolation of Genesis 49 from the Joseph cycle obscures the overall context and skews our understanding of this biblical chapter. Joseph has been blessed by Jacob in Gen. 48:18, and he garners some sort of gift (whatever *shechem apayim* means) for his sons from Jacob in Gen. 48:21–22. Joseph also looks on as Jacob makes Ephraim's and Manasseh's Israelite status official. When Joseph receives the longest blessing in Genesis 49,[18] one may conclude that Jacob still favors the firstborn son of Rachel, from whom, Samson Raphael Hirsch contends, Joseph receives his many fine qualities.[19] Jacob's vivid praise of Joseph contains much that is uncertain:

> Joseph is a wild ass,
> A wild ass by a spring
> —Wild colts on a hillside.
> Archers bitterly assailed him;
> They shot at him and harried him.
> Yet his bow stayed taut,
> And his arms were made firm
> By the hands of the Mighty One of Jacob—
> There, the Shepherd, the Rock of Israel—
> The God of your father who helps you,
> And Shaddai who blesses you
> With blessings of heaven above,
> Blessings of the deep that couches below,
> Blessings of the breast and womb.
> The blessings of your father
> Surpass the blessings of my ancestors,

> To the utmost bounds of the eternal hills.
> May they rest on the head of Joseph,
> On the brow of the elect of his brothers. (Gen. 49:22–26)

Joseph gets a long and positive review by Jacob—especially if one translates the cryptic first line, *"ben porat Yosef,"* as "Joseph is a graceful son" rather than the more usual "Joseph is a wild ass."[20] The word "blessing" (*beraha*), repeated six times in two verses (Gen. 49:25–26), serves as the dominant motif. Except for the veiled reference to Joseph's progeny, the details of the blessing do not obviously match Joseph's biography. This may be due to the sense that Joseph here means "House of Joseph," as in Joseph and all his descendants, and partly due to poetic license. Does the image in verses 23–24 of archers shooting arrows at Joseph correspond to any incident still extant? Nahum Sarna attempts to liken both arrows and slander to the interlude with Mrs. Potiphar, but it is hard to see this as the plain sense. Midrash intuits a connection between Joseph's blessing and an overarching theme of Genesis: the tension between blessing and fraternal contention. "'They shot at him and harried him' (Gen. 49:23) Interpreted: A son who made his brothers suffer, a son whom his brothers made to suffer; a son who made his mistress suffer; a son whom his mistress made to suffer. But I do not know who caused more suffering."[21]

The overall message seems to be that Joseph and his descendants will continue to enjoy blessings, especially of a material nature. Contrary to those who find Joseph alienated from Israel, we have explicit invocations of fathers and ancestors connecting Jacob and Joseph through time and tradition. In this blessing the theophorics come fast and furiously. The "mighty one of Jacob" strengthens Joseph's arms; the "Rock of Israel" (*even Yisrael*; Gen. 49:24b), a term for God used often in postbiblical literature, aids him. God is named "the Shepherd" (*ro'eh*; 49:24b), and God is named "Shaddai" (49:25b). The phrase *nazir echav*, whether translated "elect," as NJPS translates it, or "leader" or "crown" or "Nazirite," indicates separation, but definitely not denigration.[22] (Robert Alter renders this difficult phrase "set apart from." Leon Kass attempts to mitigate what is clearly praise of Joseph.) While the blessing may not be as politically charged as Judah's, Joseph receives Jacob's promise of God's full-throttled support. One midrash hangs this idea on one of the four or five theophorics used here, "*eth Shaddai*" (Gen. 49:25b):[23]

> When Jacob blessed his sons, he blessed Joseph with the words, "by the God of your father, who shall help you, and by (*eth*) the Almighty, who shall bless you." Why did he not say "and by God (*el*)"? Because this blessing which he did give is from *aleph* to *tav*, and so the full blessing would rest upon Joseph and his brothers. Had he said, "and by God (*el*)," the blessing would have only been from *alef* to *lamed*, which is half a blessing. Now, however, the blessing was complete.[24]

"And This Is the Blessing"

There are stark differences in context and canon between Jacob's Testament (Genesis 49) and Moses' Blessing (Deuteronomy 33). Jacob's words, delivered near the end of Genesis, in Egypt, by the third Patriarch to his immediate family, differs greatly from Moses' Blessing, delivered near the end of Deuteronomy, in Jordan, by the leader of an entire nation. Given these differences, I will admit to relief that biblical scholars have found it plausible to compare them.[25] My relief stems from the fact that Moses' Blessing is the only Torah passage outside of early Exodus that mentions Joseph's character—the mentions in Exodus 13 and Joshua 24 refer only to his physical remains. Canonically speaking it is a long wait to Psalms and Chronicles, Daniel and Esther. To reiterate, this passage is our last image of Joseph in the Torah. Obviously Jacob and Moses are very different characters, with vastly differing roles to play. Jacob's prophetic qualities may be hinted at; the rabbis thought so, but Scripture declares Moses a unique prophet in Israel, whose stature was never to be equaled (Deut. 34:10). As we saw, Jacob's valedictory seems sometimes personal, sometimes tribal. By the end of Moses' lifetime, we have tribal blessings pure and simple, rather than the confusing mix of the personal and the political that characterize Jacob's ambiguous valedictions.[26] Nevertheless the sons are still grouped according to their mothers in Moses' Blessing, albeit with the positions of Joseph and Benjamin noticeably reversed, and with Judah's blessing shortened to one verse. We have, once again, the literary precedent of a father's blessing of his progeny before dying; in this case with Joshua standing in as political successor (Gen. 32:44).

The themes in the blessing of Joseph in Genesis 49—bounty, favor, and completeness—are reiterated forcefully in Deut. 33:13–17. Jeffrey Tigay notes, "More than any of the other blessings, that of Joseph [by Moses] resembles its counterpart in Jacob's."[27] In place of the recurrent word "blessing," we find "bounty," always in the singular and repeated five times, and again, the description of Joseph as *nazir*." The "myriads of Ephraim" and the "thousands of Manasseh" are now named, in acknowledgment of the tribal focus. The reality that Ephraim will surpass (or has surpassed) his older brother may be referenced in verse 17, "Like a firstling bull in his majesty."

> And of Joseph he said:
> Blessed of the Lord be his land
> With the bounty of dew from heaven,
> And of the deep that crouches below;
> With the bounteous crop of the moons;
> With the best from the ancient mountains,
> And the bounty of hills immemorial;
> With the bounty of the earth and its fullness,
> And the favor of the Presence in the Bush.
> May these rest on the head of Joseph,
> On the crown of the elect of his brothers.

Like a firstling bull in his majesty,
He has horns like the horns of the wild-ox;
With them he gores the peoples,
The ends of the earth one and all.
These are the myriads of Ephraim,
Those are the thousands on Manasseh. (Deut. 33:13–17)

Many have pointed to the strong resemblance of the two blessings on Joseph. One short question will close this chapter: does Moses repeat, qualify, or extend the lengthy and positive blessing of Joseph by Jacob in Genesis 49? The answer seems apparent: the blessing that Joseph enjoyed in Egypt becomes bounty in Israel. His status as "crown of the elect," which he exercised in Egypt as Pharaoh's viceroy, has been somehow preserved. His sons, Ephraim and Manasseh, stand ready to enter the land and realized the projections Jacob foretold long ago. "And the favor of the Presence in the Bush" (*shokheni seneh*; Deut. 33:16a) offers a stamp of divine certainty on these other successes. This "Presence" (*shekhinah*) lies on the head of Joseph. Was Jacob's blessing a fluke, a vestige of his early favoritism toward Joseph? Or was it an acknowledgment of Joseph's status as a special figure with undoubted preeminence? Moses' Blessing implies the latter.

11

The Deaths and Burials of Jacob and Joseph

In Jacob's case Erich Auerbach may be understating the "vertical" development of this biblical character when he writes, "But what a road, what a fate, lie between the Jacob who cheated his father out of his blessing and the old man whose favorite son has been torn to pieces by a wild beast!"[1] Jacob has had another seventeen years in Egypt after discovering that his favorite son has *not* been torn to pieces but, in fact, administers a land with ample food where he and his children can dwell with Pharaoh's approval. Even after his adoption of Ephraim and Manasseh and a remarkable valedictory address, Jacob has one scene left to play in a long last act.

> Then he instructed them, saying to them, "I am about to be gathered to my kin. Bury me with my fathers in the cave which is in the field of Ephron the Hittite, the cave which is in the field of Machpelah, facing Mamre, in the land of Canaan, the field that Abraham bought from Ephron the Hittite for a burial site—there Abraham and his wife Sarah were buried; there Isaac and his wife Rebekah were buried; and there I buried Leah—the field and the cave in it, bought from the Hittites." When Jacob finished his instructions to his sons, he drew his feet into the bed and, breathing his last, he was gathered to his people. (Gen. 49:29–33)

Genesis 49 concludes with Jacob's final instructions to his sons, described for the first time as "the tribes of Israel, twelve in number" (Gen. 49:28 and Gen. 49:16). "Bury me" (*kivru oti*), commands Jacob, reminding them that they have ancestral rights to the vault at Machpelah, whose purchase Abraham secured in Genesis 23. We learn for the first time that Rebekah and Leah have also been buried there. While Meir Sternberg praises Jacob's death-bed comportment, the latter's failure to name Leah "my wife" (Gen. 49:31b) follows jarringly on his previous descriptions of "Abraham and *his wife* Sarah . . . and Isaac and *his wife* Rebekah" (Gen. 49:31a). What the six sons of Leah felt, scripture does not tell us. Perhaps they were stunned into silence by Jacob's strong speech. In any event "he drew [*va'ye'esof*] his feet into the bed, and breathing his last, he was gathered [*va'yei'a'sef*] to his people" (Gen. 49:33). Burying Jacob and coming to terms with a family bereft of its Patriarch constitutes the challenge faced in the last chapter of Genesis—and of the Joseph cycle. Joseph's prominent role in the burial of Jacob in Genesis 50 may be suggested by the last line of Genesis 49: "drew" and "gathered" are actually the same Hebrew verb (*asaf*), used in Rachel's naming of Joseph, in which she first thanks God for removing the reproach of her infertility, and then implores God to add another son (Gen. 30:22–24). At the end of Genesis Jacob gathers Joseph, his brothers, and the whole family. Given the looming Exodus, and the challenges this will present to all the children of Israel, this image of familial togetherness seems appropriate.

Joseph Arranges Jacob's Funeral

Genesis 50 begins melodramatically, "And Joseph flung himself on his father's face and wept over him and kissed him." The threefold verbal usage is, as usual, emphatic. This is the only case in Scripture, moreover, where we have one character literally falling on another's face, though this may be nothing more than an acknowledgement that Jacob lies in bed. (In Gen. 33:4 Esau falls on Jacob's neck in an embrace, though one midrash imagines that Esau was going to bite him.)[2] Joseph mourns for his father profoundly, wordlessly—unlike the wordy mourning of Jacob for Joseph in Genesis 37. The proper order has been restored; the child should mourn the parent, not the other way around.

One feels that after his great speech of self-revelation in Genesis 45 and after the settling of his Israelite family, Joseph has become increasingly quiet—a man who depended so much on words for his rise now finds fewer words that need saying. Given the build-up to Jacob-Israel's decease, one might have thought that the book of Genesis had found an appropriate terminus right here. Yet, as striking as Joseph's acts of mourning are in Gen. 50:1, the next verse comes as an even greater surprise.

In Gen. 50:2 Joseph orders the Egyptian physicians to embalm Jacob! Strikingly inconsistent with later traditions of Jewish burial, which mandate speedy interment in simple linen shrouds, the details of Jacob's embalming made commentators uncomfortable.[3] Early on the rabbis debated whether or not Joseph ought to have embalmed his father. Judah the Prince, editor of the Mishnah, believed that Joseph shortened his own life by such an egregious violation of Jewish law.[4] But other rabbis dissented, praising Joseph for doing what was necessary to carry out his vow to bury Jacob in Canaan immediately rather than wait for Jacob's ossification.[5] Sarna insists that this embalming had no religious significance, but rather was the necessary hygienic preparation needed for the multiday trek back to Canaan and the Cave of Mahpelah. Sarna can strengthen his case with the reference in the text to physicians rather than to priests as the actual embalmers. But Joseph is also embalmed and put in a casket, where immediate burial and subsequent reinterment would clearly do.[6] Given that Sarna insists on the authentic Egyptian provenance and basic historicity of the Joseph cycle, his desire to distance the meaning of the text from the wording of the text (the word "embalmed" is used three times) is strained.

Curiously the news of Jacob's death has a great impact on the Egyptians, who carry out the full forty day period needed for embalming and another thirty days on top of that—royal standards of mourning.[7] The Bible leaves unanswered the question of why the Egyptians would mourn Jacob at all, although midrashim provided a slew of answers. Perhaps the status of being the vizier's father sufficiently explains matters. (Joseph himself carries the title "Father of Pharaoh," if that is the meaning of "Abrek" in Gen. 41:43.) Joseph requests, albeit indirectly, that Pharaoh grant him permission to return to Canaan to bury Jacob: "Joseph spoke to Pharaoh's court" (Gen. 50:4). Do we have here the first hint of Israel's deteriorating status in Egypt? Or perhaps Joseph's secondhand request was only the function of the king's inability to come into contact with a mourner for reasons of ritual purity. Many commentators have explained the text in just these terms. But the rabbis sensed in Joseph's reassurance in the last word of the verse that he would indeed be returning (v'ashuvah) to Egypt after the burial, a note of distrust. Some commentators have gone so far as to note that the children and the property remained in Egypt—as hostages! According to this line of thought, the Pharaoh was insuring Joseph's return.

The Egyptians seem authentically sorry about Jacob's death. Yet one can easily imagine that the prosperity of Jacob's family, combined with Joseph's prominence, combined with the sharing of land and food with foreigners during the initial five years of famine, could have caused resentment on the part of the Egyptians. Aaron Wildavsky, consistently critical of Joseph, goes so far as to say that by concentrating power in Pharaoh's hands, Joseph plays a role in the national servitude of Israel in Exodus.[8] The disagreement over whether these funeral preparations are straightforward or full of dark undertones lie mainly between commentators who incline toward treating the Joseph cycle as a self-contained unit and those who read the end of Genesis in light of the beginning of Exodus.

The language Joseph uses to request the trip bears noting. He emphasizes that his father begged him to appeal to Pharaoh and made Joseph swear to him to bury him in Canaan (Gen. 50:4). Now the Egyptians were very religious, according to both the Bible and Herodotus, so this is a good rhetorical gambit. It also avoids repeating before Pharaoh the words of Jacob—potentially offensive to Egyptian ears—that while Egypt might be okay for temporary dwelling and a square meal, Jacob would not want to reside there for all eternity: "Please do not bury me in Egypt" (Gen. 47:29). These funeral politics highlight the delicate balancing act that Joseph must play once his brothers are in Egypt. He is both vizier of Egypt, a prominent figure in the court with all that implies, and a man who feels compelled to oversee the fortunes of his substantial kin group.

The Anxiety of Fatherless Brothers

Joseph's prominence in the burial of Jacob is emphasized in Gen. 50:7: "So *Joseph* went up to bury *his* father"; and again in Gen. 50:14: "After burying *his* father, *Joseph* returned to Egypt." In the state processional (Gen. 50:7), the other brothers get listed after an array of Egyptian officials. The literary suppression of the brothers' role sets up the most troubling part of this chapter—the response of the brothers to Joseph after their return from burying Jacob. The brothers "cite" the last words of Jacob, described to Joseph, tellingly, as "*your* father."[9] "Before his death *your* father left this instruction: So shall you say to Joseph, 'Forgive, I urge you, the offense and guilt of your brothers who treated you so harshly'" (Gen. 50:17). But there is absolutely no indication in the Bible that Jacob ever said these words, or indeed that he ever learned of the brothers' earlier transgression. Most commentators, ancient and modern, agree that the brothers fabricated Jacob's death-bed injunction. This of course raises a slew of questions: Why would the brothers think that Joseph still harbored hostility toward them? Does anything in the text hint at a change of attitude on Joseph's part? Does Joseph still bear a grudge? Are the brothers justified in lying—whether to save their own skins or to preserve the integrity of the family?

Rashi responds to the complex of questions raised here, "When Joseph's brethren saw that their father was dead" (Gen. 50:15). He notes that the brothers had already accompanied Joseph to Canaan on the burial mission. Thus they clearly saw Jacob dead and buried. What, then, could the verb refer to? What does the text mean by *"they saw"*? Rashi writes, "They perceived the effects of his death on Joseph, the latter keeping on close terms with them out of respect for his father. As soon as Jacob died, he ceased to be on close terms with them." Rashi understood this anomaly as a comment on the effect that Jacob's death had on Joseph's demeanor. Other sources attempt to present Joseph's reserve as modesty, not wanting to present himself as a replacement Patriarch for Jacob, especially in light of the fact of Reuben's and Judah's standing. To Rashi, by contrast, the natural effect of Jacob's passing was that the brothers each went their own way. Implicit in Rashi's remark is his view that an anemic sense of fraternity existed between the brothers. Only respect for Jacob, Rashi suggests, had kept the family together.[10]

Other sources looked for a more specific referent to the key word in Gen. 50:14, *"saw."* One midrash asks, "What had they seen? Said Rabbi Isaac: The brothers saw Joseph on his way back from burying his father, go and peep into the pit (into which they had cast him), though he had been inspired by the purest of motives."[11] Although the pit caused Joseph to reflect on the wonders of God in this incredible tale, the brothers assumed he was harboring vengeful motives. Their original words, which inspired the subsequent "quotation" of Jacob's last words, are filled with fear: "What if Joseph still bears a grudge against us and pays us back for all the wrong that we did him!" (Gen. 50:15). The doubling of the verb "to return" (*ha'shiv ya'shev*) may be read colloquially as "he will return us double trouble" for our earlier misdeeds. Of course one may look at this narrative and see little that indicates deterioration in the relationship between Joseph and brothers following the death of Jacob. After the moving reunion and resettlement of the family, *finished* by Genesis 47, nothing intervenes until the death-bed blessings of Manasseh and Ephraim in Genesis 48. These seventeen years remain a hole so complete that even the midrashic imagination cannot fill it. Joseph's prominence in the burial of Jacob, and the reaction of the brothers in 50:15, just described, gave the rabbis the sense that something about Joseph's bearing and demeanor must have changed after Jacob's death.[12]

Traditional commentators have taken a forgiving attitude toward the brothers' fabricated quote. On the whole the rabbis see the brothers' fabrication as excusable on the ground of keeping the family peace. One could push this and argue that the fate of Jacob's entire family—and hence the nation Israel—turned on Joseph's forgoing vengeance, and therefore the brothers' fabrication was justified. Modern readers often incline toward a less forgiving view on two grounds: One, the brothers seem more concerned with saving their own skins than by idealistic concerns. Two, we tend to think that the truth is the truth and that even the cause of peace must be subordinated to it. But many early Sages thought differently. Rabban Simeon ben Gamaliel said: "Great is peace, for even the tribes uttered fabrications in order to promote peace between themselves and Joseph, as it is written: 'And they sent a messenger unto Joseph saying, Thy father did command.' For where did he command? We do not find that he so commanded."[13]

Rabban Gamaliel acknowledges the brothers' falsehood, and their unwillingness to confront Joseph directly. And Abravanel notes the brothers have forfeited fraternal claims and hence appeal to Joseph's fidelity to Jacob rather than to brotherhood. The Bible conveys the brothers' anxiety powerfully:

His brothers went to him themselves, flung themselves before him, and said, "We are prepared to be your slaves." But Joseph said to them, "Have no fear! Am I a substitute for God? Besides, although you intended me harm, God intended it for good, so as to bring about the present result—the survival of many people. And so, fear not. I will sustain you and your children." Thus he reassured them, speaking kindly to them. (Gen. 50:18–21)

Astonished and mortified, Joseph hears their words and asks, "Am I a substitute for God" [*tahat elohim anokhi*]?" In the climactic scene in Genesis 45, Joseph invoked God three times (45:5, 45:7, 45:8) to emphasize that events turned out according to the divine plan. Joseph utters these words, the exact ones uttered by his father, Jacob, in different circumstances. Naturally commentators compared Joseph's declaration to Jacob's identical words to his wife Rachel when she cried out in anguish, "Give me children or I will die" (Gen. 30:1). In Jacob's case most rabbis were appalled at his lack of sensitivity to Rachel's infertility. In Joseph's case the opposite is true. If there were lingering doubts that Joseph deserves the appellation "righteous," this ought to put them to rest. Why does Joseph cry? One cannot find better words than those of the thoughtful Italian moralist Rabbi Moshe Hayyim Luzzato: "He understood that the brothers had instructed the messenger what to say; otherwise Jacob would have told him himself. Joseph therefore wept at seeing the tragic state of his brothers, going in fear of their lives and forced to such shifts to stave off his vengeance."[14]

Joseph is sad at the brothers' impaired fraternal feelings, sad to be thought of as a tyrant, sad that a true fraternity will never be achieved.[15] The details of Joseph's brief speech (Gen. 50:19–21) deserve scrutiny. The first thing Joseph does at this juncture is to reassure the brothers, "Have no fear!" (Gen. 50:19). Then Joseph repeats what he had told them years before, that it was God's plan to bring about this result. Once again, as in the past, he emphasizes the universal benefits of his long journey—"the survival of many people" (Gen. 50:20). Joseph closes with an assurance that he will support them and their children. More than that, the section ends with the narrative notice, "Thus he reassured them, speaking kindly to them" (Gen. 50:21). Perhaps the Hebrew is even stronger than the translation, for he comforted them as well as reassuring them. One could render the end of this verse, *"va'yidaber al libam,"* as "and he spoke to their hearts," to their hearts and minds, that is, not just "kindly." Compare the details of this speech to Joseph's initial self-revelation in Gen. 45:4–8. Genesis 45 does *not* contain the categorical statement "Do not fear," and Genesis 45 refers twice to the specific transgression of selling Joseph. (The verb "sold" appears twice in Genesis 45 but appears here only in the softened verb "thought to do ill.") Moreover Genesis 45 has no comparable narrative framing device explaining that Joseph spoke "to their hearts." The cumulative difference between these two speeches is striking. Joseph in Genesis 50 communicates more emphatically that he has, indeed, put the past behind him. The spoiled seventeen-year-old has become a tzadik (righteous person).[16]

Joseph's Death Reported

Although Joseph lived 110 years, and even saw his great grandchildren, he was the first of Jacob's children to die:

> At length, Joseph said to his brothers, "I am about to die. God will surely take notice of you and bring you up from this land to the land that He promised on oath to Abraham, to Isaac, and to Jacob." So Joseph made the sons of Israel swear, saying, "When God has taken notice of you, you shall carry up my bones from here." Joseph died at the age of one hundred and ten years; and he was embalmed and placed in a coffin in Egypt. (Gen. 50:24–26)

The end of our story ("So Joseph and his father's household remained in Egypt"; *va-yeshev Yosef*) recalls its first line,

"And Jacob dwelt" (va-yeshev Ya'akov; Gen. 37:1). Whether the next phrase is rendered as the second half of same verse (Gen. 50:22b) or, as with the NJPS translation, begins a new verse, "Joseph lived" (va-yehi Yosef), it certainly recalls the title of the weekly portion of the Torah cycle (Va-yehi). Together the text seems to be tying loose threads together and remind us of the Sages' insightful equation of Jacob and Joseph as spiritual twins, the son destined to replicate the father's experiences. In Rashi's abbreviated rendering of a midrash:

> Also everything that happened to Jacob happened to Joseph.
> This one was hated, and the other was hated.
> This one's brother is seeking to kill him,
> And the other's brothers are seeking to kill him.[17]

Quite pointed is the distinction between Joseph and the rest of the clan. Recalling the amorphous discussion of Joseph's other children in Genesis 48, this may allude to the distinction made here between the households of Joseph and Jacob. But it may also simply be a statement that while Joseph would protect his brothers and their offspring, he could not feel entirely one with them. In Genesis 6 God set the proper age limit at 120 years, as God allotted Moses, his special servant (Jews invoke this age in "happy birthday" greetings until today). Joseph does not quite attain ideal Mosaic longevity, but he does reach 110 years (Gen. 50:22, 26), considered the ideal age in Egypt.[18] This great age, and the report that Joseph saw the third generation of his progeny, the children of Machir, signified a fitting reward for his character and accomplishments.[19] Although we have no direct statement of Joseph being in full command of his faculties as we do with Moses, that seems to be suggested by Joseph's matter-of-fact speech, ability to address his family's concerns, and clearly articulated funeral plans.

On his death bed, Joseph assures his brothers, or perhaps his brothers' families, if we favor probability over the plain sense that his brothers outlived him, seeing that Joseph was the youngest excepting Benjamin, that God will see to their condition and bring them back up from Egypt (Gen. 50:24–25). The verb employed by Joseph in this pronouncement, "to visit, appoint, designate" (*pakod/yifkod*) can be a strong one, signaling God's direct intervention. [20] Without the prophetic insight of his father, Joseph can only affirm God's future intervention as a matter of belief, as a New Testament author reports, "By faith, Joseph made mention of the exodus of the Israelites and gave directions concerning his bones" (Heb. 11:22).

One last request of Joseph's is striking and leads to a midrashic tradition of considerable complexity: Joseph makes the Israelites swear to bring his bones up from Egypt with them to Canaan. "When God has taken notice of you, you shall carry up my bones from here" (Gen. 50:25). We do not get the exact wording of their swearing, as we did earlier with Jacob and Joseph, but we are told in the Hebrew Bible that Moses did indeed bring up Joseph's bones (Exod. 13:19) and that Joshua did indeed bury them in Canaan (Josh. 24:32). Joseph was buried in Shechem, described in Joshua as "the piece of ground which Jacob has bought for a hundred kesitas from the children of Hamor, Shechem's father, and which had become a heritage of the Josephites."

Joseph's last words in Genesis are dignified ones, as is the way his descendants live up to their oath. Ben Sirach, or "Ecclesiasticus," a second-century BCE author of a work containing a list of Jewish heroes, found this concern with Joseph's physical remains even more noteworthy than his restraint in the house of Potiphar.[21] Ben Sirach groups Joseph with the early worthies of the human race, not the Patriarchs, at the conclusion of his historical review: "Few have ever been created on earth like Enoch, for he was taken up from the earth. Nor was anyone born like Joseph; even his bones were cared for. Shem and Seth and Enosh were honored, but above every other created living being was Adam."[22]

What to Do with Joseph's Bones?

The last verse of Genesis concludes with the word "Egypt" (*mitzrayim*), and is suitably ominous. Those commentators who saw a decline in Israel's status at the end of Genesis compared the elaborate state funeral for Jacob with the quiet burial accorded Joseph: "Joseph died at the age of one hundred and ten years; and he was embalmed and placed in a coffin in Egypt" (Gen. 50:26). The Bible gives no explanation why Joseph's remains could not be transported back to Canaan as were his father's. Midrash offers three principal reasons: war, wizardry, and worthiness. First, the border between Egypt and Canaan was closed; second, Pharaoh's magicians opposed letting the remains of this good luck talisman out of the country; third, no one before Moses merited transporting Joseph's bones. James Kugel, Rivka Ulmer, and others have illuminated the intricacy with which these three reasons are woven together in the midrash to develop a full-fledged, expansive story.[23] Three verses dedicated to a character's physical remains is a lot for the Bible. Moreover the transition from Genesis to Exodus, while artful, is terse. Israel comes down, multiplies, and becomes a nation in eight verses. But since this process took four hundred years, readers naturally wanted details on the intervening years, and the more natural extension was forward from the deceased Joseph, not backward from the infant Moses.

Jubilees makes the surprising claim that only Joseph was not interred in Canaan:

> And before he [Joseph] died he gave instructions to the Israelites to take his bones with them when they went out of the land of Egypt. And he put them on oath regarding his bones, for he knew that the Egyptians would not take and bury him in the land of Canaan. For Makmaron king of Canaan, while living in the land of Assyrian, fought in the valley with the king of Egypt and killed him there, and pursued the Egyptians to the gates of

Ermon. But he was not able to get inside, because another king, a new one, had become king of Egypt, and he was stronger than he was and so he returned to the land of Canaan. And the gate of Egypt was shut, and no one went out of Egypt and no one went in. And Joseph died . . . and they buried him in the land of Egypt. And all his brothers died after him. And the king of Egypt went out to war with the king of Canaan . . . and the Israelites brought out all the bones of Jacob's children except Joseph's and they buried them in the country, in the double cave of the mountain. And most of them returned to Egypt.[24]

The "hidden bones" tradition appears first in *Testaments of the Twelve Patriarchs*, which often focuses on Joseph:

And when Simeon had finished his instructions with his sons, he slept with his fathers at the age of one hundred and twenty years. They placed him in a wooden coffin in order to carry his bones up to Hebron; they took them up in secret during a war with Egypt. The bones of Joseph the Egyptians were kept in the treasure-houses of the palace. Since their wizards told them at the departure of Joseph's bones there would be darkness and gloom in the whole land and a great plague on Egyptians, so that even with a lamp no one could recognize his brother.[25]

By the time of the Mishnah (ca. 225 CE), the special nature of Joseph's bones must have been a well-known tradition:

Joseph was the one who was found worthy to bury his father—and there were none among the brothers greater than him—as it is said, "And Joseph went up to bury his father, and there went up with him chariots and riders" [Gen. 49:7–9]. Who then was greater than Joseph? Moses was the one who took care of him, as it is said, "And Moses took Joseph's bones with him" [Exod. 13:19]. Who then do you have greater than Moses [who might in turn bury him]? God himself was the one who took care of him, as it is said, "And he buried him in the valley but no man knows the place of his burial to this day" [Deut. 34:5].[26]

A tradition of approximately the same antiquity addresses another barrier to immediate burial—nobody knew where Joseph's bones were buried!

> But whence did Moses know where Joseph was buried? They said Serah the daughter of Asher had survived from that time and she showed Moses Joseph's grave. She said to him: this is the place where they put him. The Egyptians had made for him a metal casket and dropped it in the middle of the Nile. He came and stood over the Nile, He took a pebble and cast it in the midst of the water and cried out: Joseph! Joseph! The time of the oath has come which was sworn by God our father Abraham, that he would redeem his sons. Give honor to the Lord, the God Of Israel and do not hold up your redemption, for on account we are now held up, and if not, then we are hereby free from your oath [Gen. 50:25]. Thereupon Joseph's coffin floated to the surface and Moses took it.[27]

Admittedly this is rather late to introduce another character, yet we cannot neglect "this product of the collective Jewish imagination."[28] Serah bat Asher is mentioned in Genesis 46, again in Numbers 26, and once more in 1 Chron. 7:30. The citation of a female character in two genealogical lists separated by four hundred years invited rabbinic comment. As Nahum Sarna comments: "It is inconceivable that Jacob's twelve sons, who themselves had fifty-three sons in all should have had only one daughter. In light of the general tendency to omit women from the genealogies, there must be some extraordinary reason for mentioning her in this particular one, although no hint of it is given in the text."[29] Marc Bregman explains, "the rabbinic Serah seems to provide a link between the death of Joseph and the birth of next great Israelite leader, Moses."[30]

Having settled on Serah as a righteous woman, the rabbis assigned her additional duties. The preceding midrashim focus on Serah's longevity and consequent ability to help Moses and the generation of the Exodus find Joseph's remains. The first mention of Serah, however, occurs just after Jacob learns that Joseph is still alive and after God assures Jacob that he may descend to Egypt. Serah, not the brothers, becomes the figure who lets Jacob know that Joseph is still alive. As we noted earlier in this book, the Bible's narrative at this point seems too brief, and Jacob's acceptance of their account—"'Enough!' said Israel. 'My son Joseph is still alive! I must go and see him before I die'"—seems implausible, even considering that the Bible previously told us "Jacob kept the matter in mind" (Gen. 37:11b).[31] But what if someone, say Serah, had been given the role of priming the imaginative pump? *Sefer ha-Yashar* imagines it like this:

> The brothers now had to tell Jacob that Joseph his son and their brother were still alive. Afraid of breaking this news to their elderly father too suddenly, they decided to employ Asher's daughter, Serah, since she knew how to play the harp in a soothing manner. At their instigation she sat near Jacob while he was deep in daily prayer—and sang repeatedly, "Joseph my uncle is still alive and he rules over the land of Egypt." Not only was Jacob understandably delighted with this lyric revelation, but the spirit of God came upon him and he knew all that she said was true. And so Jacob blessed Serah and said to her: My child, may death never rule over you for you brought my spirit back to life.[32]

And indeed Serah is granted eternal life, a place in a paradise, by mystical traditions from the medieval era until today.[33] But the palaces of the righteous women described in the Zohar seem like a fitting place to end this search for Serah. She is pictured here announcing Joseph, who is included, as in many mystical traditions, as being among the seven righteous visitors invited to the sukkah along with the Patriarchs, Moses, and David. Joseph spends the holiday in august company, but not only on Sukkot:

Here, three times a day a voice rings out announcing the visit of Joseph, the righteous one. Joyfully, Serah retired behind a curtain to gaze upon the light of his face and show him honor. And here, each day, she proclaims: "O happy day, that I brought the good tidings to my grandfather Jacob that you were still alive." Then Serah returns to her women companions to teach them Torah and to join with them in praise and thanks to the master of the Universe.[34]

Whether in the Zohar, in Yiddish prayer books, or in Thomas Mann's *Joseph and His Brothers*, which devotes many pages to her role in relaying the good news to Jacob that Joseph still lives,[35] Serah and Joseph remained conjoined in Jewish tradition. They link the Patriarchal and Exodus Eras, Jacob-Israel, and Moses. They are among the righteous: They are agents of the divine, though fully human. Of course Joseph is the focus of thirteen chapters, and Serah is mentioned three times total—the closest one gets to a characterization is the epithet naming her a sister of Asher's sons. Serah is an obscure figure; Joseph, an authentically enigmatic one.

12

Portraying Egypt in Joseph

Many readers have noted that the ominous last word in Genesis is *b'mitzrayim* (in Egypt). Without question the nature of Egypt is at issue as the death place of Jacob and Joseph, the birthplace of Moses, the land of slavery, and the site of God's greatest act since Creation, the Exodus. *Mitzrayim,* which can mean Egypt the land or Egypt the people, stands as a kind of biblical character in Joseph and beyond, so the significance of Egypt is worth thinking about. The parentage of Egypt, like that of Ammon and Moav, must be regarded as pejorative. Egypt is first mentioned as the second son of Ham (Gen. 10:6), who infamously left a naked, drunk Noah uncovered in his tent after the flood (Gen. 9:20–22). This counts as derogation of Egypt as well as Canaan, the principal target of this unsavory genealogy.[1] The Bible lists Ammonites, Moabites, and Egyptians as among those whose acceptance into the community of Israel must be qualified—or prohibited.[2]

Consistent with the Bible's exoticizing non-Israelites, Gen. 12:11–12 and 12:14–15 presume hypersexualized Egyptians will lust after Sarah when she and Abraham descend into Egypt. Hagar, Abraham's handmaid and mother of his eldest son, is pointedly described as Egyptian, and so is the wife that Hagar arranges for Ishmael. This reinforces the view in Genesis, supported by God's command to Abraham to heed Sarah's voice in the banning of Hagar and Ishmael, that the line of Abraham flows through Isaac, not Ishmael. Most proximately to our story, God commands Isaac in Gen. 26:2 *not* to go down to Egypt. That *yeridah*, that descent, seems more than merely directional—as confirmed by the explicit assurance God gives Jacob in Gen. 46:2–4, "I am God the God of your father. Fear not to go down to Egypt, for I will make you there into a great nation. I myself will go down with you to Egypt, and I myself will also bring you back; and Joseph's hand shall close your eyes."[3]

Reimagining Egypt: History versus Memory

The Exodus from Egypt stands in the middle of the Torah as the great linchpin—the ultimate proof of God's covenantal relationship with Israel and the historical event for which Israel must always be indebted.[4] Insistently the Torah presents enslavement as the condition that should mandate social compassion on the part of Israelites when they are the empowered people. Thus Egypt serves as a cautionary tale throughout the Torah, as in the "law of the King" passage (Deut. 17:14–20), and even the mainly negative mentions of Egypt in the prophets. In one of his important studies on the memory of Egypt in the West, Jan Assmann explains that the attribution of monotheism to Moses rather than Akhenaton, and the presentation as Egypt as the land of idolatry par excellence, constitutes a successful act of countermemory on the part of Western civilization. In Assmann's words:

> The meaning of the Biblical image of Egypt and the target of this discourse can be easily defined in retrospect. The Biblical image of Egypt means "idolatry." It symbolizes what "the Mosaic distinction" excluded as the opposite of truth in religion. By drawing this distinction, "Moses" cut the umbilical cord which connected his people and his religious ideas to their cultural and natural context. The Egypt of the Bible symbolizes what is rejected, discarded, and abandoned. Egypt is not just a historical context; it is inscribed in the fundamental semantics of monotheism.[5]

212

The Bible characterizes Egypt negatively overall, but a few items remain on the positive side of the ledger. Egypt is the quintessential land of plenty—all three Patriarchs go to Egypt for food. Under Joseph's viziership Egypt sustains life not only for the Israelites but for the entire world (Gen. 47:13). Egypt symbolizes plenty, leadership, and stability, "the gift of the Nile" in Herodotus's celebrated words. In Lot's eyes Egypt is as verdant as Eden (Gen. 13:10). In the Joseph story Egypt serves as a destination of refuge, a temporary residence, a terminal point for the generation of Jacob, and a burial place for all the Israelites in between Jacob and Exodus—not only for Joseph. Egypt will not be Israel's ultimate future; it is conspicuously absent in Jacob's valedictory speech in Genesis 49, where context would seem to invite a mention.

Egyptians as people cannot be condemned in Joseph's story, even if they are in the Bible overall, as Assmann argues. Midrash notes that women played an important role in the Exodus, Egyptians among them. The daughter of Pharaoh, of course, plays a critical role in saving Moses. So too do the "midwives to the Hebrews," if they are actually Egyptians, as many think.[6] There are righteous gentiles among the Egyptians as well. The animus in Exodus is directed mainly toward the Pharaoh of oppression, his gods, and his armies more than toward the Egyptians at large.[7] The so-called spoiling of the Egyptians passage in Exod. 12:33–36 has served as antisemitic fodder from time immemorial but seems more like back pay, willingly turned over by the Egyptian populace. At this point in the narrative, the Egyptians are mainly anxious that Israel depart before any more plagues befall them. The text says plainly, "the Lord had given the Israelites favor in the eyes of the Egyptians"—a very common idiom. However one parses the verbs "ask" (va'yishalu) and "plunder" (va'yashilum) in Exod. 12:35–36, there is not much evidence of hatred on the part of either party—the Egyptians are terrified, and the Israelites, at that moment, are obedient to Moses and Aaron. Despite the enslavement of the Israelites, it is not clear that Egyptians at large get a harder knock than most of the Bible's non-Israelites; better to be an Egyptian than an Amalekite (Exod. 17:16).

How are we to evaluate the Egyptian characters in the Joseph narrative? Pharaoh, who elevates Joseph, has been discussed previously; arguably he has been evaluated overgenerously in Jewish tradition relative to the biblical text. His overreliance on magicians and wise men seems pathetic, and anyone who finds execution a legitimate birthday celebration has a rough sense of fun. Unless one accepts Rashi's astrological exculpation, or Thomas Mann's more psychologically elaborate one, Potiphar's wife engages in sexual harassment. She certainly uses ethnic difference to stir up her household against Joseph. Potiphar's thoughts are harder to gauge. He imprisons Joseph to save face but sets him up for success. In Potiphar's house and in Pharaoh's prison and court, Egyptians seem to accept Joseph's talents despite his being a Hebrew. The steward describes Joseph as "a Hebrew, a youth, a servant" (Gen. 41:12), yet Joseph's interpretation of Pharaoh's dream "pleased him *and his courtiers*" (Gen. 41:37). The Egyptian baker seems both obtuse and a slacker; the steward remembers Joseph only when it has the potential to bring him benefit. But these characters seem all too human, not evil. (Unlike Potiphar, the *ish mitzri*, an Egyptian man, these royal servants are not described as Egyptian, though one assumes that they are.) The Egyptians in the Joseph story seem a mixed lot, like the rest of us. The negative verdict of Egypt, no doubt present in the Bible at large, seems muted in the Joseph story.

Biblical Egyptians do have a sense of superiority toward others. Leon Kass explains the Egyptian dislike of shepherds as a product of Egypt's being Nile-based farmers and in touch with nature, with Israel being animal-based vagabonds and alienated from nature. This reading of Israel coheres with the Israelite idea of God outside nature but lacks obvious support in the biblical text. While Joseph tells his brothers that Egyptians despise shepherds, neither Pharaoh nor any other Egyptian says this.[8] Outside the desperate scene in which Egyptians in Genesis 47 surrender their money, livestock, land, and freedom, the Egyptians do not act as a collective very often in Joseph's story. We have an interesting exception when the Egyptians appear through the eyes of the Canaanites at the seven-day mourning period conducted for Jacob, at the otherwise unattested site of Goren ha-Atad: "This is a solemn mourning on the part of the Egyptians" (Gen. 50:11).[9]

Whatever the original sources and canonical divisions between Genesis and Exodus, the biblical Redactor wrought a careful transition between the Bible's first two books. Again the last word in Genesis stresses the connection dramatically: "Joseph died at the age of 110 years. He was embalmed and laid to rest in a coffin in Egypt."[10] So does the equally ominous verse in Exod. 1:8, quoted nervously by Jews in Hebrew to one another whenever new rulers took over: "And a new king arose over Egypt who knew not Joseph," bitter repayment to the family of the man whose foresight saved the starving nation.[11] The second report of the death of Joseph, his brothers, and all that generation in Exod. 1:6 is a resumptive repetition, which looks back to known events in order to forward a new story. The description of the people Israel in Exod. 1:7, which "multiplied and increased," follows directly after this—juxtaposition reminds readers of the awkward situation relayed in Gen. 47:26 versus Gen. 47:27, in which the Egyptians are reduced to serfdom by Pharaoh just as Israel flourished in the land of Goshen—clearly a potential source of tension.

The embalming of Jacob and Joseph, described in the previous chapter, gave the rabbis opportunities to liken the fates of father and son. This dual mummification, the quintessentially Egyptian death practice, also serves to highlight the entanglement of Canaan and Egypt. Jacob, the eponymous father of all Israel, must have his corpse treated in an Egyptian manner. Joseph, the mighty vizier of Egypt, must remain with the enslaved children of Israel until they can all return to Canaan together. Joseph makes his descendants swear to bring his bones back to Canaan for burial—just as Jacob made Joseph swear to bury him in Canaan in Genesis 48. Exodus opens with the doubled reminder (in Exod. 1:1 and 1:5) that it was only the small Jacob clan, "seventy souls in all, that entered Egypt, *Joseph being already in Egypt*." Exod. 8:18 and 9:26 inform us that the children of Israel settled in the land of Goshen, as if to confirm that the settlement arranged by Joseph in Genesis 46–47 remained in effect four hundred years later.

At the end of Genesis Joseph clusters the three Patriarchs together for the first time in Torah: "Joseph said to his brothers, 'I'm about to die. But I'm sure that God will come to help you. He'll take you up out of this land. God will bring you to the land he promised with an oath given *to Abraham, Isaac and Jacob*'" (Gen. 50:24). By Exod. 3:6 the trio of Abraham, Isaac, and Jacob had become canonical—this formula will be used many more times in the Hebrew Bible, in the New Testament, and until today in Jewish worship.[12] Joseph, excluded from the ranks of the Patriarchs, at least is the first to name them. To summarize, the biblical text reminds us persistently that Joseph served as the bridge between the family narrative of Genesis and the national narrative of Exodus.

Joseph as Assimilationist Redux:
Moses as Counterexample?

The editorial links between Genesis and Exodus are fine grained; the contrast between the major characters of Joseph and Moses are stark and obvious. Aaron Wildavsky summarized their contrasting relationship as follows: "So Moses, born in Egypt becomes Hebraicized; Joseph, who grows up a Hebrew, becomes Egyptianized. Joseph, who leads his people into Egypt, is succeeded by Moses, who leads his people out. The opposition between the two is so great and so consistent . . . that it is difficult to believe it is unintended."[13]

Unquestionably the Bible makes Joseph an obvious precursor to Moses, but does it necessarily follow that Joseph represents a negative counterexample?

Both Joseph and Moses partake of Israelite and Egyptian identities.[14] The trajectories of the two diverge, but to deny the Egyptian elements in Moses seems forced.[15] One need not subscribe to Freud's idiosyncratic view that Moses was an Egyptian killed by Israelites who then accepted monotheism out of guilt feelings for their heinous deed. Moses remains Egyptian to the extent that he never trades in his Egyptian name for a Hebrew one. His famed reluctance to confront Pharaoh stems partly from his awareness of what it means to challenge Egypt.[16] (Like Joseph, Moses marries a non-Israelite.) From Assmann's *Moses the Egyptian* to the animated *The Prince of Egypt*, the Exodus story does not make sense without assuming some level of familiarity with Egyptian ways on Moses' part. *The Prince of Egypt* ingeniously imagines the Pharaoh and Moses as intimates—the former feels betrayed by Moses' throwing in his lot with the Hebrews despite his courtly upbringing. Joseph strikes modern readers as Egyptianized, but also as the first in a long line of Jews who ascend to problematic positions of power. These successful court Jews exercised power directly contingent on the patronage of a ruler.[17] Joseph's position is personal, not institutional, and thus precarious. The lack of ceremony attending Joseph's burial and the emergence of a new king "who knew not Joseph" testify to a decline. As Exodus makes clear, Israel's situation in Egypt was fraught with danger. While Joseph lived that danger was successfully navigated.

As any reader of the Bible knows, Joseph's success was limited, not only with respect to Israel's fortunes in Egypt, but within the dynamics of Jacob's descendants. In the astute words of Gabriel Josipovici, "What in fact happens is that if we do not artificially divide Genesis from Exodus and both from Judges, Samuel and Kings, we discover a pattern is being created to which Joseph is not privy. For the fact of the matter is that it

will be Judah's seed which will inherit and not Joseph's. . . .
In light of all this even Genesis 50 has to be thought about
again. God did mean it for good, but even Joseph could not see
what good it was that God meant."[18] Typical of modern literary readers, Josipovici brings a strong sense of the story as a
whole to bear on individual episodes. The Hebrew Bible can
be read successfully as a classical epic or as a modern novel.[19]
Judged from this perspective, Joseph's success is limited, as
all human success must be.

Early Interpreters on Joseph's Rule

Ancient Egyptians had plenty to say about Joseph's rule, mainly
negative and emphatic in denying him native status. As Louis
Feldman recounts, Joseph was derided by a variety of antisemitic authors.[20] The third-century BCE Manetho charged Osar-
siph, a variant of Joseph, as a persecutor of native religion—and
a missionary for Judaism.[21] While the biblical Joseph lauds the
God of Israel to Pharaoh, there is not an iota of biblical support for Manetho's charge of proselytism, though it probably
reflected the popularity of Judaism in the Hellenistic world.
Manetho reflects, anachronistically, the religious polemics of
his era. Jewish interpreters, not surprisingly, saw Joseph quite
differently from his Egyptian detractors; *Jubilees*, for example,
presents a harmonious picture of a popular leader and a satisfied population:

> Joseph ruled over all the land of Egypt, and all the notables of
> Pharaoh and all his attendants and all those who did the king's
> business esteemed him highly, for he walked in uprightness and
> he had no pride nor arrogance nor partiality and there was no
> bribery, for in uprightness did he judge all the people of the land.
> And the land of Egypt was at peace before Pharaoh thanks to
> Joseph, for the Lord was with him and gave him favor and mercy
> for all his family before those who knew him and those who heard

about him, and the kingdom of Pharaoh was well ordered and there was no Satan and no evil.[22]

Josephus rejected the charge of missionizing as well as the charge that Joseph cared only for his own. He emphasized the generosity of Joseph as an administrator, though he did not go so far as the imaginative Egyptian Jewish historian Artapanus, who described Joseph as "greatly loved" by the Egyptians.[23] Louis Feldman notes that Josephus adds a detail not found in the Bible—when the famine subsided, Josephus went to each city and bestowed the land to the inhabitants in perpetuity:

> But when this misery ceased, and the river overflowed the ground, and the ground brought forth its fruits plentifully, Joseph came to every city, and gathered the people thereto belonging together, and gave them back entirely the land which, by their own consent, the king might have possessed alone, and alone enjoyed the fruits of it. He [Joseph] also exhorted them to look on it as every one's own possession, and to fall to their husbandry and cheerfulness; and to pay, as a tribute to the king, the fifth part of the fruits from the land which the king, when it was his own, restored to them.[24]

Ancient Jewish commentators displayed a greater willingness to criticize biblical characters than their Christian or Muslim counterparts. When we show, then, that Jewish interpreters defended the regime of Joseph, we should not expect to find prominent critics from the other Abrahamic traditions.[25] If the Church Fathers focused mainly on the religious dimensions of Joseph's character, medieval Islamic and Christian rulers tended to see Joseph's concentration of power as laudable.[26] One of these, by Alfonso X the Wise of Castile, drew on all three exegetical traditions to expand the biblical original. Alfonso's *General History* (1272) imagines Joseph ruling efficiently, popularly, and well under the reigns of *two* Pharaohs, Nicrao and Amosis.

The reader of *General History* gets a lengthy account of Joseph's maneuverings for his masters and learns about Joseph's plans for Egypt after the famine ends. Joseph receives the praise of the author, someone blatantly well versed in courtly politics. Joseph had convinced King Nicrao of monotheism, but Amosis slipped back into idolatry. Even this challenge proved manageable by Joseph; his long rule receives the treatment it had not enjoyed since the tale of "Joseph and Asenath," composed approximately a millennium earlier.

Did Joseph Really Rule in Egypt?

In this book, now drawing to a close, I have largely avoided the question of whether there really was a Joseph who served as viceroy over Egypt.[27] Nothing excludes the possibility. One eminent contemporary scholar describes the biblical account as "historically plausible."[28] Many scholars, at mid-twentieth century, went further. Ephraim Avigdor Speiser, an extreme optimist when it came to the ultimate recovery of the facts behind Genesis, conceded that the narrative details in Joseph were still lacking corroboration, but he certainly believed a positive history would eventually be uncovered. For Speiser the plot lines, personal names, titles, and geographical location of Jacob's family in Genesis 37–50 all indicated familiarity with Egyptian life. A transition from private ownership of land, characteristic of the Middle Kingdom to titular pharonic ownership, characteristic of the New Kingdom, corresponded to both the description of Joseph's agrarian policies and the reaction to the Hyksos period.

The Hyksos period, a national scandal from an Egyptian point of view, constituted a reasonably well-documented interregnum between the Middle and New Kingdoms, during the seventeenth to sixteenth centuries BCE. This period has remained a keystone to locating a historical Joseph, since only a period of nonnative Egyptian rule could provide a plausible backdrop to the viziership of Joseph. (The Hyksos seem to have been

"Semites" or "Asiatics" from Canaan.) But all the aforementioned evidence is circumstantial—and many of these conclusions have been rejected. Just as the Bible does not even name the Pharaohs who elevated Joseph or reduced Israel to servitude, we could hardly expect Egyptian historians to dwell on the matter of foreign invaders subjugating an ancient and proud nation.

The closest we get to a truly ancient mention of the Hyksos comes in the form of the four-hundred-year stele erected by Rameses II (thirteenth century BCE). This inscription carved in stone celebrated the inauguration of the cult of Seth four hundred years earlier, during the Hyksos era, though of course the stele does not mention this explicitly. This stele, in turn, connects the biblical Zoan (Egyptian city Tanis) to a reference about the establishment and antiquity of the city of Hebron (Num. 13:22) and to the tradition of the four-hundred-year sojourn in Egypt. These elements lead historian Baruch Halpern to conclude that the Joseph narrative reinterprets the Hyksos period from an Israelite perspective. Halpern does not claim this proves a factual basis for the Joseph story; rather, this data served the biblical author as a point of departure in composing a vivid narrative.[29]

Some Hyksos influence on the biblical narrative comports with the narratives composed by the historians most engaged in the subject, namely, the rival accounts of the Egyptian anti-Semite Manetho (third century BCE) and the Jewish apologist Josephus (first century CE). Both men worked in the genre of ancient historiography and thus cared about the historicity of these events in a way that most of the early interpreters did not. But Manetho and Josephus are writing approximately fourteen hundred and seventeen hundred years, respectively, after the Hyksos were expelled; by modern standards this is hardly firsthand evidence. Ancient testimony need not be bad testimony, but it tends to be testimony about the traditions and about the era in which the text was actually written, not about the ancient history itself. Without contemporary records, archival or historiographical, an era once past cannot be easily recreated.[30] Nor did this attempt at recreation constitute the job description of the ancient historian; they generally took the facticity of oft-related events for granted. Herodotus and Thucydides truly believed that a Trojan War occurred; they did not think to question that event, some eight hundred years before the conflicts they chose to chronicle.[31]

Let us consider the views of a couple of contemporary scholars. S. David Sperling states, "I am compelled to read the Torah allegorically because it cannot be read historically. If 'historical' means that an event occurred in the time and place in which it is set, then nothing in the Torah is historical."[32] This does not mean, as some contend, that there was no historical Israel at all. On the contrary Sperling demonstrates how many narratives and characters of the Torah were inspired by actual events, but ones that took place at a much later time than that presented by the Bible. Sperling's *The Original Torah* considers Joseph's story "a thinly veiled allegory" about the politics of the Kingdom of Israel and the support afforded it by Egyptian Pharaoh Sheshonk.[33] Sperling contends that the ninth-century BCE alliance of Pharaoh Sheshonk and Jeroboam I led to an imperially inspired fusing of the common ancient Near Eastern genres and the enslavement in Egypt, though Sperling also considers the Egyptian enslavement allegorical rather than historical.[34]

As Sperling conceives of the creation of the Joseph narrative, "the propagandists of Jeroboam I did not have to create new motifs when they introduced the figure of Joseph—the eponymous ancestor of the group from which Jeroboam I claimed ancestry—into the exodus traditions. As 'Joseph,' Jeroboam I had been protected by Pharaoh and risen to great power under the ultimate protection of Yahweh."[35] For Sperling, Joseph is an allegory written in a particular place and time, not a mélange of sources nor purely fictional.[36]

222

Egyptologist Donald Redford's *A Study of the Biblical Book of Joseph* offers a different approach to placing the Joseph narrative historically.[37] Redford shares the view of the narrative's multiple authorship and like many others sees Genesis 38 and 49 as extraneous to the main story.[38] He argues for a Joseph narrative that proceeded in four stages—an original story, a Judah addition, later editions, and final redaction by the great editor of Genesis.[39] Redford is thus quite skeptical of the source-critical approach as deployed for Genesis 37–50. He finds no evidence of a "J" or an "E" source as contributors to the Joseph narrative and indeed finds the Joseph narrative so different from what comes before and afterward that he presumably sees little value in the literary, contextual reading undertaken here. Redford posits a late origin for the Joseph story indeed—only the extreme minimalists who regard the whole Bible as Persian-era fantasy would date Joseph later.[40] He holds that the core of Joseph reflects the Egyptian realities of the mid-seventh to mid-fifth centuries BCE.[41] His minimalist views have not prevailed, but the maximalism of an earlier generation has also been abandoned. One could retort: well, if not by Joseph's actions, how did Israel get down to Egypt? But of course Israel's sojourn in Egypt is also contested by many modern Bible scholars.[42] Even the narrative details surrounding King David, a later, better documented figure, have been challenged.[43]

One may take Joseph's historical reality on faith, and many do. But this misconstrues history for meaning. My own perspective is that no ancient classic could possibly be "historical" in our modern sense of the word. Nineteenth-century developments of "historicism" and "historiography," which determine our view of what "history" means, depart from ancient views of memory and mythopoeicism. The meanings and lessons of Joseph's life mattered to ancient readers; his weekly calendar did not. Our current understanding of how narrative works suggests that were a historical Joseph demonstrable, the decision how to portray his character and tell his story determined the biblical details.

With respect to the overworked word "Tradition," we have seen that this biblical story, like all biblical stories, represents only the tip of the iceberg of what people had to say about the events and persons related therein. Enormous latitude for the interpretation of that biblical text has been channeled by the particular era and religious viewpoint, but interpretation has not been limited by them. Otherwise we could not have had a flowering of Joseph literature in many different genres and in many different religious worldviews. A "Traditional" perspective on the biblical narrative, hard to define in any case, cannot possibly mean a historicist one. And a "Traditional" perspective cannot be offered as conclusive without acknowledging differing exegetical traditions with momentums of their own. Plural and lowercase, not singular and capitalized, "traditions" are to be preferred over "Tradition." And would one really like to exclude the nonrabbinic early interpreters or modern scholars on the grounds that their modus operandi and presuppositions differed from those of midrash? I find this exclusion unpalatable, and I hope readers of this volume would too.

Reading Joseph in Our Day

How to proceed from the agnostic conclusion that we cannot be sure what was historically true about Joseph?[44] A practical consequence for today's Bible reader might be that historical issues are interesting, but not decisive. I have come to that conclusion, and although I enjoy my monthly *Biblical Archaeological Review*, I think there are other equally valuable ways of reading the Bible. I am confident that past ages shared this perspective, and read accordingly. For over two centuries scholars have confronted the possibility that modern methods of inquiry challenge some presumptions of the Bible and its characters. Does this undermine the meaning of the text? Apparently not, as many professional scholars and many "amateurs" who have devoted enormous time and energy continue to explore the biblical text. (It is worth recalling that the regular synagogue-goer will actually read and probably discuss this story for four weeks running every single year.) How to account for this continued love of the Bible—which has waxed, not waned, in the modern era—is a story for another place and time. I will conclude with the words of one of the first to grasp this challenge to biblical meaning and to also formulate a response. Ahad Ha'Am, on the seven-hundredth anniversary of the death of the philosopher Moses Maimonides, penned an essay on the biblical Moses (1904). Although I do not think either Moses or Joseph traversed the ages in as uniform a manner as Ahad Ha'Am implied, and although I do not think Joseph belongs to Jews alone, I cannot improve on Ahad Ha'Am's basic formulation, which champions the figure that lives in Jewish tradition and life against a narrow conception of "archaeological" reality.[45]

And so when I read the Haggadah on the eve of Passover, and the spirit of Moses the son of Amram, that supreme hero, who stands like a pillar of light on the threshold of our history, hovers before me and lifts me out of the netherworld, I am quite oblivious to all the doubts and questions propounded by non-Jewish critics. I care not whether this man Moses really existed; whether his life and his activity really corresponded to our traditional account of him; whether he was really the savior of Israel and gave his people the Law in the form in which it is preserved among us; and so forth. This Moses, I say, matters to nobody but scholars. Jewish people have another Moses, whose image has been enshrined in the hearts of the Jewish people for generations, and whose influence on our national life has never ceased from ancient times until the present day. The existence of this Moses, as a historical fact, depends in no way on investigations. For even if we succeeded in demonstrating conclusively that the man Moses never existed, or that he was not such a man as we supposed, this would not thereby

detract one jot from the historical reality of the ideal Moses—
the Moses who has been our leader not only for the forty years
in the wilderness of Sinai, but for thousands of years in all the
wildernesses in which we have wandered since the Exodus.[46]

An Unending

We have read the ways in which Joseph and Moses differ in
the biblical account. They vary in tradition too. Joseph is not
central to Judaism. Joseph is neither lawgiver nor Patriarch nor
prophet. Yet Joseph is a fully drawn character—so much so that
in James Kugel's view his story did not demand explanation
but rather invited energetic retelling. Those retellings yielded
remarkably different results in different eras and for different
readers. In Jack Miles's view, "Joseph is the most appealing
figure yet seen in the Bible. And God for the first time, seems,
susceptible to the appeal."[47] Miles's judgment mirrors that of
many readers from the Hellenistic era until today, who have
found Joseph a gracious figure, capably living up to the edge of
his considerable talents, in Thomas Mann's presentation, ultimately with an ironic and self-knowing edge. But beginning
with midrash, and up until today, others have found Joseph a
brat, an unforgiving brother, and a despot who prepared the
way for Israel's slavery.

As an individual, as a family man, as a transitional figure
from family to nation, and as a vehicle for a subtler form of
Providence than seen earlier in Genesis, Joseph has called forth
varying judgments. We may conclude with this certainty: Joseph
remains an eternal figure in Western culture, a beautifully
composed palimpsest, a biblical canvas constantly repainted
over by a variety of authors and artists, ancient and modern,
Jewish, Christian, and Muslim, religious and secular, male
and female.[48] This book has tried to convey some small part
of that picture.

NOTES

Introduction

1. For recent examples of biblical biographies, see Weitzman, *Solomon*; Zakovitch, *Jacob the Unexpected Patriarch*; and David Wolpe, *David: The Divided Heart* (New Haven CT: Yale University Press, 2014), all in the Jewish Lives series. For recent examples of a postbiblical "career," see Jon D. Levenson, *Inheriting Abraham*; and Rabow, *Lost Matriarch*.

2. Kugel, *How to Read the Bible*, 1–46 and 662–89.

3. My method of triangulation differs from Greenberg's "holism," concisely explained in his *Anchor Bible Ezekiel*, 1–20. I think the axioms of premodern and modern biblical criticism preclude synthesis yet allow conflicting perspectives to coexist coherently.

4. Groups such as the Sadducees and Karaites delimited Judaism to the written Bible alone, rejecting rabbinic traditions and authority.

5. I do not mean to imply that traditional Christian exegesis lacked range or creativity, only that the New Testament served as exegetical point of departure. The scholarly goal of isolating an independent Old Testament theology did not precede the eighteenth century and even then played out as a predominantly Protestant and Germanic undertaking.

6. For Jews the acronym *pardes* (*peshat, remez, derash,* and *sod*) roughly corresponds to plain sense, implied sense, homiletic sense, and mystical sense. On the difference between premodern and modern commentary, see David C. Steinmetz, "Superiority of Pre-critical Exegesis."

7. Jews engaged in inward acculturation at all times, and at all levels of society, constantly employing, incorporating, and reformulating external, non-Jewish traditions. Maimonides' use of Greek philosophy as mediated by Islamic scholars is often cited as the parade example, but he was more the norm than the exception in this respect. Many examples of inward acculturation existed and exist at both the elite and folk level. I borrow the

term "inward acculturation" from Ivan Marcus, *The Jewish Life Cycle* (Seattle: University of Washington Press, 2004).

8. Alan Levenson, *Making of the Modern Jewish Bible.*

9. Benedict (Baruch) Spinoza articulated this position of the Bible as a flawed and archaic document in his *Theological-Political Treatise* (1670). Explications, defenses, and rejoinders to Spinoza's viewpoint on the Bible are too numerous to note here. Likewise there are many translations of Spinoza's works. *Martin Yaffe's Spinoza's Theologico-Political Treatise* (Newburyport MA: Focus, 2004) retains the Hebrew, which I find helpful.

10. Miles, *God*, 78.

11. The legal material in the Torah came to be called "halachic" by the early rabbis. There is legal material in Genesis and, arguably, much reflection on the narrative material in later biblical law codes.

12. Dever, *What Did the Biblical Writers Know and When Did They Know It?*

13. Halpern, "Exodus from Egypt."

14. Rendsburg, *Redaction of Genesis*, argues for this dating. See also Cyrus Gordon, *The Bible and the Ancient Near East*, 4th ed. (New York: Norton, 1997).

15. Levin, "Benjamin Conundrum."

16. Redford, *Study of the Biblical Story of Joseph*, rejects the traditional division of Joseph into J, E, and P sources, although he affirms the presence of multiple authors and texts in Genesis 37–50.

17. The classic statement remains Yerushalmi, *Zakhor.*

18. Speiser, *Anchor Bible Genesis*, 292. An avid source critic, Speiser was a proponent of the view that Genesis—Joseph included—reflected ancient historical traditions. With its northern focus and affection for dreams, scholars regard E as the principal source in Genesis 37–50, Genesis 38, and other additions as J texts, and genealogies as from P.

19. Richard Elliott Friedman, *Who Wrote the Bible?* (San Francisco: Harper & Row, 1997), 62–67. See Brettler et al., *Bible and the Believer*, 3–19.

20. Source criticism was foreign to traditional Jewish and Christian exegesis, though medieval rabbis acknowledged problems with assuming unitary authorship of Torah. Form criticism—with its interest in identifying type scenes and etiologies, epithets, and more—seems to me more fruitful for an analysis of Genesis 37–50.

21. Dating follows Feldman, Kugel, Schiffman, *Outside the Bible*, 1:272. Although reconstructing the development of the Joseph text is not my purpose, I address the politics in chapter 7, "Judah in Joseph."

22. This charge of theism lite in literary approaches has merit, especially when couched in language like Benno Jacob's *Der Verfasser*, "The Author," with upper cases resplendent, in his *Das Erste Buch Der Tora: Genesis* (Berlin: Schocken Verlag, 1934). James Kugel doubts that "literary" readers of the

Bible really do "literary criticism" as understood in other disciplines. He further questions whether the Bible ought to be read as literature: "So even if I could wave my wand and forget about J, E, P, H and D, dismissing them as if they were a single author's preliminary drafts and focusing only on the book of Genesis as it now is, nevertheless, that would not turn it into *literature* unless I were prepared to assume something about its genre that is largely inappropriate. Neither the original authors nor the final editors and canonizers of Genesis were out to create *literature*." Kugel, "Biblical Criticism Lite."

23. See Levin, "Benjamin Conundrum," note 13, for a concise overview of the various genres assigned Joseph.

24. I have relied on Simpson, *Literature of Ancient Egypt*. James Pritchard's collection *Ancient Near Eastern Texts* (Princeton NJ: Princeton University Press, 1975) includes Egyptian, Mesopotamian, and Hittite documents and provides the biblical parallels in the margins; it remains invaluable.

25. Von Rad, "Joseph Narrative and Ancient Wisdom." The Egyptologist John Wilson likened "The Instructions of Amenotep" to Proverbs, another Wisdom classic, in Pritchard, *Ancient Near Eastern Texts*, 1:237.

26. I also find the reference to Joseph (spelled here with a *yud*) in Ps. 81:6 odd since Joseph did not leave Egypt but descended there: "For it is a law for Israel, a ruling of the God of Jacob; He imposed it as a decree upon Joseph when he went forth from the land of Egypt; I heard a language that I knew not."

27. For Matthew, Joseph is Mary's husband and Jesus's legal father—an angel of the Lord appears to Joseph son of David and proclaims, "Do not be afraid to take Mary as your wife" (Matt. 1:20).

28. I rely on Rosenthal, "Josephgeschichte mit den Büchern Esther," and Gan, "Scroll of Esther in Light of Events of Joseph in Egypt."

29. For up-to-date, impeccable introductions to these works, see Feldman, Kugel, Schiffman, *Outside the Bible*. An acceptable, neutral name for this period or its literature does not exist. "Inter-testamental" seems inescapably Christian; "Second Temple" misses the point that much of this literature is post–70 CE; "Ancient Jewish Writings" strikes me as misleading, since the Bible is clearly much more ancient and arguably Jewish. Kugel's "early interpreters" is accurate, but vague for readers unfamiliar with his numerous works. I have used "Hellenistic" here only because I think it is the most familiar term.

30. Gruen, "Hellenistic Images of Joseph." The first-century BCE Jewish Alexandrian philosopher Philo Judaeus had much to say about Joseph, but his portrayal is very inconsistent, and so I exclude Philo from consideration.

31. For the early rabbis all the Hebrew Bible is grist for the midrashic mill, although Torah enjoyed preeminence.

32. BT, Berahot 16b: "The term patriarchs is applied only to three and the term matriarchs only to four."

33. Argyle, "Joseph the Patriarch in Patristic Teaching."

34. Helpful works on Rashi include: Hailperin, *Rashi and the Christian Scholars*; Pearl, *Rashi*; Shereshevsky, *Rashi*; Boncheck, *What's Bothering Rashi?*; and Grossman, *Rashi*.

35. The gold standard on Rashbam remains Lockshin's *Rabbi Samuel Ben Meir's Commentary on Genesis*. See also Moshe Berger's 1982 Harvard University doctoral dissertation, "The Torah Commentary of Rabbi Samuel Ben Meir."

36. Helpful sketches of Abraham ibn Ezra may be found in Edward Greenstein, "Medieval Bible Commentary," in *Back to the Sources* (New York: Simon & Schuster, 1984), 249–52; and Barry Wallfish, "Medieval Jewish Interpretation," *The Jewish Study Bible*, ed. Adele Berlin and Marc Zvi Brettler (New York: Oxford University Press, 2004), 1876–99.

37. Nachmanides (or Ramban), a Spanish exegete, takes Rashi and Abraham ibn Ezra as his exegetical starting points but often takes issue with their conclusions. The most helpful introductions for the general reader are Charles (Chaim) Chavel, *Ramban: His Life and Teachings* (New York: Feldheim, 1960); and Chavel's introduction to Nachmanides, *Commentary on the Torah*.

38. That said, the medieval commentators were especially critical regarding Joseph's failure to let his father know he was still alive.

39. Mann, *Joseph and His Brothers*, 815.

1. Joseph: Favored Son, Hated Brother

1. Not every woman who had trouble bearing was called an *akarah*. Ruth, for instance, is not, though she was married for ten years in Moav without children, nor is Tamar called an *akarah* in Genesis 38, though she did not get pregnant through Er.

2. Each of these attempts by Rachel to become pregnant has generated considerable discussion. Zakovitch, *Jacob the Unexpected Patriarch*, makes the point that Leah and Rachel's negotiating over the mandrakes (*dudaim*), a negotiation of food for sex, mirrors the red pottage negotiation of Jacob and Esau, a negotiation of food for birthright.

3. As far as double-naming at birth, I can think of only Ben-oni/Benjamin and Yedidyah/Solomon as other examples.

4. The characters of Jacob and Rachel are analyzed by Fokkelman, who named Rachel "Jacoba" in *Narrative Art in Genesis*. Pardes, *Countertraditions in the Bible*, pushed this matter further in her correct judgment that one can portray Rachel as a side character to Jacob's but not the other way around. One may imagine Rachel as a "Jacoba," but not Jacob as "Rachela." See Zakovitch, *Jacob the Unexpected Patriarch*, 74–75, on Rachel's naming speech.

5. Two examples will suffice: in Genesis 34 Dinah gets no lines. She is a rape victim; her brothers are agents of retribution. In David's double introduction God and Samuel speak about David (1 Sam. 16), and then David delivers long set speeches to Saul, Goliath, and the assembled Israelites (1 Sam. 17). In this second chapter David emerges as a public figure.

6. Greenspahn, *When Brothers Dwell Together*, lodges an important qualification: Benjamin is called *ha-Katan* (the littlest or youngest son), which Joseph is not. Additionally the age gap between the brothers and Joseph cannot be that great; the theme of youngest serving eldest does not appear in Joseph's dreams. Greenspahn argues against making too much of either first-birth or last-birth status.

7. The painting *Joseph Recognized by His Brothers* (1789) by Anne-Louis Girodet de Roucy-Trioson shows Benjamin in front of the pack, embracing his full brother, who wears the adornments of royal power.

8. "*Ger v'toshav*" is often rendered "stranger and sojourner."

9. *Midrash Rabbah Bereshit* 84:3: "*ya'akov avinu al yadei sh'bikesh leishev b'shalvah b'olam ha-zeh nizdaveg lo satano shel yosef*," 2013–14.

10. This paragraph break is unsupported by the Masoretic text: there is no *petuchah* or *setumah* in between Jacob and Joseph, and the cantillation signals a pause (*gershayim*) after Joseph, not in between Jacob and Joseph.

11. The Hebrew *toldot* may be rendered as "line," "story," or even "history."

12. *Midrash Rabbah Genesis* 84:6.

13. Midrashim and modern scholars alike see parallels: Miscall, "Jacob and Joseph as Analogies." While presuppositions about composition and modes of scholarly discourse differ, good readers, ancient and modern, often respond to similar textual features.

14. There are important exceptions to this Hebrew-Hebrew rule, including translations such as the Aramaic Targumim, Saadyah Gaon's Arabic *Tafsir*, the Ladino commentary *Me'am Lo'ez*, the Yiddish *Tzenah U'renah*, etc. Nevertheless it remains true that the best-known rabbinic Bible commentators read in Hebrew and wrote in Hebrew.

15. Rashbam [Rabbi Samuel ben Meir], *Commentary on Genesis*, 240–45, 413.

16. Today the term *peshat* may include consideration of cognate languages; ancient Near Eastern texts; the existence of textual variants in Greek, Aramaic, or early Hebrew versions such as the Samaritan Pentateuch; or even consideration of presumed earlier sources (J, E, P, D, H, R) as they shaped the canonized text. Unless otherwise noted, I am using *peshat* in the earlier sense.

17. Pharaoh and Potiphar do not deceive, but they have power and so do not have to deceive. The baker is deceived by his dream. The cupbearer does not deceive Joseph but fails to follow through on his promise to him.

18. Kugel, *Bible as It Was*, 247–48.

19. Rachel's beauty is described as a reason for Jacob's preference for her over Leah; Joseph's beauty, just before he becomes the object of Mrs. Potiphar's lust. The brothers envy Joseph, but not because he is attractive.

20. Alter, *Art of Biblical Narrative*, called attention to the use of clothing in the early part of the Joseph story. In Genesis 37 the coat is used to deceive Jacob. In Genesis 38 Tamar used clothing to deceive Judah into thinking that she was a prostitute. In Genesis 39 Mrs. Potiphar grabs Joseph's cloak, then charges him with attempted rape, using his cloak as "evidence."

21. Thomas Mann, *Die Geschichten Jaakobs*, 6:294, as cited in Koelb, "Coat of Many Colors," 479, 472–84.

22. Speiser, *Anchor Bible Genesis*, 290.

23. For a recent analysis of Auerbach's continuing influence on Bible scholars, see James Adam Redfield, "Behind Auerbach's "Background": Five Ways to Read What Biblical Narratives Don't Say," *Association of Jewish Studies Review* 39, no. 1 (April 2015): 121–50. Redfield observes that the phrase "fraught with background" (*hintergründig*) benefited from Willard Trask's translation.

24. Pardes, *Countertraditions*, 63–66.

25. *The Brown-Driver-Briggs Hebrew and English Lexicon of the Old Testament* (Oxford: Clarendon, 1951), lists eight possible meanings for *"asher."* The prefixed *khaf* does not eliminate the ambiguity.

26. The Bible text reverses the order of Rachel and Joseph in Gen. 33:2 versus Gen. 33:7 when the family approaches Esau, prompting them to imagine a preternaturally chivalrous Joseph protecting his attractive mother from the probing eyes of his lascivious Uncle Esau.

27. Jon Levenson, "Genesis," in Berlin and Brettler, *Jewish Study Bible*, 75.

28. Greenspahn, *When Brothers Dwell Together*; Carmichael, *Law and Narrative in the Bible*; Fishbane, *Biblical Interpretation in Ancient Israel*.

29. In Genesis 49 Simeon and Levi are grouped together and scored by Jacob for using weapons of violence—a clear reference to the slaughter at Shechem. So Jacob emphatically disapproves of their deed.

30. Zakovitch, *Jacob the Unexpected Patriarch*, 152.

31. With respect to Jacob and Israel, the alternating name choice often seems intentional (Jacob to emphasize personal relationships; Israel to emphasize familial-national matters, as in this passage). For a dogged attempt to make the alternation of Jacob and Israel into a narrative rule, see Jacob *Quellenscheidung und Exegese im Pentateuch*.

32. "His father" highlights Jacob's overfocus on Joseph. The use of epithets in biblical characterization is widely accepted. For example it makes

a difference if Michal is described as "David's wife" or "Saul's daughter," or if Benjamin is described as "his brother" or "our father's son."

33. Erich Auerbach, "Odysseus' Scar," *Mimesis* (Princeton NJ: Princeton University Press, 1953), 9. In the cases of Jacob (Gen. 43:46) and Moses (Exod. 3:4) the name ("Jacob, Jacob" or "Moses, Moses") is used twice, unlike the call to Abraham and Joseph, although "Abraham, Abraham" appears at Gen. 22:11. I think this variation only strengthens the Jewish midrashic understanding of the word *hineni* as more than simple acknowledgment.

34. My speculation is admittedly simplistic, since Rashbam lived in Rashi's part of the world yet employed the *peshat* method relentlessly. For a wonderful discussion of the argument among Rashi, ibn Ezra and Nachmanides on "the man" in Gen. 37:15, see Leibowitz, Studies in Genesis–Deuteronomy, 394–99.

35. Nachmanides, *Commentary on the Torah*, 455–57.

36. Nachmanides, *Commentary on the Torah*, 458–59.

37. This rather strange self-declared Orthodox translation may be found on the website biblegateway.com.

38. Leibowitz, *Studies in Genesis–Deuteronomy*, 400–409, can be consulted in order to find the best rabbinic attempts at reconciling these narrative discrepancies, none of which seemed conclusive to Leibowitz on this point.

39. The Qur'an presents Jacob and the brothers imagining that a wolf will devour Joseph. The Qur'an also presents the brothers as the initiators of Joseph's mission to Dothan, not Jacob. See Goldman, "Joseph."

40. Leibowitz, Studies in Genesis–Deuteronomy, 407.

41. Speiser, *Anchor Bible Genesis*, 291. I came upon Joel Baden's excellent book *The Composition of the Pentateuch: Renewing the Documentary Hypotheseis* (New Haven: Yale University Press, 2012), 34–44, after completing this manuscript. As the title promises, Baden offers an excellent updating of the source critical method. His approach to the sale of Joseph remains fundamentally the same as Speiser's: dissection of the various sources.

42. Greenstein, "Equivocal Reading of the Sale of Joseph," 123.

43. The brothers' guilt forms a major theme of the *Testaments of the Twelve Patriarchs*. See Feldman, Kugel, and Schiffman, *Outside the Bible*. Regrettably I came across these volumes after this manuscript was written; my citations are generally to earlier editions.

44. In recent times in synagogues that have bar-mitzvah and bat-mitzvah ceremonies, this is a part of the service nobody wants to miss as the bar or bat mitzvah will often read the haftarah. (On Shabbat and holy days, the Torah service includes a prophetic reading, or haftarah, from the root *peh-tet-resh* "to complete," or "to be exempted from," not "half torah.") How this practice got started or who assigned the Torah reading its particular pro-

phetic complement is obscure. As Michael Fishbane writes, "The origin of the haftarah recitation is obscured both by the paucity of ancient evidence and by later medieval legend." Fishbane, *JPS Bible Commentary: Haftarot*, xxiii.

45. That all four *haftarot* for Joseph have a thematic connection with their Torah portion will be brought out below.

46. The Torah and haftarah portions remain the same no matter the denomination, no matter whether a whole parashah or only a third of the Torah portion, or even less, is read. The upside-down feature of sermons was expounded by Joseph Heinemann, "Proem in the Aggadic Midrashim."

47. Kugel, *Bible as It Was*, 251–52.

48. *Jubilees* 34:28–29, in Feldman, Kugel, and Schiffman, *Outside the Bible*, 414.

49. God's dictum "These I recall" (*eleh azkarah*) became part of the Mussaf service for Yom Kippur service. According to *Pirke de Rabbi Eliezer*, the sin expiated by the ten martyrs is the sale of Joseph: "Said he [the emperor], 'then what of your ancestors who sold their brother, to a caravan of Ishmaelites they peddled him, and gave him away for shoes?'"

50. Fox, *Five Books of Moses*, 181.

51. I owe this insight to Devora Steinmetz, *From Father to Son*, 44. I was privileged to study midrash with Professor Steinmetz.

52. Jon D. Levenson, *Death and Resurrection of the Beloved Son*, 143.

2. Joseph the Dreamer

1. Sigmund Freud, *The Interpretation of Dreams: The Method of Interpreting Dreams*, trans. Alix Strachey and Alan Tyson (London: Hogarth, 1953), 4:197. Freud's consuming interest in dreams is evidenced by the 6,113 entries on the subject in *Concordance to the Standard Edition of the Complete Psychological Works of Sigmund Freud*, 2:258–314 (Boston: G. K. Hall, 1980).

2. Freud, *Interpretation of Dreams*, 4:334.

3. Identifying the Jewish factor in Freud has become a cottage industry, including fine contributions by Frieden and Yerushalmi, among many others.

4. A good summary of responses to Freud's psychoanalytic methods of interest to the nonspecialist may be found in Ritchie Robertson's introduction to Freud, *The Interpretation of Dreams*, translated by Joyce Crick (New York: Oxford University Press, 1999), vii–xxxvii.

5. Joseph's own dream—also a double dream—does not seem to include any difficult-to-interpret material. Jacob, Joseph, and his brothers immediately grasp its meaning.

6. Adolph Leo Oppenheim, *Dreams and Their Interpretation in the Ancient Near East* (Philadelphia: Translations of the American Philosophical Society, 1956), 209–10.

7. Oppenheim, *Dreams and Their Interpretation*, 206.

8. Scott Noegel, review of Ruth Fidler's *Dreams Speak Falsely? Dream Theophanies in the Bible* (Jerusalem: Hebrew University, 2005), *Journal of Hebrew Scriptures* 6 (2006). For a comprehensive overview on biblical dreams see Noegel's *Nocturnal Ciphers*. Freud's Jewishness has become a scholarly cottage industry of such proportions that citing all contributors would yield an overly lengthy endnote.

9. Bar, *Letter That Has Not Been Opened*, 223–32. Bar places much emphasis on the incubation dream that takes place at a sacred site.

10. Bar, *Letter That Has Not Been Opened*, 1.

11. Bar, *Letter That Has Not Been Opened*, 3.

12. The Bible's hostility to professional dream interpreters is easily documented: Deut. 18:15–22, Jer. 23:23–32, 27:9–10, Zech. 10:2, Eccles. 5:1–7, and the humiliation of the professionals by "amateurs" such as Joseph and Daniel.

13. The *text* of prayers appear rarely in earlier biblical sources. Joseph's prayers are found only in postbiblical literature, not in the Bible. See Greenberg, *Biblical Prose Prayer*.

14. Bible scholars agree that Daniel 1–6 and Daniel 7–12 differ greatly in genre and origins. See Lawrence Wills "Daniel," in Berlin and Brettler, *Jewish Study Bible*, 1640–42.

15. This "waking" of the two kings, Pharaoh (Gen. 41:4) and Solomon (1 Kings 3:15), presumably encouraged the choice of this passage as the prophetic reading for parashah Mikkets.

16. Among the scholars who date Joseph's composition to the Solomonic era or slightly later are Benjamin Mazar, *The Early Biblical Period* (Jerusalem: Israel Exploration Society, 1965); Rendsburg, *Redaction of Genesis*, Brettler, *Bible and the Believer*, and Sarna, *JPS Torah Commentary: Genesis*, xi–xvi.

17. Von Rad argued for Joseph as a piece of Wisdom literature with great impact in many publications, including "The Joseph Narrative and Ancient Wisdom," in *Problem of the Hexateuch*, 292–300.

18. Speiser's comment, "This section is made up of all three major sources," sheds limited light on the literary purpose of the passage. *Anchor Bible Genesis*, 346.

19. Speiser, *Anchor Bible Genesis*, 346.

20. In the source-critical tradition dreams are often considered a specialty of the Elohist (E) source.

21. The doubling of "go up" and the use of the word "also" (*gam*) in Gen. 46:4 serves to make God's assurance unambiguous and certain. On the nature of this promise, on God's corporeality, and on the freedom to depart from the literal meaning of Scripture, Maimonides *Guide of the Perplexed*, 1:28, and Nachmanides, *Commentary on the Torah*, 541–53, differ.

22. Kugel, "Literary Criticism Lite." In this case I find the wordplay intentional, as does Bar, *Letter That Has Not Been Opened*, 172–73.

23. The word used here for fear (*yirah*) combines fear and awe. Unlike "*pachad*," another word for fear, "*yirah*" may have a positive connotation, as in Prov. 1:7, "The fear [*yirah*] of God is the beginning of wisdom."

24. Nachmanides, *Commentary on the Torah*, 541–53.

25. Naphtali Zvi Yehuda Berlin (acronym: the Netziv), a nineteenth-century commentator and an early supporter of Zionism, read a modern parable into this situation.

26. Leibowitz, Studies in Genesis–Deuteronomy, 507.

27. There is no explicit mention of stones here (vs. Genesis 32), but there is the phrase "and he sacrificed sacrifices" (*va'yizbah zevahim*). The set-up for offering sacrifices in that part of the world often involved erecting a stone fireplace.

28. Jacob "kept the matter in mind" (Gen. 37:11), enabling him later in the story to accept as true the report of Joseph's fate and stature in Egypt. Rashbam recognizes the Torah's tendency to relate critical pieces of information for the purpose of subsequent narrative—prolepsis. Edward Greenstein, "Medieval Bible Commentary," in Barry Holtz, ed., *Back to the Sources* (New York: Simon & Schuster, 2006), 213–59.

29. The "*vav*-consecutive" is a terribly important construction in biblical Hebrew.

30. In this case the medieval division of Genesis into chapters works better than the traditional Jewish division into *parshiyot*; chapters 40 and 41 belong together.

31. Noegel, *Nocturnal Ciphers*, 128–32, stresses that the wording of the baker contains undertones of violence and discord.

32. Noegel, *Nocturnal Ciphers*, 128–32.

33. This is the third use of the phrase "and he lifted up his head," this time by the narrator rather than Joseph.

34. A wedding night (*mishteh*) also leads Jacob to sleep with Leah—the "wrong" sister (Gen. 29:21).

35. Leibowitz, *Studies in Genesis–Deuteronomy*, 453.

36. Rashi to Gen. 41:12.

37. Learning Talmud remains a vocal, dialogical endeavor. Unpacking talmudic argumentation, sometimes terse and formulaic, sometimes meandering and inconclusive, requires much practice. My comments rely on Rabbi Adin Steinsaltz, *Biblical Images*, and *The Essential Talmud* (New York: Basic Books, 1976).

38. Rabbi Samuel Edels (the Maharsha, 1555–1631) adds that authority requires the support and agreement of the community. Maharsha reflects the consensus that Joseph ruled fairly, but at personal cost.

39. This is as opposed to the many "message" dreams delivered to the Patriarchs and Rebecca or Abraham's "covenant between the pieces" vision in Genesis 15. Isaac Heinemann's discussion of "biblical firsts" as a key to rabbinic interpretation remains unsurpassed. *Darchei ha-Aggadah.*

40. I am reassured in making this association by the *Iyyun Ya'akov*, as cited by Adin Steinsaltz, *Koren Bavli* (Jerusalem: Koren, 2012) 1:356.

41. Frieden, *Freud's Dream of Interpretation*, 73–93.

42. There may be an implication of Joseph's laxness in matters Judaic— the other two things the sages say shorten a man's life are his failure to take an *aliyah* to the Torah and the failure to say Grace after Meals. These are Jewish rituals and positive, time-bound mitzvot, whereas "assuming airs of authority" is clearly not. But Nachmanides defends Joseph's religious observance in the strongest terms.

43. Steinsaltz, *Biblical Images*, 69.

44. Steinsaltz, *Biblical Images*, 71.

3. Tamar, a Difficult Hero

1. Bat-Shua does not seem to be a proper name in Genesis 38; in 1 Chron. 2:3 it does. The English reader should recall that Hebrew has no uppercase or lowercase letters. For a recent analysis of scholarship on this chapter, see Leuchter, "Genesis 38 in Social and Historical Perspective."

2. Bat-Shua's quick-paced procreation contrasts to narratives where barrenness will be a major theme. Sarah, for instance, is introduced as barren in Gen. 11:30; her dilemma is not resolved until Gen. 21:2. My colleague Dr. Lifsa Schachter notes that every woman named an *"akarah"* by the Bible winds up giving birth to a male child, so the usual translation is misleading.

3. The narrator uses indirect speech, or putting it more crassly, gossip, twice in this passage (Gen. 38:13, 38:24) to convey how the notice of Tamar's pregnancy was delivered to Judah.

4. Distinguishing the view of the narrator and that of God in the Hebrew Bible is not simple. The scholarship on this is overwhelming—I find the comments in Alter, *Art of Biblical Narrative*, 157, and Josipovici, *Book of God*, 85, helpful. See also Miles, *God*.

5. All Mann translations are Woods's, in Mann, *Joseph and His Brothers*, 1254. See Mann's "Sixteen Years," his account of the genesis of *Joseph and His Brothers*, xxxviii.

6. Von Rad, *Genesis*, 356–57.

7. This sort of variation in spelling in biblical Hebrew is common. See following note.

8. The Midrash Rabbah Genesis 63:8, 562, does not quite explain the orthography of the variously spelled "twins," Gen. 38:27 versus Gen. 25:24. It looks like the missing letter is an *aleph*, not a *vav*.

9. Ancient Hebrew script is consonantal—this creates challenges of textual criticism, translation, and interpretation. See Seidman, *Faithful Renderings*, 153–98.

10. BT, Berachot 31a–b.

11. Alan T. Levenson "Christian Author, Jewish Book? Methods and Sources in Thomas Mann's *Joseph*," *German Quarterly* 71, no. 2 (Spring 1998): 166–78. (I thought I had made a great discovery—until I read the Hebrew preface to Mann's tetralogy.)

12. Speiser, *Anchor Bible Genesis*, 299.

13. Niditch, "Wrong Woman Right," notes that "views of the function and purpose of Genesis 38 have remained relatively static" (147–49).

14. That Genesis 38 has been included on the basis of J's great interest in Judahite themes remains the consensus among source-critical scholars. For an explanation of Genesis 38 and Genesis 49 as chiastic "partners," see Rendsburg, *Redaction of Genesis*, 79–90.

15. Alter, *Five Books of Moses*.

16. David Berger, "Interpreting Bible," *Commentary* 63, no. 3 (1976): 15; Kugel, "Biblical Criticism Lite."

17. Mann, *Joseph and His Brothers*, 1255–56.

18. Michael Fishbane, *Inner Biblical Exegesis* (Oxford: Clarendon, 1985); Levinson, *Deuteronomy and the Hermeneutics of Legal Innovation*.

19. Since Tamar's and Ruth's levirate marriages both depart from the legal text, this passage was a ready-made invitation to expound a mysterious custom. The levirate requirement itself conflicts with the prohibition against incest with sisters-in-law, spelled out in the Holiness Code of Leviticus (Lev. 18:16, 20:21). Levirate laws possibly emerged from the abhorrence of seeing Israelite names and lines abolished. Ruth and the daughters of Zelophahad narratives suggest an interest in preserving family land allotments, as do the provisions concerning the sabbatical year and the Jubilee year (Leviticus 24–25). See Weisberg, *Levirate Marriage and the Family in Ancient Judaism*.

20. Carmichael, *Women, Law, and the Genesis Traditions*, 66.

21. Nachmanides, *Commentary on the Torah*, 469–70.

22. 1 Chron. 2:3 does not contain this information. Carmichael, *Women, Law, and the Genesis Traditions*, and others emphasize that this stricture applies only to the firstborn son.

23. Nachmanides' language on this verse, 38:8 (*va'yabaym otah*), is elusive (*Commentary on the Torah*, 468–70). See also Jon D. Levenson, *Resurrection and Restoration of Israel* (New Haven CT: Yale University Press, 2006), and Neil Gillman, *Death of Death* (Woodstock VT: Jewish Lights, 1997).

24. Frymer-Kensky, *Reading the Women of the Bible*, 266; "no longer know": Mann, *Joseph and His Brothers*.

25. Jacob, *First Book of the Bible, Genesis*, 261. Jacob notes that we have examples of negative exogamy in Genesis 34 (Dinah) and Genesis 36 (Esau) counterbalanced here by a positive example of exogamy. Observations like these fed Jacob's distaste for the source-critical tendency to "read-out" parts of scripture as appendages.

26. The sale of Joseph was a major theme for later exegetes, Jewish and Christian, and the varied payment amount reported in the Hebrew Bible and the Septuagint suggests that exegetical work began early. The sale of Joseph for the price of sandals, reflected in the choice of the haftarah, is also reflected in the Yom Kippur martyrology *"eleh azkarah."* In Christianity this sale was often seen as foreshadowing Judas's betrayal of Jesus. This perspective, of course, fed the anti-Jewish tradition of the Church Fathers.

27. Sacred prostitution played no role in ancient Israel (Deut. 22:20–21; 23:18), and Priests were explicitly forbidden to marry prostitutes (Lev. 19:29, 21:7). There were, however, sacred prostitutes in surrounding societies, and the text reflects that with the word *kedeshah*. A well-known example of dual language is the use of "household gods" and "idols" in Genesis 31. When Jacob or Rachel speaks to Laban, the objects are referred to as household gods; when the narrator speaks, they are idols (*terafim*).

28. "Rabbi said: We searched the whole of Scripture and found no place named Petach Enaim. What then is the purport of Petach Enaim? It teaches that she lifted up her eyes to the gate to which all eyes are directed and prayed: 'May it be Thy will that I do not leave this house with naught.'" Midrash Rabbah Genesis 86:7.

29. Bloom and Rosenberg, *Book of J*, 222.

30. Tamara Cohn Eskenazi, ed., *The Torah: A Women's Commentary* (URJ, 2007), 219.

31. Ochs, *Sarah Laughed*, xvi.

32. Pardes, *Countertraditions in the Bible*, 39–59.

33. The claim of female authorship had already been forwarded as a possibility by R. E. Friedman and others. One cannot prove the identity of any of the sources—though source critics including Friedman deserve much credit for plausibly narrowing the field.

34. Bloom and Rosenberg, *Book of J*, 220, 223.

35. Cited in Fields, *Torah Commentary for Our Times*, 96.

4. Potiphar's Wife Vilified and Redeemed

1. The literature on Joseph and the wife of Potiphar is overwhelming. Some works worth consulting: Bernstein, *Stories of Joseph*; Kalimi, *Early Jewish Exegesis*; Goldman, *Wiles of Women/ Wiles of Men*; Kugel, *In Potiphar's House*; Yohannan, *Joseph and Potiphar's Wife*.

2. The story of Lot's daughters is at least partly a negative etiology of Moab and Ammon, traditional enemies of Israel.

3. Mann, *Joseph and His Brothers*, 815.

4. Al Thalabi, in the name of Abd al Akhbar, an eighth-century CE Yemenite Jewish convert to Islam, cited in Goldman, *Wiles of Women/ Wiles of Men*, 83. Joseph has been rendered as both Yusuf and Yusef. One talmudic tradition claims that of the ten portions of human beauty bestowed by the Almighty, Joseph possessed ten of them (BT, Yoma 35b).

5. The Hebrew word *bayit* can mean house, household members, or even dynasty.

6. *Midrash Rabbah Genesis* 2:86–87 includes several versions of Joseph's beauty. See Ulmer, *Egyptian Cultural Icons in Midrash*.

7. Although Potiphar is mentioned only once in Genesis 39, he is mentioned by name at the end of Genesis 37.

8. On anonymous characters in the Hebrew Bible, see Reinhartz, *Why Ask My Name*.

9. The "Story of the Two Brothers" (Anpu and Bata) may be found in Yohannan, *Joseph and Potiphar's Wife*, in James Pritchard's collection *Ancient Near Eastern Texts* 1:12–16, and in Simpson et al.'s *Literature of Ancient Egypt*. The similarities between this tale, dated on the basis of a manuscript from the thirteenth century, and the biblical account of Joseph and Potiphar has long been acknowledged. Yohannan doubts direct borrowing, since the story of "the chaste youth and the lustful stepmother" seems nearly universal (*Joseph and Potiphar's Wife*, 23). But the possibility should not be dismissed for the tales share bags of goods, food supply issues, female hair combing, male physical strength and good looks, the role of work, and jealousy of the younger brother on the part of his elder(s).

10. The Epic of Gilgamesh, which precedes the biblical account by several centuries, includes a version of the flood story that has been found in part at Megiddo in the center of Israel. In addition to the direct parallels between the Genesis Flood account and the Gilgamesh account, and the theme of flooding generally, more frequent in Mesopotamia than in Canaan, these tablets leave little doubt that the Genesis Flood story is written with Gilgamesh in mind. I adhere to the view of Sarna, *Understanding Genesis*, that the biblical account constitutes a polemical joinder.

11. Yohannan, *Joseph and Potiphar's Wife*; Kugel, *In Potiphar's House*; Goldman, *Wiles of Women/ Wiles of Men*.

12. Redford, *Study of the Biblical Story of Joseph*, considers Genesis 39 an independent unit. I agree with Rendsburg, *Redaction of Genesis*, that Genesis 39 fits well within the Joseph story.

13. Alter, *Art of Biblical Narrative*, remains unsurpassed in its exposition of the biblical type scene.

14. Kugel, *In Potiphar's House*, 16n7, concludes the name Zulaika derives from post-Qur'anic Persian authors. By the Middle Ages Zulaika is well attested in Jewish, Muslim, and Christian sources.

15. On Joseph in the Qur'an, see Baidawi, *Commentary of Sura 12 of the Qur'an* (Beeston's translation); Al-Thalabi, *Lives of the Prophets* (Brinner's translation); and Mustansir Mir, "The Qur'anic Story of Joseph."

16. *Pirkei de-Rabbi Eliezer*, 38, cited in Goldman, *Wiles of Women/Wiles of Men*, 106.

17. Rashi to Gen. 39:1. Throughout this book I have cited Rashi only by the verse he comments on; traditionally one may cite Rashi by the "opening word" (*dibbur ha-matchil*), also referred to as the opening (*pitchon peh*).

18. Leah and Dinah are considered gadabouts in some midrashim.

19. Mann, *Joseph and His Brothers*, follows rabbinic tradition here: making Mrs. Potiphar Joseph's age or younger adds piquancy to his marriage with Asenath in Genesis 41.

20. Jami, "Yusuf and Zulaikha," cited in Yohannan, *Joseph and Potiphar's Wife*, 220.

21. *Midrash Rabbah Bereshit* 137:6. Compare Rashi to 39:2 and Zohar, *Book of Enlightenment*, 1:84–90.

22. Leibowitz notes that Joseph mentions God often in his speeches to both Madam Potiphar and Pharaoh; this reading of Joseph may sound apologetic, but it is consistent. She makes a plea here for Torah education and *aliyah*. "But what of those who have caught only second- or thirdhand glimpses of their ancient traditions and shadows of their ancestral image during moments of Torah study in their childhood. Do they similarly stand a chance of being saved amid alien cultures and climes." *Studies in Genesis–Deuteronomy*, 415.

23. Flavius Josephus, *Antiquities*, 2:4:2.

24. *The Koran*, Sura 12:25–30 (ed. N. J. Dawood; Hammondsworth: Penguin Classics, 1974), 40.

25. *Koran*, Sura 12:41.

26. Ginzberg and Szold, *Legends of the Jews*, 2:58–60.

27. Kugel, *In Potiphar's House*, 66–124.

28. Kugel, *Bible as It Was*, 257–58.

29. Budd, "Mark Twain on Joseph the Patriarch."

30. Twain cited in Budd, "Mark Twain on Joseph the Patriarch," 579; Kass, *Beginning of Wisdom*, 541–45.

31. BT, Sotah 36b. See Kugel, *In Potiphar's House*, 95. The Jewish tradition is ambivalent over whether Joseph gave in to temptation: Second Temple literature, *Midrash Rabbah Genesis*, BT, Yoma 35b, and Zohar, *Book of Enlightenment*, 1:189b, stress Joseph's ability to resist sin; Rav Samuel and others insisted that Joseph intended to sin.

32. *Midrash Rabbah Genesis* 86:3 assumes Potiphar purchases Joseph for sex, is punished by God, and becomes a eunuch. On the use of *saris* as an emasculate, see Tigay, *JPS Torah Commentary: Deuteronomy*, 210n2.

33. Sarna, *JPS Torah Commentary: Genesis*, 271.

34. Each of these three descriptions of Potiphar drew exegetical attention. Was Potiphar a eunuch? If so Mrs. Potiphar's sexual desire needs less explaining. Was he head of the cooks, or of the executioners? These seem like two very different jobs.

35. Sarna, *JPS Torah Commentary: Genesis*, 271.

36. Hirsch, *Hirsch Chumash*, 730–31.

37. Sarna, *JPS Torah Commentary: Genesis*, 275.

38. The epithet "Joseph's master" here is in a construct state, and also chanted with a *kadma-azla*, which joins the two words.

5. Joseph from Rags to Riches

1. David Wolpe and others have sensed similarities in David's rise and Joseph's rise. David's family life, of course, goes downhill after his adulterous relationship with Bathsheba and criminal treatment of Uriah. Moses, like Joseph, experienced sibling rivalry when Miriam and Aaron complained about his special status. The Patriarchs were successful in worldly terms, but Joseph and David achieved national leadership. David Wolpe, *David: The Divided Heart* (New Haven CT: Yale: University Press, 2014).

2. Rendsburg, *Redaction of Genesis*, 79–97, argues that this continuation of policy prescriptions in Genesis 47 closes a chiasm (a, b, c, c', b', a') begun in Genesis 41. Rendsburg considers these editorial features critical to the structure of Joseph and Genesis.

3. Aaron Wildavsky, *The Nursing Father: Moses as a Political Leader* (Tuscaloosa: University of Alabama, 1984); Wildavsky, *Assimilation versus Separation*.

4. The method called inner biblical interpretation had already been recognized by Sandmel, "Haggadah within Scripture," and in the works of the nineteenth-century German Jewish scholar Abraham Geiger (*Abraham Geiger and Liberal Judaism*, ed. Max Wiener [Philadelphia: JPS, 1962] 216–43).

5. Kraemer, *When Asenath Met Joseph*. See also the discussions of Docherty, "Joseph and Aseneth"; Gruen, "Hellenistic Images of Joseph"; and Hicks-Keeton, "Rewritten Gentiles." I am grateful to Dr. Hicks-Keeton for sharing her manuscript.

6. In Gen. 39:1 the passive *hufal* is used: "Joseph is brought down [*hurad*] to Egypt." Scholars disagree over whether the phrase "*ve'hurad mizraymah*" is a moral judgment or only a geographical designation, Egypt lying to the South of Canaan.

7. On Zulaika see Kugel, *In Potiphar's House*, 61n7: "The name Zulaika for Mrs. Potiphar does not appear in early Jewish sources, nor even in the Qur'an."

8. Joseph's new name, "Zaphenath-paneah," is cryptic. Jewish exegesis connects the name with Joseph's dream interpreting: "to hide" and to "elucidate"; he is, that is, "revealer of hidden things." But the name may be an etymological Egyptian transcription of "God speaks; he lives." Sarna, *JPS Commentary: Genesis*, 288. Abraham ibn Ezra frankly acknowledged that if it is an Egyptian word, scholars do not know it, and if it is a Hebrew translation of part of Joseph's name, that part is unclear. Nachmanides, *Commentary on the Torah*, 503, ingeniously proposes that Pharaoh asks Joseph, "What's Canaanite for secret revealer?" thus prompting Joseph to name himself.

9. Joseph's age is given three times in the narrative: in Gen. 37:2 he is called a seventeen-year-old *na'ar*. At Gen. 41:46 we are told that "Joseph was thirty years old when he entered the service of Pharaoh king of Egypt," which marks his growth in intervening years. Pertinent, perhaps, is this verse: "David was thirty years old when he became king and he reigned forty years" (2 Sam. 5:4). The third time we told Joseph's age in Genesis is at his death at 110, the same age attained by Joshua, Joseph's descendant.

10. *Jubilees*, Pseudo-Philo, Ben Sira, *Wisdom of Solomon*. On these works see the texts and introductions in Feldman, Kugel, Schiffman, *Outside the Bible*.

11. Quoted in Niehoff, *Figure of Joseph in Post-biblical Jewish Literature*, 48–49.

12. Philo's position on Joseph is notoriously ambivalent. See Gruen, "Hellenistic Images of Joseph," 79–87.

13. Josephus's *Antiquities*, written about twenty years later than *Jewish War*, showed more awareness of widespread pagan hostility toward Jews; Josephus wrote the first anti-antisemitic tract, a refutation called *Against Apion*. Josephus's defense of Judaism was mounted mainly against two Egyptian priests, Apion and his predecessor, Manetho. My view of Josephus draws mainly from Feldman, *Josephus's Interpretation of the Bible*, 335–73; Niehoff, *Figure of Joseph in Post-biblical Jewish Literature*; and Gruen, "Hellenistic Images of Joseph." The three biblical pericopes that interested Joseph

most, in Feldman's appraisal, were his dreams, the episode with Potiphar's wife, and his testing of the brothers.

14. Josephus, *Antiquities*, 2:20. I have used Whiston's antiquated translation for its King Jamesian qualities.

15. A fluid interpreter of the Bible, Josephus remains an important source too for first-century CE Judaism and an enduring subject of scholarly inquiry. His story has been recently retold by the versatile novelist, scholar, and playwright Frederic Raphael in *A Jew among Romans*.

16. Von Rad, *Wisdom in Israel*; von Rad, "Joseph Narrative and Ancient Wisdom."

17. "The Joseph narrative is a novel through and through, and the material is in no way associated at any point with genuine local traditions." Von Rad, "Joseph Narrative and Ancient Wisdom," 292, 294–95. Von Rad dissented from the view of Hermann Gunkel that Joseph originated as an oral saga; Gunkel, *The Legends of Genesis* (New York: Schocken, 1964).

18. Joseph's humiliation in the pit came at the hands of his own brothers. Midrash picked up on this in its imagining that Joseph revisited that very pit on the way back to Egypt after burying Jacob in Canaan.

19. *Jubilees* is a midrashic-style pseudepigraphic book that comments on Genesis and Exodus, now available in Feldman, Kugel, Schiffman, *Outside the Bible* 1:272–465.

20. Gen. 47:13–15 uses the phrase "there was famine in the land of Canaan" three times. This is curious since: (1) Jacob's family has already been relocated to Goshen, and (2) it is unlikely that a river-based agriculture (Egypt) and a rain-based agriculture (Israel) had famines of equal duration.

21. Caine, "Numbers in the Joseph Narrative."

22. Nehama Leibowitz, Studies in Genesis–Deuteronomy, 526. See also Jacob, *First Book of the Bible*, 318–19.

23. Midrash Rabbah Genesis 95:1–4.

24. I borrow this phrase from Samuel's chapter title in *Certain People of the Book*.

25. I believe *temiyah* and *hitbollelut* are the most common modern Hebrew words for assimilation.

26. *Tanna Devrei Eliyahu* 23:4. The threesome of distinctly Jewish names, language, and clothing reemerged as a creed of ultraorthodoxy in the nineteenth century.

27. The brothers may assume that Joseph has died or been enslaved.

28. On the Egyptian context, the rabbis were somewhat at a loss, not being privy to much knowledge of ancient Egypt. This generated some especially fanciful midrash, such as their derivation of the name Zaphenath-paneah; see Kasher, *Encyclopedia of Biblical Interpretation*, 5:157–58.

29. Wildavsky, *Assimilation versus Separation*, contrasts Joseph and Moses.

30. Zornberg, *Genesis*, 286–90.

31. Joseph's naming speeches for his sons invoke God, but it is significant here that Joseph invokes the "Elohim" name of God, rather than the more specifically Israelite name (i.e., the Tetragrammaton, pronounced "Adonai" or "Ha-Shem," usually translated as "Lord" in English).

32. Assimilation, the inevitable shedding of foreign elements by an immigrant, and assimilationism, an ideology that this phenomenon is a positive good, ought to be distinguished.

33. Pava, "Joseph and the Use of Inside Information," esp. 141. Pava uses Austrian economist Frederick Hayek's analysis to good effect in this essay.

34. Caine, "Numbers in the Joseph Narrative," 9–10.

35. Jacob, *First Book of the Bible*, 318–19, translation amended.

36. Pirson, *Lord of Dreams*, 3.

37. Carmichael, *Law and Narrative in the Bible*, 142–46; 278–91, 299–303.

38. Rosenthal, "Die Josephgeschichte mit den Büchern Esther und Daniel verglichen"; Gan, "Scroll of Esther in Light of Events of Joseph in Egypt." Other scholars, including Humphreys, *Joseph and His Family*, have built on these seminal articles.

39. Hebrew, or *Ivri*.

40. Wildavsky, *Assimilation versus Separation*, 126–29.

41. Samuel, *Certain People of the Book*, 244–345.

42. Jon Levenson, "Beloved Son as Ruler and Servant," in *Death and Resurrection of the Beloved Son*, 143–45.

43. Absalom kills his half brother Amnon, who raped his half sister Tamar. Absalom is subsequently killed in a rebellion against his father. Adonijah, another son, is put forward as a candidate to inherit David's throne and is killed by his half brother Solomon, the "winner" of this dynastic struggle.

44. Kraemer, *When Asenath Met Joseph*; Kraemer, "How the Egyptian Virgin Asenath Converts to Judaism."

45. Hicks-Keeton, however, argues for the earlier date assigned this work by Marc Philolenko and Randall Chesnutt; see Hicks-Keeton, "Rewritten Gentiles." I thank Dr. Hicks-Keeton for calling my attention to Docherty, "Joseph and Aseneth."

46. The text of this version of "Asenath and Joseph" comes from Charlesworth, *Pseudepigrapha*, cited in Kugel, *In Potiphar's House*. I recommend comparison with Patricia Ahearne-Kroll's more recent rendering, "Joseph and Asenath," in Feldman, Kugel, and Schiffman, *Outside the Bible*, 2528–81.

47. Kraemer, *When Asenath Met Joseph*, argues that the tradition that makes Asenath halachically Jewish, the daughter of Schechem and Dinah, is late.

48. "Asenath and Joseph," Charlesworth, *Pseudepigrapha*, cited in Kugel, *In Potiphar's House*, 88. Joseph said to Pentepheres, "Who is this woman who is standing on the upper floor by the window? Let her leave this house," because Joseph was afraid, saying, "This one must not molest me too." For all the wives and daughters of Egypt used to molest him [, wanting] to sleep with him, and all the wives and daughters of the Egyptians, when they saw Joseph suffered badly because of his beauty. But Joseph despised them; and the messengers whom they sent to him with gold and silver and valuable presents Joseph sent back with threats and insults, because Joseph said, " I will not sin before the Lord God of my father Israel."

49. Kraemer, "How the Egyptian Virgin Asenath Converts to Judaism," 279.

50. The Rembrandt (or school of Rembrandt) oil painting *Jacob Blessing the Children of Joseph* hangs in the Museumslandschaft Hessen-Kassel.

51. Ginzberg and Szold, *Legends of the Jews*, 2:76.

6. Testing, Dreaming, Punishing

1. I am not convinced by those who credit Reuben with realizing that the law of equivalence (*lex talionis*) requires two for two, meaning Reuben's two sons for Joseph and Benjamin.

2. Among the classical commentators, Isaac Abravanel: punishment; Nachmanides: dreams; Rambam: testing.

3. Sternberg, *Poetics of Biblical Narrative*, 286.

4. My reading of Genesis 42–45 is beholden to Sternberg's book and to Ackerman, "Joseph, Judah, and Jacob," 85–113. See also Alter, *Art of Biblical Narrative*, 155–77.

5. The theme of sexual impropriety and violent retribution is imagined in a midrashic conversation between Joseph and the brothers. The brothers claim they tarried in Egypt three days to seek their lost brother, whom they assume may have been sold into sexual slavery. Ginzberg and Szold, *Legends of the Jews*, 2:82–85.

6. A worldwide famine, as noted, is hardly likely. Midrash takes a more literary approach: the famine heightens the sense of Joseph's overwhelming power and Israel's desperation.

7. The Hebrew word *amar* can represent actual words or internal thought. Hence "*ki amar*" can be rendered either "for he said" or "so he thought."

8. On the term *ha-shalit*, see Sarna, *JPS Torah Commentary: Genesis*, 292n6. Hamashbir was the name of modern Israel's most popular department store a generation ago.

9. Note that even in Genesis 47:1 Joseph comes unsummoned into Pharaoh's presence and announces in three verbs the arrival of his family. Sam-

son Raphael Hirsch notes that Joseph is called *adon* not *ba'al*. For Hirsch the former term denotes noble rule; the latter, one who dominates by power. Hirsch's etymologies have been criticized philologically. Often, though, they seem responsive to the situation.

10. Ginzberg and Szold, *Legends of the Jews* 2:81, 85–86. "The brethren of Joseph knew not that the viceroy of Egypt understood Hebrew, and could follow their words, for Manasseh stood and was an interpreter between them and him."

11. "To regard, recognize" (*nun-khaf-resh*) is an irregular verb that does not appear in the *kal* form. It is used in this sense only one other place in Scripture. See *The Brown-Driver-Briggs Hebrew and English Lexicon of the Old Testament* (Oxford: Clarendon, 1951) 647–48.

12. Joseph's chin is interesting: he shaves before he attends Pharaoh, and we know from archaeology that Egyptian officials were beardless, while "Asiatics" wore beards. Did Joseph ever let his whiskers grow back? Nachmanides writes: "Now in this matter of recognition our rabbis have said that Joseph recognized his brothers because he had left them bearded, but they did not recognize him because when he left them he had no beard and now they found him with a beard." Nachmanides, *Commentary on the Torah*, 511.

13. *Brown-Driver-Briggs Hebrew and English Lexicon* lists this use of "*vayitnaker*" in Gen. 42:7, also at 1 Kings 14:5–6, in the phrase "feign to be a stranger."

14. Nachmanides stresses this connection in his comment to Gen. 42:7–9.

15. I cannot agree that this fulfills both dreams, as per Sarna, *JPS Torah Commentary: Genesis*, 292.

16. The first dream is overly fulfilled, since it is in Joseph's second dream that everyone bows down to him "to the ground" (*artzah*). This clues the reader to Joseph's connecting dreams one and two and acting accordingly.

17. Sternberg, *Poetics of Biblical Narrative*, 288. Nakedness in the Bible is connected to shame more than to eros; however, the sexual undercurrent here is undeniable.

18. Ginzberg and Szold, *Legends of the Jews*, 2:85.

19. The brothers' words here in Gen. 42:14b, "he is not" (*aynenu*), echo Reuben's anguished cry in Gen. 37:30, "The child is not" (*aynenu*).

20. Matt. 28:1. See Aubrey W. Argyle, "Joseph the Patriarch in Patristic Teaching."

21. Sacks, *Commentary on the Book of Genesis*, 366.

22. Sacks, *Commentary on the Book of Genesis*, 383.

23. Sarna, *JPS Torah Commentary: Genesis*, 302.

24. Nachmanides, *Commentary on the Torah*, 516.

25. The threefold repetition, in midrashic practice, can be associated with three referents: Joseph, Jacob, and the brothers as a collective.

26. See Leibowitz, *Studies in Genesis–Deuteronomy*, 464.

27. Reuben's offer is somewhat defensible on the grounds that he realizes that *two* sons of Jacob have been jeopardized.

28. Nachmanides, *Commentary on the Torah*, 521.

29. Lieber, et al., *Etz Hayim*, 266.

30. Sarna, *JPS Torah Commentary: Genesis*, 275.

31. Two oddities appear here: One, Joseph has already seen Benjamin in Gen. 43:16, so it is unclear why he is brought to tears on this occasion. Two, after asking whether or not the boy is Benjamin, Joseph does not wait for a verbal answer from the brothers—we may infer nods of assent.

32. Kasher, *Encyclopedia of Biblical Interpretation*, 5:231. Rabbi Melai likened Joseph's separation in Gen. 49:26 to the separateness of the *nazir*, who may not drink wine.

33. Reinhartz, *Why Ask My Name?*

34. Levin, "Benjamin Conundrum."

35. Anne-Louis Girodet de Roucy-Trioson, *Joseph Recognized by His Brothers* (1789), may be found in the Musée des Beaux Artes collection in Paris.

36. My Jewish students generally find the frequent equation of Jesus with so many OT heroes reductionist. What I appreciate here is Ambrose's use of Benjamin as a prefiguration of Paul.

37. For both Judaism and Christianity a fourfold sense of reading Scripture is formalized in the medieval world but employed much earlier. In Judaism this is encapsulated in the familiar acronym *pardes* (literally: orchard). A rhyme attributed to Nicholas of Lyre holds:

> Littera gesta docet,
> Quid credas allegoria,
> Moralis quid agas,
> Quo tendas anagogia.

38. Ambrose, "Seven Exegetical Works," 226. Meyer Schapiro, *The Joseph Scenes on the Maximianus Throne in Ravenna* (New York: G. Braziller, 1979); Adam Kamesar, "Ambrose, Philo and the Presence of Art in the Bible," *Journal of Early Christian Studies* 9, no. 1 (Spring 2001): 73–103.

39. Ambrose, "Seven Exegetical Works," 220–21. Ambrose was a harsh antagonist of the Jews. "Joseph" and "The Patriarchs" were composed by Ambrose during his tenure as archbishop of Milan, which included a disgraceful effort to let Christians escape punishment for their burning of the synagogue at Callinicum in 388 CE.

40. This anonymous servant, in some midrashic traditions, is Manasseh.

41. Leibowitz, *Studies in Genesis–Deuteronomy*, 357.

42. Samuel, *Certain People of the Book*, 312.

43. Samuel, *Certain People of the Book*, 320.

44. Alicia Suskin Ostriker, *The Nakedness of the Fathers: Biblical Visions and Revisions* (New Brunswick NJ: Rutgers University Press, 1994), 113–14.

45. Leibowitz, Studies in Genesis–Deuteronomy, 468.

46. In Abravanel's view this addition of grain and money proved to the brothers that Benjamin was indeed innocent since they too had been "framed" in this way. On Arama and Abravanel, see Leibowitz, *New Studies in Genesis*, 457–62.

47. Hirsch, *Hirsch Chumash*, 776–77, explains that Joseph could have chosen "to remain a prince and nothing but a prince in the eyes of his father and brothers" but instead changed their minds about him as he had changed his mind about them.

48. Wiesel, *Messengers of God*, 151.

49. Wiesel, *Messengers of God*, 168. I incline to Josipovici's emphasis, in *Book of God*, that Joseph did not know the tribe of Judah would overshadow the tribes of Joseph.

50. In line with Greco-Roman tradition, Josephus expands these biblical speeches greatly in his rendering.

7. Judah in Joseph

1. Devora Steinmetz, *From Father to Son*, 130.

2. The Babylonia Talmud links Judah's name to his publicly righteous deed. Rabbi Hanin ben Bizna said in the name of R. Simeon the Pious: "Because Joseph sanctified the heavenly Name in private one letter [*heh*] was added to him from the name of the Holy One, blessed be He, but because Judah sanctified the heavenly Name in public, the whole of his name was called after the name of the Holy One, blessed be he."(BT, Sotah 10b, and BT, Sotah 36b)

3. Pardes, *Countertraditions in the Bible*, 63–64.

4. Sarna, *JPS Torah Commentary: Genesis*, 96, observes there were no domesticated camels until the twelfth century BCE. In my view the camels are there to signal the Joseph's impending voyage.

5. Goldin, "Judah"; Ackerman, "Joseph, Judah, and Jacob," 2:100–101.

6. Sarna, *JPS Torah Commentary: Genesis*, notes that this repeated use of "the boy" emphasizes Benjamin's youth—even Joseph, his brother, will bless him as "my son" (43:29).

7. Leibowitz, *Studies in Genesis–Deuteronomy*, 474.

8. See Exod. 6:3: "I appeared to Abraham, Isaac and Jacob as El Shaddai."

9. On the threefold repetition, see Leibowitz, *Studies in Genesis–Deuteronomy*, 466.

10. Half verse is hemistich in academic.

11. The difficulty in rendering *nefesh* into English is manifold. The doubling of *nafsho*, meaning both Jacob and Benjamin, requires elucidation in English to make the meaning clear. Old Jewish Publication Society adds "the lad's soul," which clarifies matters, but at the expense of losing the equation—which is the point the verse.

12. Eliezer Benmozegh, cited in Leibowitz, *Studies in Genesis–Deuteronomy*, 475.

13. Maimonides, *Mishneh Torah*, Hilchot Teshuva, 2:1.

14. Joseph Soloveitchik, *Halakhic Man* (Philadelphia: JPS, 1983), 115.

15. Sternberg, *Poetics of Biblical Narrative*, 308.

16. Rashi, seconding a tradition from *Avot de Rabbi Natan*, assumes the Holy Spirit prompted Jacob to include Joseph when the former says, "And may El Shaddai dispose the man to mercy toward you, that he may release to you your other brother, as well as Benjamin. As for me, if I am to be bereaved, I shall be bereaved" (Gen. 43:14).

17. Benno Jacob maintains that Judah knew it was Joseph. *First Book of the Bible*, 298.

18. Kass, *Beginning of Wisdom*, 603.

19. As cited in Kasher, *Encyclopedia of Biblical Interpretation*, 6:3.

20. Tradition imagines Joseph reproaching Judah for this speech: "Joseph said to him [Judah] Why do you speak so much? I see your older brothers standing and saying nothing. Is not Reuben older than you? Are not Simeon and Levi older than you? Yet they are silent. Why then do you speak so much?" Kasher, *Encyclopedia of Biblical Interpretation*, 6:2.

21. *Midrash Rabbah Genesis* 93:1–7 (Soncino translation 2:860–61).

22. *Midrash Tanhuma*, vol. 1, Va-yiggash 1–8, ed. Solomon Buber (New York: Sefer, 1946), 204–8; cited in Leibowitz, *Studies in Genesis–Deuteronomy*, 491–93.

23. Leibowitz, *Studies in Genesis–Deuteronomy*, 493.

24. It is not clear to me why the text tells us that Egyptians and the house of Pharaoh heard Joseph crying.

25. Zornberg, *Beginning of Desire*, 333–36, sagely comments that the brothers never could speak to Joseph.

26. Nachmanides, *Commentary on the Torah*, 560–61.

27. Hirsch, *Hirsch Chumash*, 831.

28. Alter, *Five Books of Moses*, 271.

29. Cited in Kasher, *Encyclopedia of Biblical Interpretation*, 6:72–73. "Five" is the number most sources settle on as the amount intended by *miqtseh*.

30. Miles, *God*, 78–84.

31. For instance: "The sons of Judah: Er, Onan and Shelah. These three were born to him by a Canaanite woman, the daughter of Shua. Er, Judah's firstborn, was wicked in the Lord's sight; so the Lord put him to death. Judah's daughter-in-law Tamar bore Perez and Zerah to Judah. He had five sons in all."

32. Josipovici, *Book of God*, 85. Solomon has Shimei killed, at David's instruction (1 Kings 2:36–46).

33. In Ps. 78:67–71 Judah's ascent comes directly at the expense of Joseph's descendants: "for the Lord despised the tent of Joseph, and preferred not the tribe of Ephraim."

34. Compare the image of Aaron's blossoming staff in Num. 17:16–26.

35. Tamar, not Judah, is the hero of Genesis 38. "Better for a man to cast himself in a fiery furnace rather than to shame his fellow in public. Whence is this? From Tamar" (BT, Sotah 10b). What gave Judah the right to propose immolation? Nachmanides, *Commentary on the Torah*, 475–76, conjectures, "It appears to me that since Judah was a tribal chief, an officer, and a ruler of the land, his daughter-in-law who committed harlotry against him was not judged by the same law as other people, but as one who degraded royalty."

8. The Return of Rachel

1. Gerhard von Rad, *Genesis*, 1st ed. (1944), cited in Dresner, *Rachel*, 140. See also Speiser, *Anchor Bible Genesis*, 359, "verse 7 would seem to be irrelevant at first glance. On closer probing, however, its pertinence is easily vindicated. Death had robbed Jacob of his beloved Rachel. . . . Hence Jacob feels justified in substituting two of Rachel's grandsons for such other sons as fate may have her prevented from bearing."

2. Torah bans this kind of memorial pillar (*matzevah*), but this is not the only halakhic problem in this verse.

3. Where *is* Rachel buried? Bethel is in the land of Canaan, and the way from Bethel to Bethlehem can be only in the land of Canaan. Despite traditions that place the site of Rachel's tomb south of Jerusalem, a later text (1 Sam. 10:2) supports Jeremiah's prophecy that "a voice is heard in Ramah," several miles to the north of Jerusalem (Jer. 31:14–15). Sarna, in *JPS Torah Commentary: Genesis*, 408, prefers this Benjaminite location, as we are told that Jacob continues to Migdal-Eder, a site Micah identifies as a section of Jerusalem.

4. Abraham ibn Ezra disagrees that the *peshat* is elusive: "He [Jacob] mentioned this to Joseph that he should not be angry for asking him for something which he had not done on behalf of his mother." Leibowitz, *Studies in Genesis–Deuteronomy*, 539.

5. All three sentiments may be found in the rabbinic tradition, which generally focus on the word *alai*, "on me" or "unto me." *Pesikta Rabbati* 83 emphasizes the enormity of the loss, as does BT, Sanhedrin 22b, where the adage "a man is dead only to his wife" is inverted. *Midrash Ruth Rabbah* 82:7 focuses on the numerous travails in Jacob's life, noting that Rachel's death surpassed them all. *Midrash Leket Tov* and *Midrash Yelamdenu* hold Jacob accountable for the imprecation that whoever stole the idols of Laban would die. Cited in Kasher, *Torah Shlemah* 7:1747–50.

6. Robert Alter offers this explanation of the verse, but Jacob has already begun the adoption process, so even if Jacob was trying to compensate the Rachel by offering a portion to both Joseph's sons, it does not explain why the utterance occurs here. Speiser's view that the resumption the narrative from verse 8 forward combines the theophoric Elohim and the proper name Israel demonstrates "the fusion of both narrative sources" (J and E). *Anchor Bible Genesis*, 357, 359. This is the sort of circular reasoning that frustrates those who cannot find the source-critical approach the be-all and end-all of exegesis.

7. Technically: Ephratah—the first mention includes the directional *heh* ending, that is, "to Ephrat."

8. To be sure, Gen. 48:7 repeats only the second half of this passage beginning with "She was buried on the road to Ephrath."

9. Rabow, *Lost Matriarch*, 184–85.

10. Pardes, *Countertraditions in the Bible*, 107–12, characterizes the mention of Rachel and Leah in Ruth 4:11 as the reconciliation of the two sisters and of female commensality in general.

11. Laban, unlike Jacob, continues to respect the biological birth order when searching for his household idols, visiting Leah's tent first and then Rachel's.

12. Steinberg, *World of the Child in the Hebrew Bible*, 40. Although *na'ar/ na'ara* is the most frequently used term for childhood (about three hundred occurrences) as opposed to *yeled/yalda* (ninety-three occurrences), Steinberg concludes, "lexical study alone is insufficient to clarify the understandings of the meaning of childhood in biblical Israel."

13. Rashi mitigates Reuben's sin by reporting that Jacob moved his bed from Rachel's tent to Bilhah's, not Leah's. For a novel partly inspired by these Genesis narratives, I recommend Margaret Atwood's dystopian *The Handmaid's Tale*. For a scholarly treatment of the handmaid, see Savina Teubal's works *Sarah the Priestess: The First Matriarch of Genesis* (Athens: Ohio University Press, 1984), and *Hagar the Egyptian* (San Francisco: Harper Collins, 1990).

14. Dinah is never heard from in Genesis 34 and never heard about after her rape at Shechem's hands. Anita Diamant's *The Red Tent* (New York: St Martin's, 1997) reimagines Dinah's tale in novelistic form.

15. For a wonderful novelistic retelling of the Joseph story with female principals, I recommend Dara Horn's *Guide for the Perplexed*. Since there is only one sibling in Horn's novel, who deeply regrets her betrayal of Josepha, Horn's insights might also be applied to the relationship between Leah and Rachel.

16. Bloom and Rosenberg, *Book of J*, 209–19.

17. It has been suggested that there might be a *resentful* reaction toward this physical reminder of Rachel in Joseph's person. But this does not seem supported by the text. One colleague suggested a homoerotic relationship between Jacob and Joseph, if not an outright incestuous one. In this reading the brothers are actually trying to remove Joseph from Jacob's abuse. Jacob crossed many ethical borders in his life and acted disreputably on several occasions, but I do not find this charge convincing.

18. Jeremiah is a prophet, but the line between revelation and interpretation, between the divine message and the human understanding of that message, has been proven to be less hard and fast than one might suppose. See BT, Baba Batra 14b, on the order of the prophetic books.

19. Jeremiah came from Anatoth, but his ancestors were priests at Shiloh, described as destroyed 1 Samuel 3–4 and recalled by Jeremiah during his famous Temple Sermon (Jeremiah 7 and 28). Thus his acute, prophetic sense that further disasters would befall Judah and Jerusalem stems in part from his awareness of the desolation of his family's ancestral shrine—he told contemporaries that disaster had happened before and could happen again. For most of the book of Jeremiah, the sense of warning overwhelms the consolation, adumbrated by four verbs of destruction to two of rebuilding in God's initial call (Jer. 1:10). Many scholars have questioned whether this optimistic prophecy of consolation comes from Jeremiah, from his scribe Baruch, or from an even later author.

20. Abravanel comments on the oddity of Jer. 31:8b, which describes Manasseh as the firstborn son.

21. Fackenheim addresses the differing Jewish and Christian responses to Jeremiah 31 in his luminous "New Hearts and Old Covenants." This essay remains a must-read for anyone interested in the dynamics of ecumenical readings of Scripture.

22. Rashi to Gen. 48:7.

23. Nachmanides, *Commentary on the Torah*, 332 and 573. Carmichael, *Law and Narrative in the Bible*, considers the various divergences between patri-

archal practice and later legislation a motivating factor behind much of the wording of Deuteronomy.

24. Nachmanides, *Commentary on the Torah*, 332. Nachmanides considered Jacob's actions questionable: marrying sister-wives; setting up a pillar; even marrying Bilhah and Zilpah, regarded by some traditions as sisters of Rachel and Leah.

25. Jeremiah regards himself as an intercessor, as we must conclude from God's admonition, "Even if Moses and Samuel were to intercede with Me, I would not be won over to that people" (Jer. 15:1).

26. *Lamentation Rabbah*, Proem 24, found also in *Pesikta Rabbati*, 83. See Pardes, *Countertraditions in the Bible*, 116; Dvora Weisberg, "Men Imagining Women Imagining God," in *Agendas for the Study of Midrash in the Twenty-First Century*, ed. Marc Lee Raphael, 63–83 (Williamsburg VA: College of William and Mary Press, 1999).

27. Dresner, *Rachel*, 135.

28. *Lamentations Rabbah*, Proem 24. This midrash has been interpreted with great insight by Dresner, *Rachel*; Weisberg, "Men Imagining Women Imagining God"; Pardes, *Countertraditions in the Bible*; and Zornberg, *Beginning of Desire*.

29. The Maharal of Prague, cited in Zornberg, *Beginning of Desire*, 376.

30. "The victory of Rachel reaches beyond clan and epoch. It is not limited to the spectacular successes of her son Joseph and Joseph's son Ephraim, who along with his brother Manasseh, was raised to the rank of leader of one of the twelve tribes of Israel, and who became the most influential of them all." Dresner, *Rachel*, 175.

9. Adopting Ephraim and Manasseh

1. A useful source-critical analysis of Genesis 48 may be found in Dr. Zev Farber's "Va-yehi" discussion on Project TABS (The Torah: A Historical and Contextual Approach), an online Torah study site that employs biblical critical approaches and Jewish perspectives (accessed March 10, 2016).

2. The division into verses is often credited to Bishop Stephen Langton in the fourteenth century.

3. The following paragraph is indebted to Sternberg, *Poetics of Biblical Narrative*, who is, in turn, indebted to the Jewish exegetical tradition.

4. On Friday nights it is customary for fathers to bless boys in the same order that Jacob blesses them: "May God make you like Ephraim and like Manasseh."

5. Sternberg, *Poetics of Biblical Narrative*, 352.

6. Nachmanides, *Commentary on the Torah*, 541, endorses the midrashic tradition that neither Joseph nor the brothers told Jacob about the sale of Joseph.

7. An oath, *sh'vuah* (root: *shin-vet-ayin*), is different from a vow, *neder* (root: *nun-dalet-resh*).

8. Ephraim comes first in Jacob's speech. Reuben has long since been replaced narratively as the leading brother.

9. Deut. 21:15–17: "If a man has two wives, one loved and the other unloved, and both the loved and the unloved have borne him children, but the first-born [*bekhor*] is the son of the unloved one. . . . He may not treat as first-born the son of the loved one in disregard of the unloved one who is older."

10. For instance, Rashbam, ibn Ezra, Nachmanides, and Radak.

11. For instance, Saadyah Gaon and Rashi.

12. Sarna, *JPS Torah Commentary: Genesis*. Gen. to 48:6. Gen. 48:15 presents a similarly troubling verse: "And he [Jacob] blessed Joseph," which makes little sense in this context, since the whole chapter focuses on Joseph's descendants. No surprise, then, that the Septuagint renders "he blessed them" and the Vulgate added "the sons of."

13. Zornberg, *Beginning of Desire*, 371. NJPS renders the simple verb for "seeing" as "And Jacob noticed."

14. Zornberg, *Beginning of Desire*, 371.

15. Kass, *Beginning of Wisdom*, 636–59. Modern critics of Joseph include Maurice Samuel, Moses Pava, Ivan Caine, Leon Kass, Aaron Wildavsky, Yoram Hazon, and Anita Diamant. Why these modern scholars differ so greatly from their Hellenistic (and even rabbinic) predecessors in their evaluation of Joseph invites speculation.

16. David Rothstein, "Chronicles," in Berlin and Brettler, *Jewish Study Bible*, 1729.

17. Mann, *Joseph and His Brothers*, 1461.

18. Kugel, *Bible as It Was*, 269–72.

19. On 1 Chronicles 5 see Jacob Myers, *Anchor Bible Chronicles I* (New York: Doubleday, 1964): 32–39.

20. Sarna, *JPS Torah Commentary: Genesis*, 329.

21. The rabbis took the plural form in Gen. 48:15, "The God in whose ways my fathers Abraham and Isaac walked," to imply that all three Patriarchs went out into the world and spread knowledge of God. Kasher, *Encyclopedia of Biblical Interpretation*, 6:123.

22. One can think of other Hebrew words for portion, including *helek* and *ahuza*. This word choice (*shechem*) brings part of the Jacob story full circle, since he purchases land in Shechem in Gen. 33:19.

23. Kasher, *Encyclopedia of Biblical Interpretation*, 6:134.

24. Abraham's purchase of Machpelah in Genesis 23 initiates a biblical concern for resting places.

25. Alter, *Five Books of Moses*, 280–81.

26. See *Midrash Rabbah Genesis* 48:22 in connection to Joseph's double portion.

27. Scholars sometimes call this section of Jeremiah 31 the "scroll of consolation."

10. Jacob's Valedictory

1. Sarna, *JPS Torah Commentary: Genesis*, 331.

2. Among the formal structures of Genesis 49 linking it to the Joseph story are the prose opening and prose closing at 49:1 and 49:28, a chiastic rendering of the mothers' sons (Leah, Bilhah, Zilpah, Bilhah, Rachel), and the alternating use of Jacob and Israel five times each in the course of the chapter. Such facets support a view of Genesis 49 as "the product of careful design."

3. Sarna, *JPS Torah Commentary: Genesis*, 337.

4. See the essays in Amy Jill Levine and Marc Zvi Brettler, eds., *The Jewish Annotated New Testament* (New York: Oxford University Press, 2010). Later Jewish writers in this case include the authors of the New Testament. It is likely that three of the four Gospel writers were Jews, as was Paul. I cannot find an allusion to Gen. 49:10 in the New Testament, but it was widely used as a messianic proof text by Christian disputants in the Middle Ages.

5. See Josh. 17:1 and Judg. 5:14–15.

6. In addition to the phrase *"aharit ha-yamim,"* which can mean "in days to come" or "at the end of days," the context of the valedictory address of the last Patriarch in the land of Egypt invites such speculation, as does the parallel to Moses' valedictory address in the last portion of the Torah, "And this is the blessing."

7. BT, Pesachim 56a.

8. *Deuteronomy Rabbah* 2:35, cited in Lawrence Schiffman, *Texts and Traditions* (New York: KTAV, 1998), 678.

9. A Torah reader would naturally pay attention to the physical layout of the Torah text, the cantillation notes, and the opening and closing of the weekly sections.

10. Zornberg, *Beginning of Desire*, 355.

11. Rashi to Gen. 47:28. Rashi's second answer that Jacob wanted to reveal the end of time to his sons, but could not, comes from *Midrash Rabbah Genesis* 96:1. See also Nachmanides, *Commentary to the Torah*, 580.

12. *Midrash Rabbah Genesis* 98:3. These parables of a "king of flesh and blood" are a common midrashic trope for speaking of God. But Zornberg's striking contrast between this midrash with the talmudic view of "depar-

ture of the Shekhina" in BT, Pesachim 56a, is original. Zornberg, *Beginning of Desire*, 358–59.

13. *Sefat Emet* was written by Yehudah Leib Alter (1847–1905), the founding rabbi of the Ger Hasidim. As with many Hasidic classics, the author is commonly called by his most famous work, hence "the Sefat Emet," or "the Kedushat Levi."

14. *Midrash Rabbah Genesis* 98:7. I am persuaded by those who connect "choice vine" (*soreka*, Gen. 49:11) to the Wadi of Sorek, where Judah and Tamar had their sexual encounter. I am also persuaded that the image in 49:11b, "He washes his garment in wine," alludes to the dipping of Joseph's long-sleeved garment in goat's blood. If so Jacob's blessing of Judah contains some personal barbs with its promise of political dominance.

15. The last Hebrew word for "tools of lawlessness" (*klei hamas mikhrotei-hem*) in this phrase (Gen. 49:5b) is difficult to render. Perhaps "piercings," or "wares." If the latter the Hebrew root would be *mem-khaf-resh*, the same root for to the verb "to sell" (*limkhor*) and thus a reference to Simeon and Levi's role in Genesis 37.

16. Hirsch, *Hirsch Chumash*, 864.

17. Nachmanides, in Leibowitz, *Studies in Genesis–Deuteronomy*, 543.

18. Jacob's two pronouncements are usually described as being of equal length since they comprise five verses each, sixty-one words for Joseph versus fifty-five words for Judah.

19. Hirsch, *Hirsch Chumash*, 881.

20. Robert Alter notes that several terms and phrases, including "ben porat Yosef," could be human, vegetable, or mineral. I follow Rashi's "ben hen" (graceful son), and—although Nachmanides never likes it when Rashi uses another language, in this case Aramaic, to explain the Hebrew—Nachmanides concurs with Rashi that the phrase is praise and implies abundance or fruitfulness.

21. *Midrash Rabbah Genesis* 98:19. Unless one were to take this reference to arrows as a metaphor for the brothers' jealousy (as in Hamlet's speech, "the slings and arrows of outrageous fortune"), this is an unknown referent.

22. Compare Deut. 33:16.

23. We can read four or five theophorics depending on whether "the Shepherd, the Rock of Israel" (*ro'eh even Yisrael*) is counted as one or two. Kass, *Beginning of Wisdom*, 644–45; Alter, *Five Books of Moses*, 288.

24. Kasher, *Encyclopedia of Biblical Interpretation*, 6:206. I find it very significant that four or five theophorics are used in Jacob's blessing on Joseph (e.g., "Mighty One of Jacob," "Shepherd, Rock of Israel," "God of your father," "Shaddai"), as if to eliminate any doubt that God endorses Jacob's favorite.

25. Sarna, *JPS Torah Commentary: Genesis*, 342; Tigay, *JPS Torah Commentary: Deuteronomy*, 519–24; Zakovitch, *Jacob*, 174–75.

26. Of course the introduction to this poem refers to Moses' "have blessed the Israelites" (Deut. 33:1); and again the use of the simple past in "When Moses charged us with the Teaching" (Deut. 33:4) suggests this poem came well after Moses' lifetime, as does the comparative between Moses and all other prophets in Deut. 34:10. Tigay, *JPS Torah Commentary: Deuteronomy*, offers a likely dating in between the reign of Solomon and the fall of the Northern Kingdom, 720 BCE.

27. Tigay, *JPS Torah Commentary: Deuteronomy*, 327.

11. The Deaths and Burials of Jacob and Joseph

1. Erich Auerbach, *Mimesis* (Princeton NJ: Princeton University Press, 1953), 17.

2. Every letter of the verb "and he kissed him" (*va'yishakehu*; Gen. 33:4) is pointed—meaning the vowels are considered uncertain by the Masoretes.

3. Jewish tradition emphasizes speedy burial, with the cleaning of the body and the wrapping of it in simple linen (*tachririn*).

4. *Midrash Rabbah Genesis* 100:3. Rabbi Judah the Prince is credited with editing the Mishnah, the first written document produced by rabbinic Judaism, approximately 225 CE.

5. See additional sources in Kasher, *Encyclopedia of Biblical Interpretation*, 222; and Fields, *Torah Commentary for Our Times*, 1:121.

6. The Hebrew *aron* for casket in 50:26 is a singular use of that word, which usually means cabinet or ark, as in the *aron ha-kodesh*, the Holy Ark used to house or transport the Torah.

7. The Greek historian Diodorus Siculus prescribes a thirty-day dressing of the corpse and seventy-two-day mourning period for royalty. The Egyptians' reactions, Pharaoh's formal permission, and the details of corpse preparation attest to a royal burial for Jacob—in contrast to the sparse narrative for Joseph (Gen. 50:26).

8. Wildavsky, *Assimilation versus Separation*.

9. Abravanel notes that the brothers forfeited their claims to fraternal loyalty, but could still invoke Joseph's filial obligations.

10. Rashi gives credence to a tradition that Jacob did not actually die—the wording at Gen. 49:33 is curious.

11. Leibowitz, *Studies in Genesis–Deuteronomy*, 558.

12. Freud, who termed his father's death the most momentous event in his life, would not have been surprised by Joseph's reaction.

13. *Midrash Rabbah Genesis* 100:8–9, cited in Leibowitz, *Studies in Genesis–Deuteronomy*, 565.

14. Leibowitz, *Studies in Genesis–Deuteronomy*, 563.

15. Ackerman, "Joseph, Judah, and Jacob," and Sternberg, *Poetics of Biblical Narrative*, agree that the brothers moved to a plane of more than ordinary fraternal solidarity. I find more ambiguity, though I disagree with Kass, *Beginning of Wisdom*, 456–57, that Joseph does not forgive the brothers.

16. Pirson, *Lord of the Dreams*, 144, sees positive and negative traditions about Joseph that have been woven together. I believe that biblical writers were capable of transcending black-and-white portraiture, and that scripture is adept at showing character development.

17. Rashi on Gen. 50:22, based on a more extended comparison in Midrash Rabbah Genesis 84:6.

18. Joshua also lives to 110 (Josh. 24:29). See Sarna, *Understanding Genesis*, 226.

19. Joseph saw "the children of Machir, son of Manasseh, were likewise born upon Joseph's knees" (Gen. 50:23).

20. The infinitive absolute works like the adverb "very"—a doubled form used for emphasis.

21. Scholars agree that Ben Sirach originally composed in Hebrew, but disappeared from the Jewish canon in the first millennium. A Hebrew text of Ben Sirach's composition was discovered in the Cairo Geniza in the 1890s.

22. This translation of Ben Sirach is taken from the NSRV New Oxford Annotated Bible.

23. Kugel, "Joseph's Bones," in *In Potiphar's House*, 125–55; Ulmer, *Egyptian Cultural Icons in Midrash*, 107–42.

24. *Jubilees* 46:5–10.

25. "Testament of Simeon," 8:1–3, in Feldman, Kugel and Schiffman, *Outside the Bible*, 2: 1715–23.

26. *Mishnah*, Sota 1:9.

27. *Mekhilta Beshallah*, 1.

28. Bregman, "Serah bat Asher."

29. Sarna, *JPS Torah Commentary: Genesis*, 315.

30. "I [Serah] linked one faithful leader of Israel Joseph, who is called faithful (Gen. 39:4), with the next faithful leader of Israel, Moses, who is called faithful." *Pesikta de Rav Kahana*, Bashallach 1, as rendered by Bregman, "Serah bat Asher."

31. There is a lengthy tradition that the wagons sent ahead by Joseph for portage make the case. See Rashi and Nachmanides on Gen. 45:27. I prefer the Serah story.

32. *Sefer ha-Yashar* (Va-yiggash) as cited in Bregman, "Serah bat Asher." See the parallel version in *Midrash ha-Gadol* as cited and discussed in McGaha, *A Coat of Many Cultures*.

33. Bregman, "Serah bat Asher."

34. Zohar, *Book of Enlightenment*, 3:167b.

35. Mann, *Joseph and His Brothers*, 1391–405, a subsection whimsically named "Annunciation."

12. Portraying Egypt in Joseph

1. Ps. 105:23, one of the most prominent mentions of Joseph beyond Genesis, also recalls the Hamite origins of Egypt.

2. Neh. 13:1; Ezra 9:1.

3. One "goes down" (*yud-resh-dalet*) to Egypt, which lies south of Israel. But the word *yeridah* takes on a negative connotation. Readers know that Israel will be enslaved in Egypt for four hundred years, but we should not assume all characters in the Joseph story do. God told this piece of information to Abraham in Gen. 15:13 but tells Jacob only that he (singular) will return to Canaan (Gen. 46:4).

4. See Greenberg, *Understanding Exodus*, and Sarna, *Exploring Exodus*, on the wide variety of themes associated with the Exodus.

5. Assmann, *Moses the Egyptian*, 209. Assman uses the term "mnemo-history" to explore the difference between history "as it really was" and history as remembered. In Assmann's view the evidence suggesting that Akhenaton's monotheistic-tending iconoclasm clashes with the Bible's representation of Egypt as the land of idolatry.

6. Nehama Leibowitz, *New Studies in Shmot/Exodus* (Jerusalem: Hemed, 1996), 31–38. Philo, Josephus, Abravanel, Shadal, and Leibowitz all think the midwives are Egyptian.

7. The unnamed Pharaoh of oppression in Exodus is paranoid and evil— perhaps the first fully characterized villain in the Bible. Genesis has plenty of losers, but the earth's evildoing before the flood has no leader, nor do the builders of Babel's tower. Cain is guilty of manslaughter, and his descendants (Lamech, Tuval-Cain, and Nimrod) seem predisposed to violence.

8. A sharp critique of Joseph on the grounds of betraying the "shepherds' ethic" championed by Hebrew Bible, and exemplified by the people Israel may be found in Hazony's *Philosophy of Hebrew Scripture*, 103–39. On shepherd ethics see the exchange between Yoram Hazony and Jon Levenson in *Jewish Review of Books*, Fall 2012 and Winter 2013.

9. Scholars call such verses etiologies, stories told to draw attention to a place, person, or custom. The weeping at Goren ha-Atad probably should not be overinterpreted narratively. See Kugel, *How to Read the Bible*, and Friedman, *Torah: A Commentary*, on Genesis 3.

10. One should not overstate the *Egyptian* coloration of the narrative. Joseph is thirty years old when he stands before Pharaoh; when thirty is

added to twice forty (forty being the traditional number of years equal to one generation), it totals 110.

11. Exod. 1:8 has been a much commented-on verse. Rashi reports the debate of Rav and Shmuel (BT, Sotah 11a) and in *Midrash Shmot Rabbah* 1:8 over whether the king was new or only his decrees were new. Hirsch, *Hirsch Chumash*, read this verse as indicating a foreign regime, not just a new king.

12. Abraham, Isaac, and Jacob are collectively called the *avot*: the invocation is an identifier for supplicants, "we are Israel," and a reminder of the merits of our ancestors (*zekhut avot*). As noted, BT, Berachot 16b, limits the Patriarchs to three and the Matriarchs to four.

13. Wildavsky, *Assimilation versus Separation*, 1.

14. The absence of a narrative concerning Moses' childhood makes his identification with the enslaved Israelites in Exod. 2:11 a rich topic for midrash.

15. Etymologically Moses' name is Egyptian in origin, but etiology trumps etymology in the Bible. Pharaoh's daughter, speaking imperfect Hebrew, names the infant Moses because "I drew him out of the water" (Exod. 2:10).

16. On Rashbam's understanding of Exod. 3:11, see Edward Greenstein, "Medieval Bible Commentaries," in *Back to the Sources*, ed. Barry Holtz (New York: Simon & Schuster, 2006), 256.

17. Raphael, *Jew among Romans*, 118.

18. Josipovici, *Book of God*, 85.

19. Josipovici, *Book of God*; Alter, *Art of Biblical Narrative* and *Five Books of Moses*; Northrop Frye, *The Great Code: The Bible and Literature* (San Diego: Harcourt, Brace, Jovanovich, 1982); Frank Kermode, *The Literary Guide to the Bible*, ed. Robert Alter and Frank Kermode (Cambridge MA: Harvard University Press, 1987); and Bloom and Rosenberg, *The Book of J*, all make solid cases for the applicability of different literary genres to the Bible.

20. Feldman, *Josephus's Interpretation of the Bible*, 355–73.

21. Leibowitz also suggests this missionary motive in *Studies in Genesis–Deuteronomy*, 439–42.

22. *Jubilees* 40:8–9, cited in Niehoff, *Figure of Joseph in Post-biblical Jewish Literature*, 45.

23. In Artapanus's *Jewish History*, Joseph regulated the state's operations, protected the weak, increased the amount of arable land, and more. Cited in Niehoff, *Figure of Joseph in Post-biblical Jewish Literature*, 48–49.

24. Josephus, *Antiquities*, 2:7 150. I rely on William Whiston's eighteenth-century translation.

25. I am sure a more adept researcher could find such critics; I have not.

26. Alfonso quoted in McGaha, *Coat of Many Cultures*, which introduces and reproduces Jewish, Christian, and Muslim texts on Joseph from medieval Spain.

27. Zakovitch, *Jacob the Unexpected Patriarch*, concedes that his portrait of Jacob is a "biography based on a biography" (7–8). Zakovitch is more confident than I am that one can establish the earliest strata of a biblical story.

28. Ronald Hendel and P. Kyle McCarter, "The Patriarchal Age," in *The Rise of Ancient Israel*, ed. Herschel Shanks (Upper Saddle River NJ: Prentice Hall, 1999), 27–30.

29. Halpern, "Exodus from Egypt"; see also Speiser, *Anchor Bible Genesis*, introduction.

30. Finley, *Use and Abuse of History*, 22.

31. Herodotus chronicled the Persian War; Thucydides, the Peloponnesian War. Both wrote fundamentally contemporary history. They accepted the Trojan War as actual and made no attempt to interrogate those ancient events in the rigorous manner they did the conflicts of their own times.

32. Sperling, *Original Torah*, 8–9.

33. Sperling, *Original Torah*, 91–102.

34. Sperling's position should not be confused with that of the minimalists, often associated with universities of Copenhagen and Sheffield. Sperling thinks the Bible stories were inspired by actual events and ancient models.

35. Sperling, *Original Torah*, 99.

36. See Feuchtwanger, *House of Desdemona*, on the uses of historical fiction.

37. Redford, *Study of the Biblical Book of Joseph*, esp. 244–53.

38. Redford, *Study of the Biblical Book of Joseph*, 180–82.

39. Redford, *Study of the Biblical Book of Joseph*, considers Genesis 39 the most ancient—but in his view, clearly interpolated—part of the Joseph narrative.

40. Redford, *Study of the Biblical Book of Joseph*, dissents from Speiser's seventeenth-century dating of the historical Joseph (*Anchor Bible Genesis*), from Gary Rendsburg's tenth-century BCE dating (*Redaction of Genesis*), from Richard Elliot Friedman's ninth-to-tenth-century BCE dating of J and E (*Torah*).

41. We might imagine Redford's view the exact opposite of Speiser's. Speiser, *Anchor Bible Genesis*, had great confidence that the different sources J, E, and P all contributed to Joseph but believed in the great antiquity of the germinal tale. Redford, *Study of the Biblical Book of Joseph*, doubts the antiquity of the older (hypothetical) sources (J and E), concedes P's fingerprints, but considers the Egyptian details literary verisimilitude, intended to give the story an ancient feel.

42. On Egyptological evidence supporting the Exodus, see Ulmer, *Egyptian Cultural Icons*, 1n1.

43. The Tel Dan Inscription famously mentions a "House of David" but sheds no additional light on his character.

44. We also cannot draw the line precisely between what "the "Bible says" and what "the Bible suggests."

45. Ahad Ha'Am draws on a Nietzschean distinction between three types of history.

46. Leon Simon, *Selected Essays of Ahad Ha'Am* (Cleveland: Meridien, 1962), 308–9.

47. Miles, *God*, 84.

48. Dara Horn's novel *Guide for the Perplexed* retells the Joseph story with sibling competition at the core.

SELECTED BIBLIOGRAPHY

Ackerman, James. "Joseph, Judah, and Jacob." In *Literary Interpretations of Biblical Narratives 2*, edited by Kenneth Gros-Louis. Nashville: Abingdon, 1982.

Alter, Robert. *Art of Biblical Narrative*. New York: Basic, 1981.

———. *The Five Books of Moses*. New York: Norton, 2004.

Al-Thalabi. *Lives of the Prophets*. Translated by William Brinner. Brill: Leiden, 2002.

Ambrose. *Seven Exegetical Works*. The Fathers of the Church 9, no. 47. Washington DC: Catholic University of America Press, 1972.

Argyle, A. W. "Joseph the Patriarch in Patristic Teaching." *Expository Times* 67, no. 7 (1956): 199–201.

Assmann, Jan. *Moses the Egyptian*. Cambridge MA: Harvard University Press, 1997.

Baidawi, Abd ibn Umar. *Commentary of Sura 12 of the Qur'an*. Translated by A. F. L. Beeston. New York: Oxford University Press, 1963.

Bar, Shaul. *A Letter That Has Not Been Opened*. Cincinnati OH: Hebrew Union College Press, 2001.

Berlin, Adele, and Marc Zvi Brettler, eds. *The Jewish Study Bible*. New York: Oxford University Press, 2004.

Bernstein, Marc S. *Stories of Joseph: Narrative Migrations between Judaism and Islam*. Detroit: Wayne State University Press, 2006.

Bloom, Harold, and David Rosenberg. *The Book of J*. New York: Vintage, 1990.

Boncheck, Avigdor. *What's Bothering Rashi?* New York: Feldheim, 2005.

Braude, William. *Tanna debe Eliyahu: The Lore of the School of Elijah*. Translated by Israel Kapstein. Philadelphia: Jewish Publication Society, 1981.

Bregman, Marc. "Serah bat Asher: Biblical Origins, Ancient Aggadah and Contemporary Folklore." Bilgray Lecture presented at the University of Arizona, 1996.

Brettler, Marc Zvi, et al. *The Bible and the Believer*. Oxford: Oxford University Press, 2012.

Budd, Louis. "Mark Twain on Joseph the Patriarch." *American Quarterly* 16, no. 4 (Winter 1964): 570–80.

Caine, Ivan. "Numbers in the Joseph Narrative." In *Jewish Civilization: Essays and Studies*, edited by Ronald A. Brauner, 3–17. Philadelphia: Reconstructionist Rabbinical College Press, 1979.

Carmichael, Calum. *Law and Narrative in the Bible*. Ithaca NY: Cornell University Press, 1985.

———. *The Laws of Deuteronomy*. Ithaca NY: Cornell University Press, 1974.

———. *Women, Law, and the Genesis Traditions*. Edinburgh: Edinburgh University Press, 1979.

Dever, William. *What Did the Biblical Writers Know and When Did They Know It?* Grand Rapids MI: Eerdmans, 2003.

Docherty, Susan. "Joseph and Aseneth: Rewritten Bible or Narrative Expansion?" *Journal for the Study of Judaism* 35, no. 1 (2004): 27–48.

Dresner, Samuel. *Rachel*. Minneapolis: Fortress, 1994.

Fackenheim, Emil. "New Hearts and Old Covenants." In *The Jewish Thought of Emil Fackenheim*, edited by Michael Morgan, 223–34. Detroit: Wayne State University Press, 1988.

Feldman, Louis. *Josephus's Interpretation of the Bible*. Berkeley: University of California Press, 1998.

Feldman, Louis, James Kugel, and Lawrence Schiffman, eds. *Outside the Bible: Ancient Jewish Writings Related to Scripture*. 3 vols. Philadelphia: Jewish Publication Society, 2014.

Feuchtwanger, Lion. *The House of Desdemona: The Laurels and Limits of Historical Fiction*. Detroit: Wayne State University Press, 1963.

Fields, Harvey. *A Torah Commentary for Our Times*. Vol. 1, *Genesis*. UAHC Press, 1990.

Finley, Moses. *The Use and Abuse of History*. London: Penguin Books, 1975.

Fishbane, Michael. *Biblical Interpretation in Ancient Israel*. Oxford: Clarendon, 1985.

———, ed. *JPS Bible Commentary: Haftarot*. Philadelphia: Jewish Publication Society, 2002.

Fokkelman, Jan P. *Narrative Art in Genesis*. Eugene OR: Wipf & Stock, 2004.

Fox, Everett. *The Five Books of Moses*. New York: Schocken Books, 1995.

Frieden, Kenneth. *Freud's Dream of Interpretation*. Albany: State University of New York Press, 1990.

Friedman, Richard Eliot. *The Torah: A Commentary*. San Francisco: Harper Collins, 2001.

———. *Who Wrote the Bible?* New York: Summit Books, 1987.

Frymer-Kensky, Tikva. *Reading the Women of the Bible*. New York: Schocken, 2002.

Gan, Moshe. "The Scroll of Esther in Light of Events of Joseph in Egypt." *Tarbiz*, Winter 1961, 144–49.

Ginzberg, Louis, and Henrietta Szold. *Legends of the Jews (1909)*. 7 vols. Baltimore: Johns Hopkins Paperbacks, 1998.

Goldin, Judah. "Judah: The Fourth Son; or, Where Does Genesis 38 Belong?" In *Studies in Midrash and Related Literature*, edited by Judah Goldin et al., 27–44. Philadelphia: Jewish Publication Society. 1988.

Goldman, Shalom. "Joseph" In *Encyclopedia of Islam*, 3:55–57. Leiden: Brill, 2001.

———. *The Wiles of Women/The Wiles of Men: Joseph and Potiphar's Wife in Ancient Near Eastern, Jewish and Islamic Folklore*. Albany: State University of New York Press, 1995.

Greenberg, Moshe. *Anchor Bible Ezekiel*. New York: Doubleday, 1964.

———. *Biblical Prose Prayer*. Berkeley: University of California Press, 1983.

———. *Understanding Exodus*. New York: Behrman House, 1969.

Greenspahn, Frederick. *When Brothers Dwell Together*. Oxford: Oxford University Press, 1994.

Greenstein, Edward. "An Equivocal Reading of the Sale of Joseph." In *Literary Interpretations of the Bible 2*, edited by Kenneth Gros-Louis and James Ackerman, 117–24. Nashville: Abingdon, 1974.

Grossman, Avraham. *Rashi*. Oxford: Littman Library of Jewish Civilization, 2012.

Gruen, Erich. "The Hellenistic Images of Joseph." In *Heritage and Hellenism: The Reinvention of Jewish Tradition*, 73–131 Berkeley: University of California Press, 1998.

Hailperin, Hermann. *Rashi and the Christian Scholars*. Pittsburgh: University of Pittsburgh Press, 1963.

Halpern, Baruch. "The Exodus from Egypt: Myth or Reality?" In *The Rise of Ancient Israel*, edited by Herschel Shanks, 88–106. Washington DC: BAS, 1992.

———. *The First Historians: The Hebrew Bible and History*. University Park: Pennsylvania State University Press, 1996.

Hazony, Yoram. *The Dawn*. Jerusalem: Shalem, 2000.

———. *The Philosophy of Hebrew Scripture*. New York: Cambridge University Press, 2012.

Hazony, Yoram, and Jon. D. Levenson. "Category Error." *Jewish Review of Books*, Winter 2013, no. 12.

Heinemann, Isaac. *Darkhei ha-Aggadah* (The methods of the *aggadah*). Jerusalem: Magnes-Massadah, 1949.

Heinemann, Joseph. "The Proem in the Aggadic Midrashim—A Form-Critical Study." *Scripta Hierosolymitana* 22 (1971): 100–122.

Herodotus. *The Persian Wars.* Translated by George Rawlinson. New York: Modern Library, 1942.

Heschel, Abraham Joshua. *Heaven Torah as Refracted through the Generations.* Translated by Gordon Tucker. New York: Continuum, 2004.

Hicks-Keeton, Jill. "Rewritten Gentiles: Conversion to Israel's 'Living God' and Jewish Identity." Ph.D. diss., Duke University Divinity School, 2012.

Hirsch, Samson Raphael. *The Hirsch Chumash: Commentary to the Five Books of Torah.* Translated by Daniel Haberman. Jerusalem: Feldheim, 2000–2009.

Horn, Dara. *Guide for the Perplexed.* New York: W. W. Norton, 2013.

Humphreys, W. Lee. *Joseph and His Family.* San Diego: University of Southern California Press, 1988.

Jacob, Benno. *The First Book of the Bible: Genesis.* Translated by Ernest Jacob and Walter Jacob. New York: KTAV, 1974.

———. *Quellenscheidung und Exegese im Pentateuch.* Leipzig: M. W. Kaufmann, 1916.

Josephus, Flavius. *The Works of Flavius Josephus.* Vol. 2, *Antiquities.* Translated by William Whiston. Grand Rapids MI: Baker Book House, 1974.

Josipovici, Gabriel. *The Book of God.* New Haven CT: Yale University Press, 1988.

Kalimi, Isaac. *Early Jewish Exegesis and Theological Controversy.* Assen, Netherlands: Royal Van Gorcum Press, 2002.

Kasher, Menachem. *Encyclopedia of Biblical Interpretation.* Vols. 5–6, translation of *Torah Shlemah.* New York: American Biblical Encyclopedia Society, 1962–65.

———. *Torah Shlemah.* Vols. 6–7. Jerusalem: Azriel, 1945–47.

Kass, Leon. *The Beginning of Wisdom: Reading Genesis.* New York: Free Press, 2003.

Koelb, Clayton. "Coat of Many Colors." *German Quarterly* 49, no. 4 (November 1976): 472–84.

Kraemer, Ross S. "How the Egyptian Virgin Asenath Converts to Judaism and Marries Joseph." In *Maenads, Martyrs, Matrons, Monastics.* Philadelphia: Fortress Press, 1988.

———. *When Asenath Met Joseph.* New York: Oxford University Press, 1998.

Kugel, James. *The Bible as It Was.* Cambridge MA: Belknap Press of Harvard University Press, 1997.

———. "Biblical Criticism Lite." jameskugel.com, accessed March 10, 2016.

———. *How to Read the Bible: A Guide to Scripture Then and Now.* New York: Free Press, 2007.

————. *In Potiphar's House: The Interpretive Life of Biblical Texts.* Cambridge MA: Harvard University Press, 1990.

Leibowitz, Nehama. *Studies in Genesis–Deuteronomy.* 7 vols. Jerusalem: Hemed, 1954–66.

Leuchter, Mark. "Genesis 38 in Social and Historical Perspective" *Journal of Biblical Literature* 132, no. 2 (2013): 209–27.

Levenson, Alan "Christian Author, Jewish Book? Methods and Sources in Thomas Mann's *Joseph.*" *German Quarterly* 71, no. 2 (Spring 1998): 166–78.

————. *The Making of the Modern Jewish Bible.* Lanham MD: Rowman & Littlefield, 2011.

————. "Samson Raphael Hirsch's Bible Project." *Reform Jewish Quarterly,* Fall 2010, 68–83.

Levenson, Jon D. *The Death and Resurrection of the Beloved Son.* New Haven CT: Yale University Press, 1993.

————. *Inheriting Abraham.* Princeton NJ: Princeton University Press, 2012.

————. "Category Error." *Jewish Review of Books,* Fall 2012, no. 11.

Levin, Yigal. "The Benjamin Conundrum." ZAW 116, no. 2 (2004): 223–41.

Levinson, Bernard. *Deuteronomy and the Hermeneutics of Legal Innovation.* New York: Oxford University Press, 1997.

Lieber, David, et al., eds. *Etz Hayim: Torah and Commentary.* New York: Rabbinical Assembly, 2001.

Luzzato, Solomon David. *The Book of Genesis.* Translated by Daniel Klein. Northvale NJ: Jason Aronson, 1998.

Maimonides, Moses. *The Guide of the Perplexed.* 2 vols. Translated by Shlomo Pines. Chicago: University of Chicago Press, 1963.

————. *Mishneh Torah* (The code of Maimonides). New Haven CT: Yale University Press, 1949.

Mann, Thomas. *Joseph and His Brothers.* 4 vols. Translated by John Woods. New York: Alfred A. Knopf, 2005.

McGaha, Michael. *Coat of Many Cultures: The Story of Joseph in Spanish Literature 1200–1492.* Philadelphia: Jewish Publication Society, 1997.

Menn, Esther. *Judah and Tamar in Ancient Jewish Exegesis.* Leiden: E. J. Brill, 1997.

The Metsudah Chuamsh/Rashi. Monsey NY: Eastern Book Press, 2006.

Midrash Rabbah Bereshit. Vol. 2, *Va-Ye'ra-Va-Yehi.* Jerusalem: Vagshal, 2000/2001.

Midrash Rabbah Genesis. Translated by Israel Friedlander. London: Soncino, 1951.

Miles, Jack. *God: A Biography.* New York: Alfred A. Knopf, 1995.

Mir, Mustansir. "The Qur'anic Story of Joseph." *Muslim World* 76, no. 1 (January 1986): 1–15.

Miscall, Peter. "Jacob and Joseph as Analogies." JSOT 6 (1978): 28–40.

Morgan, Michael. *The Jewish Thought of Emil Fackenheim: A Reader.* Detroit: Wayne State University Press, 1987.

Nachmanides [Ramban]. *Commentary on the Torah.* Translated and with commentary by Charles "Chaim" Chavel. New York: Shilo, 1971.

Niditch, Susan. "The Wrong Woman Right: An Analysis of Genesis 38." HTR 72, no. 1 (1979): 147–49.

Niehoff, Maren Ruth. *The Figure of Joseph in Post-biblical Jewish Literature.* Leiden: Brill, 1992.

Noegel, Scott. *Nocturnal Ciphers: The Allusive Language of Dreams in the Ancient Near East.* New Haven CT: American Oriental Society, 2007.

Ochs, Vanessa. *Sarah Laughed.* New York: McGraw-Hill, 2004.

Pardes, Ilana. *Countertraditions in the Bible.* Cambridge MA: Harvard University Press, 1992.

Pava, Moses. "Joseph and the Use of Inside Information: An Exploration of the Joseph Narrative." *Torah U'Madda Journal* 4 (1993): 134–47.

Pearl, Chaim. *Rashi: Jewish Thinkers.* New York: Grove, 1988.

Pesikta de-Rab Kahana. Translated by William Braude and Israel Kapstein. Philadelphia: Jewish Publication Society, 1975.

Pesikta Rabbati. 2 vols. Translated by William Braude. New Haven CT: Yale University Press, 1968.

Pirkei de Rabbi Eliezer. Translated by Gerald Friedlander. New York: Hermon, 1965.

Pirson, Ron. *The Lord of Dreams.* Sheffield: Sheffield Academic Press, 2002.

Prince of Egypt. Dreamworks Productions, 1998.

Rabow, Jerry. *The Lost Matriarch: Finding Leah in the Bible and Midrash.* Philadelphia: Jewish Publication Society, 2015.

Raphael, Frederic. *A Jew among Romans: The Life and Legacy of Flavius Josephus.* New York: Pantheon, 2013.

Rashbam [Rabbi Samuel ben Meir]. *Commentary on Genesis: An Annotated Translation.* Translated by Martin Lockshin. Lewiston NY: Edwin Mellen, 1989.

Redford, Donald. *A Study of the Biblical Book of Joseph.* Leiden: E. J. Brill, 1970.

Reinhartz, Adele. *Why Ask My Name?* New York: Oxford University Press, 1998.

Rendsburg, Gary. *The Redaction of Genesis.* Winona Lake IN: 1986.

Rosenthal, Ludwig. "Die Josephgeschichte mit den Büchern Esther und Daniel verglichen." ZAW 15 (1895): 278–84.

Sacks, Robert. *A Commentary on the Book of Genesis.* Lewiston NY: Edwin Mellen, 1990.

Samuel, Maurice. *Certain People of the Book.* New York: Alfred A. Knopf, 1955.

Sandmel, Samuel. "The Haggadah within Scripture." JBL 80 (1961): 105–22.

Sarna, Nahum. *Exploring Exodus*. New York: Schocken Books, 1986.

———. *JPS Torah Commentary: Genesis*. Philadelphia: Jewish Publication Society, 1989.

———. *Understanding Genesis*. New York: Jewish Theological Seminary, 1966.

Satlow, Michael. *How the Bible Became Holy*. New Haven CT: Yale University Press, 2014.

Seidman, Naomi. *Faithful Renderings*. Chicago: University of Chicago Press, 2006.

Shereshevsky, Ezra. *Rashi: The Man and His World*. Northvale NJ: Aronson, 1992.

Simpson, William Kelly, et al. *The Literature of Ancient Egypt*. New Haven CT: Yale University Press, 2003.

Sommer, Benjamin, ed. *Jewish Conceptions of Scripture*. New York: New York University Press, 2012.

Speiser, Ephraim Avigdor, ed. *Anchor Bible Genesis*. New York: Doubleday, 1964.

Sperling, S. David. *The Original Torah: The Political Intent of the Bible's Writers*. New York: New York University Press, 1998.

Steinberg, Naomi. *The World of the Child in the Hebrew Bible*. Sheffield: Phoenix, 2013.

Steinmetz, David C. "The Superiority of Pre-critical Exegesis." *Theology Today* 37, no. 1 (1980): 27–38.

Steinmetz, Devora. *From Father to Son*. Louisville KY: John Knox, 1991.

Steinsaltz, Adin. *Biblical Images*. New York: Basic Books, 1984.

———. *The Talmud* (Tractate Berachot). First Hebrew/English ed. Jerusalem: Koren, 2012.

Sternberg, Meir. *The Poetics of Biblical Narrative*. Bloomington: Indiana University Press, 1985.

Tigay, Jeffrey. *JPS Torah Commentary: Deuteronomy*. Philadelphia: Jewish Publication Society, 1989.

Ulmer, Rivka. *Egyptian Cultural Icons in Midrash*. Berlin: De Gruyter, 2009.

von Rad, Gerhard. *Genesis*. Revised ed. Philadelphia: Westminster, 1972.

———. "The Joseph Narrative and Ancient Wisdom." In *The Problem of the Hexateuch and Other Essays*, 292–300. Edinburgh: Oliver and Boyd, 1966.

———. *Wisdom in Israel*. Nashville: Abingdon, 1972.

Weisberg, Dvora. *Levirate Marriage and the Family in Ancient Judaism*. Hanover NH: Brandeis University Press, 2009.

Weitzman, Steven. *Solomon: The Lure of Wisdom*. New Haven CT: Yale University Press, 2012.

Wiesel, Elie. *Messengers of God*. New York: Random House, 1976.

Wiesel, Elie. *Sages and Dreamers*. New York: Simon & Schuster, 1999.

Wildavsky, Aaron. *Assimilation versus Separation*. New Jersey: Transaction Books, 1993.

———. "Joseph the Administrator." *Political Science and Politics* 22, no. 4 (December 1989): 779–88.

Yerushalmi, Yosef. *Zakhor: Jewish History and Jewish Memory*. Seattle: University of Washington Press, 1982.

Yohannan, John. *Joseph and Potiphar's Wife in World Literature*. Norfolk: New Directions, 1968.

Zakovitch, Yair. *Jacob the Unexpected Patriarch*. New Haven CT: Yale University Press, 2012.

Zakovitch, Yair, and Shinan Avigdor. *Gam lo kach katuv b'Tanakh* (Once again: That's not what the good book says). Tel Aviv: Yedioth Ahranot, 2009.

———. *Lo kach katuv b'Tanakh* (That's not what the good book says). Tel Aviv: Yedioth Ahranot, 2004. (Published in English translation as *From Gods to God: How the Bible Debunked, Suppressed, or Changed Ancient Myths and Legends*. Philadelphia: Jewish Publication Society, 2012.)

Zohar. *The Book of Enlightenment*. Translated by Daniel Chanan Matt. Mahwah NJ: Paulist Press, 1980.

Zornberg, Aviva Gottlieb. *The Beginning of Desire: Reflections on Genesis*. New York: Doubleday, 1995.

INDEX

Abraham: death and burial of, 171, 172, 173, 195–96; Egypt and, 211; Genesis and, xxv, 30, 31, 216; *hineni* and, 12–14, 255n24

Abravanel, Don Isaac: on Jeremiah 31, 253n20; on Joseph and brothers, 133, 134–35, 201, 249n46, 258n9; on Pharaoh's dream, 40

Absalom, 63, 245n43

acculturation, inward, 227–28n7

acharit ha-yamim, 184, 256n6

Ackerman, James, 119, 126, 142, 259n15

Adonijah, 245n43

adoption of Ephraim and Manasseh, 159, 160–61, 170, 175–79, 255n8

Against Apion (Josephus), 243n13

Ahad Ha'Am, 225, 263n45

akarah, 1, 230n1, 237n2

Akedat Yitzhak (Arama), 134

alai, 160, 165, 252n5

Alfonso X, 219–20

Alter, Robert, xxvi, 153; on adoption of Ephraim and Manasseh, 252n6; on clothing, 232n20; on Jacob's blessings and inheritance, 180–81, 182, 191, 257n20; on Judah and Tamar story, 50, 57–58, 67, 70; on looking into heads of characters, 116–17; on revelation of Joseph, 150, 152; on sale of Joseph, 20; type scenes and, 241n13

Alter, Yehudah Leib, 186–87, 257n13

amar, term of, 114, 246n7

Ambrose, 129–31, 248n36, 248n39

Amnon, 8, 245n43

Anchor Bible Genesis (Speiser), 228n18, 262nn40–41

"And he lived," 171, 186

Antiquities (Josephus), xxiv, 80, 92–93, 243n13

"Any Dream Will Do" (Rice and Weber), 23–24

Arama, Isaac, 134

Artapanus, 92, 219, 261n23

The Art of Biblical Narrative (Alter), 57–58, 232n20, 241n13

ascendance of Joseph, 41, 87–88, 90–92

Asenath: about, 89–90, 109, 128, 182, 245n45; Joseph and, 91–92, 107–9, 245–46nn46–48; in *Joseph and Asenath*, xxiv, 78–79, 107; Potiphar's wife and, 77–79

Asenath, 107

"Asenath and Joseph" (Charlesworth), 107, 245n46

Asenath and Joseph (Jami), 78–79

Asher, 138, 187, 208. *See also* brothers of Joseph

asher, 9, 232n25

aspiration, 23–24

assimilation, term of, 99, 244n25, 245n32

Other works by Alan T. Levenson

An Introduction to Modern Jewish Thinkers (Jason Aronson, 2000)

Between Philosemitism and Antisemitism (University of Nebraska Press, 2004)

The Making of the Modern Jewish Bible (Rowman & Littlefield, 2012)

The Wiley-Blackwell History of Jews and Judaism (2013)